Drawn to the Deep

UNIVERSITY PRESS OF FLORIDA

Florida A&M University, Tallahassee
Florida Atlantic University, Boca Raton
Florida Gulf Coast University, Ft. Myers
Florida International University, Miami
Florida State University, Tallahassee
New College of Florida, Sarasota
University of Central Florida, Orlando
University of Florida, Gainesville
University of North Florida, Jacksonville
University of South Florida, Tampa
University of West Florida, Pensacola

Drawn to the Deep

The Remarkable Underwater Explorations of Wes Skiles

Julie Hauserman

For Patrice,
Enjoy the adventure!
Julie Hauserman

UNIVERSITY PRESS OF FLORIDA

Gainesville / Tallahassee / Tampa / Boca Raton / Pensacola / Orlando / Miami / Jacksonville / Ft. Myers / Sarasota

FRONTISPIECE: Wes geared and ready, Blue Spring, Merritt's Mill Pond.
Photo by Mark Long. Courtesy of Terri Skiles.

This book may be available in an electronic edition.

23 22 21 20 19 18   6 5 4 3 2 1

Library of Congress Control Number: 2018933358
ISBN 978-0-8130-5698-2

The University Press of Florida is the scholarly publishing agency for the
State University System of Florida, comprising Florida A&M University,
Florida Atlantic University, Florida Gulf Coast University, Florida
International University, Florida State University, New College of Florida,
University of Central Florida, University of Florida, University of North
Florida, University of South Florida, and University of West Florida.

UNIVERSITY PRESS OF FLORIDA
15 Northwest 15th Street
Gainesville, FL 32611-2079
http://upress.ufl.edu

To Terri Skiles, the heroine in our hero's story

I was adding it up recently, and I have surpassed 500 miles of virgin exploration in my career. I've been in, and laid line— the first line ever—in 500 miles of virgin cave. That's a lot of going places no human being has ever been before. In a world where most everything on the planet has been explored, it's like discovering a state the size of Florida and being the first person on Earth to walk its entire length from the Panhandle to the Florida Keys. I've done this all underground, under water.

WES SKILES, MAY 2010

Contents

Introduction

I ran face-to-face into an 8-foot alligator. Most likely he sank down trying to escape our bubbles. Dropping down, he headed straight down on top of me. The light must have confused him as well. At first I thought it was a log, but then I realized it was a big, fat, black gator. Both of us freaked! I swung my arm and he did a 180 and bolted. . . . We returned into the siphon to map the passage. I flinched at several gator-ghosts along the way. Great dive.

WES SKILES JOURNAL, NOVEMBER 1995

WHEN WES SKILES DIED on July 21, 2010, in a diving accident, news traveled fast among those of us who work to protect and document Florida's remarkable springs—one of the largest stores of fresh water on the planet.

In the days afterward, people e-mailed around a story from the *Washington Post*, the one with the headline that none of us could wrap our heads around yet: "Wes Skiles, Photographer Who Captured Vivid Worlds Underwater, Dies at 52."

The *Post* story described how the striking underwater photographs and films Wes did for PBS, IMAX, and the Discovery Channel revealed "a dark, alien world," how Wes had once escaped after being buried alive in an Australian cave, how he was the first to set foot on the largest iceberg in Antarctica, and how he used his bulky camera in South Africa to fight off a great white shark that barreled right through his (supposedly) protective metal cage and ended up with "close-up photos of the great white's jagged teeth as a token of his survival."

The *Post* reported that Wes's pictures of stalactite-filled underwater Bahama caves called blue holes were, coincidentally, the cover story of that month's *National Geographic*. It went on to say:

> Such adventures were the reason Mr. Skiles became a photographer. In an online profile, he quoted an ad from Sir Ernest Shackleton, who was seeking men for his Antarctic expedition: "Men wanted for hazardous journey. Low wages, bitter cold, long hours of complete darkness. Safe return doubtful. Honour and recognition in event of success."
>
> Under it, Mr. Skiles wrote, "pretty much reflects my life."

With his *National Geographic* cover story, which had a much-coveted but infrequently published pull-out photo section, Wes had reached the top spot of adventure journalism. Remarkably, he had become one of the best photographers in the world by practicing his art in places with no light. He started making pictures before digital cameras were invented, using film and flashbulbs, and rigging up homemade equipment to survive the dangerous, deep places that most people wouldn't ever think of going. We were all rooting for him. Now, dammit, he was gone.

When I drove back to Tallahassee after Wes's funeral in tiny High Springs, Florida, I grieved for his family—his wife of twenty-nine years and his two teenaged children. I was still contacting environmental colleagues to try to make sense of it. To those who knew him, and even those who just knew *of* him, it was not really surprising that Wes would meet his end while diving. But dying during a routine open-water dive in 75 feet of water, not back in some unexplored underwater cave miles below the Earth's surface? Nobody expected that.

The coroner listed the cause of death as drowning. That didn't explain much. Wes had just spent two weeks on a shoot for television's premier science program, *NOVA*, filming for a segment called *Speed Kills*, which featured footage of high-speed predators. This one focused on the ocean. Wes was hired to film schools of a large, ugly fish called the goliath grouper.

He wasn't happy with the footage he'd shot. But *NOVA* was moving on. So ten days after leaving the *NOVA* shoot, Wes went back for another dive with scientists studying the fish, on his own time and on his own dime, to try to get better footage off Boynton Beach, near Palm Beach.

He was using borrowed diving equipment, a computerized rig called a rebreather. The device allows divers to recycle their own breaths by scrubbing out the carbon dioxide. It also produces no bubbles, which is chiefly why Wes was using it. Bubbles tended to scare off fish. No bubbles meant better footage.

They'd gone to a reef about a mile out, and were shooting, when Wes signaled to them that he was going up to the surface because his digital tape needed replacing. Not long afterward, the scientists swam by and found him on the ocean floor, his breathing regulator out of his mouth.

"There was nothing to indicate natural causes or outside forces," the medical examiner's chief investigator told the *Palm Beach Post*.

Some of Wes's closest friends thought they knew what might have happened: the rebreather had malfunctioned somehow, and Wes passed out and drowned. At least, they thought, he never knew what hit him. At least he didn't die back in some cave, lost or trapped, waiting for his air to run out. Like so many others they had known.

"You lose a good friend, and especially doing what we loved to do, we always have to take a step back and say, you know, why am I doing this again?" Wes's Bahamas dive buddy Brian Kakuk told me. "And then it always comes back, every time—some of us *have to* keep doing it. It's in our blood. We can't stop it."

History is full of explorers, and this is the story of one, a homegrown Florida boy who saw a watery cave in the palm-filled forest and knew right then that he had to go inside.

WHEN YOU START TALKING about cave diving to people who aren't cave divers, you get interrupted right away.

"No way!" they say, shaking their heads. "Those people are crazy. I would *never* do that! *Never!*"

You don't hear people saying that when you talk about other explorers of extreme environments, like astronauts, because most people can't imagine themselves on the Moon. But many people have swum and snorkeled over underwater caves. They've looked down into those depths, and it stirs something uncomfortable in their bellies.

Face it: there is just a visceral difference between those of us who would swim down into a stony hole in the bottom of a dark river and those of us who would not. If we topsiders are claustrophobics, maybe the best way to describe these extreme cave divers is to use a word a friend of mine made up: claustrophiliacs.

Cave divers will tell you that they actually like it down there. They like how the Earth cocoons them in inky darkness and perfect silence. They especially enjoy the feeling that, like astronauts, they are the first ever to see a place that was once unreachable to humans—virgin territory known among hard-core underwater explorers like Wes as "cave booty."

Neuroscientists who study extreme risk say that for some people, the thirst for adventure may be biological, determined by levels of the pleasure chemical, dopamine.

"Dopamine helps elicit a sense of satisfaction when we accomplish tasks: the riskier the task, the larger the hit of dopamine," writes Peter Gwin in a 2013 *National Geographic* article. "Part of the reason we don't all climb mountains or run for office is that we don't all have the same amount of dopamine. Molecules on the surface of nerve cells called autoreceptors control how much dopamine we make and use, essentially controlling our appetite for risk."

One Vanderbilt University study found that people who had fewer autoreceptors in the part of the brain that is linked to reward, addiction, and movement were more prone to novelty-seeking behavior like exploration.

"Think of dopamine like gasoline. You combine that with a brain equipped with a lesser ability to put on the brakes than normal, and you get people who push limits," neuropsychologist David Zald said.

I always assumed that cave divers had to wrestle down their fear before going inside the underwater tunnels—because that's what I would certainly have to do if I were to take up the sport. But the cave divers I interviewed say they never had fear; they were drawn inside at first sight. They describe being in the underwater caves as "church," "the womb," and "Mother Earth"—a pure place where they experience unrivaled peace and a singular focus.

"Generally, if you had some nervousness about a particular dive," one cave diver told me, "the minute you get in the water and take off down that dive, it all goes away. Just goes away. You swim in, the water's crystal clear and it's pretty. It doesn't feel dangerous."

It's a state Hungarian psychology professor Mihaly Csikszentmihaly calls "flow," which he describes as "being completely involved in an activity for its own sake. The ego falls away. Time flies. Every action, movement, and thought follows inevitably from the previous one, like playing jazz. Your whole being is involved, and you're using your skills to the utmost."

The only time fear enters the picture, the cave divers I've interviewed say, is when things go awry underground. A heavy boulder falls and blocks an entrance. Fins stir up silt into a whiteout. Something malfunctions with their equipment. When that happens, they have to resist giving in to emotion.

"The alligator brain takes over, and the back of your head starts getting hot," one diver says. "I mean honest to God, literally, it's warming up. Hair is standing up on the back of your neck. You just cannot stop being productive. You have got to do the right thing. And you absolutely are sitting on top of emotions that will kill you if you let them go. So you conquer your fear."

When asked why he was drawn to cave diving, Wes put it this way:

Cave diving is really a dangerous sport in a way. In other ways it's benign; it's easy if you have the right training and equipment. There's no reason for cave diving to be dangerous. I ride a dual sport motorcycle on mountain dirt roads and on clay in rain and lightning storms. I look at going on a cave dive and some of the things I do on a motorcycle, and I go, "Whoa, motorcycle riding at the level I do it is much, much more dangerous." The problem with cave diving is it's totally unforgiving.

When something happens, it tends to create this cascade, this series of events, and if you manage them perfectly you stay alive. If you fail to have total focus on solving the problem, you often die. The challenge of cave diving is task loading, that you have to follow these very strict rules and preserve them all the time, stay one hundred percent in the moment. You've got to be *there*. You can't drift off and think about the relationship with the girlfriend or the boss, or the stress of a new scenario. When you're down there, the physical danger, the reality is that if something goes wrong, you can count how long you have from that moment to hopefully getting to the surface in breaths.

There are not a whole lot of sports like that. There are a lot of sudden-death sports. Climbing a mountain, free climbing—slip, you're dead. Cave diving deaths are much more hideous.

When things go wrong, you realize it, and you have thirty, forty minutes, an hour, hour and a half—yet you're not going to survive. In that respect it's really agonizing that you're trapped, you're lost, you can't see to find your way out. You run out of air and die a very agonizing, ugly death.

Really, what it's all about is comprehending that we have sometimes hundreds and hundreds of feet of rock above us and hundreds and hundreds of feet of rock below us. We're diving in this very narrow void inside the spaces of the rock. You don't want to think about it a lot when you're down in the caves, because when you *do* think about it, you can feel the weight of the Earth pressing down upon you.

You can only get to the level of photography that I do by having the sport be second nature. That, everything you do within it, you're comfortable thinking ahead and planning and knowing what you're going to do and how you're going to approach it and contingency plans for survival. Only when you can do that can you pick up a camera and take a picture. . . . You have to put together a phenomenal number of things as far as light and coordination and direction and depth and action to create these images. While you're doing that, you also have to be reminding yourself that you're cave diving and doing one of the most dangerous things on Earth.

The truth is, we are all better off because Wes had that biologically innate drive to explore, and because he also wanted to communicate what he saw. Some of the wonders that he and other cave divers discovered could be documented only by going down there into the deep black unknown. No GPS or X-ray machine or penetrating radar would do the job. The words "environmental hero" get tossed around too much, but Wes was one. Despite a tight-lipped, clannish culture of secrecy among his peers, despite people calling him crazy and warning him not to go further toward danger, Wes became one of the rare cave divers who climbed out of the depths to tell us where our water comes from, where it's going, and what we need to do to keep it clean.

1

Swimming under Sonny's Barbecue

AT THE SONNY'S BARBECUE RESTAURANT outside Gainesville, the lunch crowd is downing sweet iced tea, chicken, and ribs when three men come in the door, looking so odd that every head swivels to get a better look.

The men carry an unusual assemblage of equipment. The first man is small and prototypically nerdy; he wears glasses, a floppy sun hat, shorts, and black socks. His pale skin in midsummer Florida makes him instantly recognizable as Not From Around Here. He's carrying what looks like two pieces of plywood stuck together with a homemade wire handle.

The next man looks local; he's tan, big-armed, and beefy, with a stuffed backpack that has two things sticking out of it—a clutch of red flagging stakes and the hilt of a very large knife. Despite the knife, the man doesn't look menacing. In fact, he has a huge grin and a sense of expectant exhilaration about him.

The last of the three men carries a movie camera and a microphone.

As they move between the booths, they peer at the floor.

"I think they're going this way," says the nerdy one, Brian Pease, eyeing the contraption he's carrying. Between the pieces of plywood, Pease has a coiled antenna that is detecting magnetic signals from a six-inch-long rod of a metallic compound called ferrite.

Below the restaurant, under the ground, beneath a layer of ancient limestone, two expert cave divers carry the ferrite as they swim through inky black caverns and tunnels in the groundwater that flows under Sonny's

Barbecue, four-lane Highway 441, and the strip-mall landscape around the restaurant.

The loop antenna emits a low-frequency magnetic field, so low that it can penetrate the earth.

In the restaurant, the three men look expectant as they peer at the floor.

"'Scuse us," the beefy one, Wes Skiles, says to the crowd. "Underground survey in progress."

Wes says "underground survey" matter-of-factly, but really the whole enterprise is something brand-new and astonishing. This is the first real-time experiment of its kind in Florida, an attempt to explore the course of the state's drinking water from both above and below the ground and to film it for everyone to see.

"They're heading towards the salad bar," Pease reports, eyes down, rushing past bewildered diners.

"Heading towards the salad bar!" Wes echoes. You can hear the "Holy crap!" wonder in his voice. This is actually happening; his wild idea is coming true.

Under Sonny's, the cave divers are swimming through the pitch-black labyrinth, their handheld lights exposing a limestone wonderland that few humans have seen. Florida's aquifer is a place with craggy stone cathedrals big enough to park jumbo jets in; fossilized coral heads from when Florida was a barrier reef under a prehistoric sea; remnant bones of ancient mastodons, whales, sloths, and camels; and rare, specialized life-forms that live without light.

"Next time I dive here, I'll be enjoying the fact that I'm diving underneath my favorite restaurant," Wes says.

The underground signals identifying the divers' positions now lead out of the restaurant. Wes and Pease and the cameraman come out of Sonny's, and sheets of rain suddenly confront them. It was dry just a few moments ago when they went in.

"Oh, great," Wes says, peering at the sky. "It's classic Florida. I mean, how long were we in there, like one minute?"

Where does the water go when it falls from the sky and sluices off underground? This has been Wes's lifelong question. He is one of the best underwater cave divers on the planet, and one of the few who feels a sense of urgency to show us (by "us" I mean those of us confined, by choice, to the planet's surface) what lies beneath our feet.

The film Wes is creating this day at Sonny's Barbecue is called *Water's Journey: Hidden Rivers*, and it is going to become his most memorable and important work. The divers will swim under more than just Sonny's Barbecue. Wes and Pease track them under a golf course, under houses and streets, under the lanes at a bowling alley, and—to really bring it home—the divers swim by someone's wellhead, which is sucking drinking water deep from the aquifer straight to someone's kitchen faucet.

Wes's unusual storytelling approach has made him one of the most effective environmental educators in the state's history. Once you saw *Water's Journey: Hidden Rivers*, which eventually would air on PBS stations across the United States and around the world, you couldn't forget it. You couldn't forget watching scuba divers Jill Heinerth and Tom Morris rising up from a cave through a sinkhole to the surface, where Wes filmed them pawing their way through discarded tires, scary-looking corroded metal drums, and plastic motor oil containers.

In the film, Wes is the friendly explorer and narrator, learning along with us. He looks down at the sinkhole and says: "People are obviously backing up to this place and dumping their garbage right into the sink. And people have no idea, do they? They are thinking that they are getting rid of this, that they're getting it out of their lives. And what they're actually doing is putting it down into their drinking water where they are going to re-consume the very poisons they are trying to run away from."

This message has been percolating in Wes's consciousness in the years since he first set eyes on the liquid blue bowl called Ginnie Spring, just a few miles down the road from Sonny's Barbecue. Ginnie Spring has captivated Wes his whole life, and it will be, in the end, the site of his funeral.

2

Water Boy

WES'S FIRST VISIT TO North Florida's Ginnie Spring is on a winter's day in 1971. He is thirteen, and here on a special mission.

It's a wild place then, and first he has to bushwhack through the thick green tangle that is Florida, spiderwebs hitting his eyes, bugs buzzing his ears, and prickers snagging his shins. Then he's at the edge of a 100-foot-wide swimming hole that looks like some Hollywood movie set of the mythical paradise Shangri-la.

The sun glints off a baby-powder-white sand bottom. Florida's domed sky tints the pool impossibly blue. It's so clear you can see everything—swimming fish, turtles, waving water plants, fallen tree branches; it's as if there's no water there. Below the water's surface, outcroppings of pale craggy limestone shimmer, the prehistoric reef that is Florida's bones.

Then the spring grows deeper and darker toward a shadowy cave entrance at its bottom. Swim into it, and the force of the water coming out of that cave will blow you back.

Cartoony cypress knees poke up around the spring's forested edges, and in the upper branches, gray-green Spanish moss makes lacy veils. The spring empties into the Santa Fe River in a lovely sand-bottomed stream that's lined with arching trees. Where the river meets the spring, there's a visible line between the clear spring flow and the dark, tannin-stained river water.

When Wes looks into that reflecting spring, he knows with sudden certainty that he wants to do more than swim on its surface. He wants to go inside it.

His two companions have sternly warned against it. Wes is with his older brother, Jim, and the Skileses' adult neighbor, Kent Markham. They've traveled here from Jacksonville, where they live in a low-slung middle-class neighborhood that is typical of Florida in the mid-twentieth century. Revolutions may have been unfolding around them—civil rights demonstrations, people protesting the Vietnam War, and the flowering 1960s counterculture—but in the Skiles family it was still a buttoned-up, God-and-country, Baptist church world. Wes and his brother Jim wore buzz cuts; big sister Shirley wore saddle shoes and bobby socks.

Their family life revolved around water. In those days, Jim Skiles remembers, "Mom not only drove us to the beach all the time, but I have vivid memories of walking out of junior high school at the end of the day, where the bus pickup was, and seeing Mom in her blue Valiant with three surfboards loaded on top of the car, waving, like, 'Come on, the surf is good, let's go surfing.' She didn't surf, but she was that good of a mom that she would load up our boards—and the boards were, of course, nine foot six inches. I mean, they were big longboards back then, you know? I was small enough I couldn't even get the board on top of the car by myself. So yeah, that was the kind of mom she was, she constantly put us ahead of her. Wes was young, but I took Wes surfing with me, and Wes fell in love with surfing, too."

Wes's sister Shirley says: "The hardest thing was getting those boys out of the water. Mom and Dad would be giving them the evil eye, you know, 'Now! Get out now!'"

When he reached driving age, Jim would load up surfboards and buddies in his slick black 1953 Ford Fairlane.

"One of the surfing trips, Wes comes running out. 'I want to go! I want to go!'" Jim says. "And I'm thinking, Ugh. And I said, 'All right, Wes, the only spot we have is if you can squat down on the floorboard of the car,' and he goes, 'Okay!' I mean, it was only a twelve-minute ride to the beach or something. He actually got down and crouched on the floorboard under all of the guys' legs. Wes got accustomed at an early age to be in tight spots."

Wes was wild about the outdoors, but in school he was an unmotivated student and had trouble sitting still. He was athletic and might have dedicated himself to the surfer's life, but the coincidence of living near Mr. Markham changed his trajectory.

Kent Markham was a teacher and, in his off time, an inventor. In the mid-1960s, just down the street from the Skiles house, he was creating an unusual device, a futuristic, portable, one-man "sport submarine." Fashioned of plywood, metal tubing, fiberglass, and plastic, it looked like it belonged on the TV cartoon *The Jetsons*. The craft was space-age cool, and if you look at pictures of it today, you see a quirky artifact native to that particular time and place. Just 165 miles down the Atlantic coast, scientists and astronauts at Cape Canaveral were readying the Apollo ship to rocket men up into space and walk on the Moon for the very first time.

Powered by a marine trolling motor, the Markham Sport Submarine had delta wings, a pointed nose, and a pop-up clear bubble over the diver's seat. Coolest of all, an onboard air tank and a battery pack made it possible for a diver to explore underwater without putting on a scuba mask. Markham called it a "semi-dry submarine," because the user's upper body remained dry but the legs and much of the torso were under water. The diver sat breathing comfortably in the air-filled chamber while watching the underwater scenery pass by through a clear "dashboard."

Before Markham could unveil his invention, he had to field-test it. He turned to his enthusiastic young surfer neighbor, Jim Skiles, for that task. Jim was in junior high school and on his way to becoming a YMCA swim teacher and Jacksonville Beach lifeguard when Markham asked him and another teen from the neighborhood to help test-drive the Sport Submarine.

"I think he had two daughters who weren't very interested," Jim explains. "Wes and I were both water bugs. We were fascinated with Jacques Cousteau, and that was the very early days of Jacques Cousteau's show on TV." But Wes was too small to go on the submarine test, and he was crestfallen that he'd been left out of the adventure.

The test run went perfectly. *Popular Mechanics* did a cover story on Markham's invention in June 1968 with the banner "Build This One-Man Sub!" Markham made his plans widely available. If you sent him $6, he'd mail you the details on how to build the Sport Submarine.

Once Markham finished his sub, he started working on something more portable to help scuba divers explore farther and faster through the depths.

By 1971, Wes had taken snorkeling classes at the YMCA pool and was so focused that he got his scuba diving certification at age thirteen. When Markham needed test drivers that year for his underwater scooters, he asked Wes and Jim to come along. Jim recalls:

"Because Wes was so disappointed that he didn't get to go out on the initial trip on the submarine, Mr. Markham said, 'Okay, I'm working on something else.' And it was these little, handheld, early underwater scooters."

In Jacksonville, Markham loaded up Wes, Jim, and the scooters and drove seventy-five miles inland to Ginnie Spring.

"It was wintertime," Jim recalls, "and Mr. Markham had got us full wetsuits."

Ginnie Spring is a constant 72 degrees year round. In the hot summer, the spring water seems freezing, and people squeal with shock when they jump in. In winter, the cold air makes the spring water seem warm.

"You would get down there with that scooter and start scooting along and having so much fun," Jim recounts. "We didn't have tanks on, and all of a sudden you go, 'I'm out of breath!' and have to surface. It was so neat to go out of that spring and swim to the river and do a U-turn back to the spring, because you go from this brown, cold river water and start going back through the spring, and it's like you're going through a warm bath."

A *Popular Mechanics* photographer brought something that day: a Super 8 movie camera. He had made a special Plexiglas box to fit around the camera so he could shoot film underwater. (Up in New England, off Martha's Vineyard, Steven Spielberg was also using a Plexiglas box around his camera to get the haunting swimming shots, half above water and half below, for the landmark shark horror movie *Jaws*.)

Wes was fascinated, and he recalled later:

The photographer had five or six cameras, and he went, "Here, take one of my Nikons and take some pictures." The first thing I did was, I went in the cave. Everyone told me, "Don't go in the cave," but I went in the cave. I got this shot of [my brother] scootering past the entrance, and the shot came out really good. I was hooked from that point on.

That day at Ginnie Spring was the day Wes and the underwater world got hitched for life.

3

The Caves Below

A YEAR AFTER THE SCOOTER test run, a St. Petersburg developer named Robert Wray and his wife, Bobbie, bought the riverfront land that would become Ginnie Springs camping resort.

It was a fine piece of wild Florida. That part of the Santa Fe River is lined with shady cypress swamps and supernatural, undulating limestone formations. Some of the massive bell-bottomed cypress trees have stood there with their pointy knees sticking out of the river's edges for hundreds, if not thousands, of years. Dozens of springs—none as large as Ginnie—pop up all along its length; some are black from forest tannins and some are sky blue.

The Santa Fe is also known among fossil hunters for the treasure trove of prehistoric bones and teeth found on the river bottom and in the springs. Even though it's illegal to remove them without a permit, one house I visited along the Santa Fe had garden beds that were lined with what looked like limestone rocks. But the homeowner pointed out to me that they weren't rocks at all—they were large fossilized mastodon bones and the enormous teeth of prehistoric sharks. His best specimens were inside the house, but he had collected so many in the Santa Fe over the years he used the "extras" in the garden.

The Santa Fe is also famous for a curious natural feature: it abruptly stops at one point and pours down into a large sinkhole. It's an arresting sight to stand at that spot and watch all the debris—leaves, branches, and trash—

swirling slowly into this remote portal leading to Florida's underworld. The river flows underground for the next three miles before popping up again.

This is the crazy-quilt landscape of Florida's karst geologic region, a Swiss-cheese topography where rivers disappear and springs pop up in the middle of deep woods. The only certainty of karst is uncertainty.

For example: At about eleven p.m. on February 28, 2013, a thirty-six-year-old man named Jeremy Bush woke to an explosive sound at his house in the Tampa suburb of Seffner. Then he heard screaming from the room where his brother Jeffrey slept.

"I ran in there, and all I see is this big hole!" he told a local TV reporter. "All I see is the top of his bed. I didn't see anything else, so I jumped in the hole and tried getting him out. The floor was still giving in and the dirt was still going down, but I didn't care. I wanted to save my brother. I could hear him screaming for me, hollering for me. I couldn't do nothin.'"

When the sheriff's department got there, a deputy ran in and pulled the hysterical Jeremy out of the hole that had been his brother's bedroom, likely saving Jeremy's life. Rescuers carefully picked their way around the edges of the damaged house and dangled detection equipment into the hole to look for signs of life, but found none. Jeffrey Bush, a thirty-seven-year-old maintenance worker, had simply vanished into the earth. His hats still hung on the walls next to the dark, yawning sinkhole. His body was never found.

Authorities condemned the house and the houses on either side of it. All were eventually demolished. Government workers filled the hole with gravel, the county bought the land, and the area was fenced off for good.

Two years later, however, it was clear the land was still unstable, because another sinkhole opened there.

IN THE DAYS AFTER the sinkhole swallowed Jeffrey Bush, Jonathan Arthur was on the phone in his Tallahassee office for, it seemed, a solid week. Arthur was Florida's state geologist, and reporters were calling from all over the world about the bizarre event. Patiently Arthur told them what he told everyone, all the time: sinkholes happen, and, most times, you can't predict when or where.

Arthur recalls one notable incident that happened while he was in Tallahassee attending graduate school at Florida State University in the early 1990s. The local fire departments kept the university's geology department phone number handy in case they needed help with sinkholes or other geologic emergencies that might come up. Arthur got the call. About ten miles from the state's Capitol Complex, a woman was tending children in the yard outside a trailer at a day care center in the tiny sand-road community of Woodville.

"She just heard this sound, and looked around, and she saw fingertips at grass level," Arthur said. "The child had punched through the sod, right there behind her."

The woman was able to pull the child—understandably freaked out but thankfully unhurt—out of the hole, which was now deep and steep sided, shooting through limestone that was 10 to 100 million years old.

Florida's limestone substrate is constantly being eroded by slightly acidic groundwater and rainwater. The limestone gets eroded from both above and below, forming the tiny fissures, giant arches, massive caves, and miles-long tunnels that Wes and his dive buddies lived to explore. Florida's so-called basement rocks, which lie a mile under the state's sunny surface, were once part of Africa. They formed even before the Atlantic Ocean. On top of the bedrock lie massive sheets of limestone, dolomite, clays, sands, and gravels.

The limestone is made primarily from the compacted remains of ancient sea creatures. You can sit on a rocky outcropping near a Florida spring, like Ginnie, and spy marine fossils embedded there. Within this limestone labyrinth lies one of the most significant natural resources on the planet, the massive underground reservoir called the Floridan aquifer.

"As much water as you can see in Florida, there is even more of it you cannot," Cynthia Barnett writes in her book *Mirage: Florida and the Vanishing Water of the Eastern U.S.* All told, the Floridan aquifer holds an amount estimated by the Florida Geological Survey at 2.2 quadrillion gallons, equal to about 36 percent of the water in all five Great Lakes.

"Basically, Florida is one giant aquifer," says Gary Knight of the Florida Natural Areas Inventory, a state-funded group that maps Florida's natural resources. "You've got all this pressure in the aquifer, and it is popping up all over the state as springs."

More than a thousand springs have been documented in Florida, and, combined, they pump out more than eight billion gallons of water every day. The region that's ground zero for this fascinating karst landscape lies around the Suwannee, Ichetucknee, and Santa Fe Rivers.

The property that the Wrays bought in 1972 outside High Springs is one of the Santa Fe's most awe-inspiring stretches. Only about twenty miles from the bustle of the University of Florida's Gainesville campus, it is another world. It has five springs with those narrow, sugar-white spring runs leading out to the Santa Fe. Scientists say these little streams are biological powerhouses, like mini aquatic rain forests. Ginnie is the biggest of the springs, with its blue limestone bowl 100 feet across. Just upstream are the craggy, scary-looking holes called Devil's Eye, Devil's Ear, and Little Devil Springs. The Wrays didn't know it in 1972, but the Devil's system would become one of the most popular cave diving destinations in the world, with thirty thousand feet of explorable underground passageways. Every day the springs pump out some eighty million gallons of water—enough to fill more than 120 Olympic-sized swimming pools.

In 1972 there was only one problem in this paradise: it was being trashed. Locals drove in and spent the weekends partying at the springs. They'd drink and throw their bottles in the springs, then shoot bullets into the clear water and smash the bottles to bits, covering the bottoms of the idyllic swimming holes with broken glass. It's hard to believe, but people dumped—and still dump—pickup truck loads of trash straight into the springs. Divers find vehicles (once, an ambulance), washers and dryers, toilets, antifreeze, motor oil, and 55-gallon drums inside spring caves. The Wrays had quite a bit of cleaning up to do.

One day about two years after they bought the property, they drove up from St. Petersburg to spend the weekend sprucing up the place and camping with their three kids, Rhonda, Mark, and Risa.

"There was a young man with a garbage bag, picking up garbage," says Bobbie Wray. "We stopped and talked to him and told him: 'You are trespassing.' And he said: 'Well, yes, I know, but I am trying to be useful. I am going to pick up all the garbage I can.' He said: 'This place is too beautiful to be trashed the way it is.'"

It was Wes, age sixteen.

"We would come up here on the weekends," Bobbie says, "and Wes would be living in a little tent."

At the time, Wes was in high school, working at a dive shop in Jacksonville, and he was coming over to Ginnie with older divers he had met through the shop. All of them were in the vanguard of the new sport of cave diving, and all were obsessed with solving the unpredictable karst landscape's riddles.

"We had a little trailer that we were living in on the weekends," Bobbie Wray says. "Didn't have electricity, didn't have plumbing, but it had a lot of good cooking going on, and Wes would show up at mealtimes, sit on the picnic table with knife and fork in his hand, and I would feed him right along with the rest of the kids.

"He was very self-assured and he always acted older than he was. He was just a really neat kid. And different. Before we opened Ginnie, we hauled twenty-one dump-truck loads of garbage out. Wes was the smart one to pick up the broken glass off the bottom. There were junk cars, old refrigerators, stoves."

There was another problem at Ginnie Springs. Some people were going inside the underwater caverns without proper equipment or training, and they were not coming out alive.

"We asked Wes what he was doing with the scuba diving, because at that point in time there had been probably twenty deaths in Ginnie. It was just a very, very dangerous cave," Bobbie Wray says. "He said that he was teaching himself how to cave dive because there were no schools at the time. No training that was 'official training' in order to survive and learn how to cave dive. So he taught himself. He was very systematic. If he did it and survived, he would do the same thing the next time. He did his first body recovery that summer. He was probably sixteen or seventeen. Wes went in and got the guy out that had trespassed and died.

"We had a meeting that summer with all of the friends of Wes, the cave divers. We asked them: 'What could we do to make it a safe dive?' And they showed us a map of inside Ginnie, and how it could be barred off safely."

Wes hand-penciled a map that painstakingly charted the underwater tunnels and caverns. On a series of dives, he used a compass, a protractor, and a rope that was tied with equally spaced knots to measure distance. Above the map, Wes wrote:

Reason for this fence: 23 men have died past this location. None have died from fence location to entrance. Heavy clay silt is beyond fence location which has help[ed] cause deaths in past along with the extensive cave system causing people to get lost. Most deaths were caused from not having proper equipment and training. Ginnie is a beautiful dive, if at all possible it should remain open. June 26–27, 1976.

The Wrays decided to put a steel grate inside Ginnie Spring to keep divers away from its most treacherous reaches.

"Inside Ginnie Spring, there was a huge ballroom, and then at the backside of the ballroom there was a narrowing of the cave, and then it split after that, narrowing in to multiple passages, which is why it was so dangerous," Bobbie says.

Ginnie Spring's caves also had fine, silty sand. If divers were not careful with their fins, they could stir up an immediate whiteout. Disoriented, confused about which way was up or down, they could die.

"The consensus of all the divers at the time was that if you wanted to make it safe, you could put bars across that narrow opening. And when I say narrow, it was eight feet high and twenty-two feet across down inside of the cave, at the back wall of the cave," Bobbie Wray says. "There were a group of twelve or fourteen divers that volunteered. They came and worked around the clock, putting in the grid, as we call it. We had to special-order the steel. It can't be cut with a hacksaw. The only way you can cut it is with a torch, and no one is likely to be taking a torch down underneath the water. They built three sections of it, and then they drove these spikes in to the ceiling, the sides, and the bottom floor. It looked like teeth."

The metal bars worked to cut the number of dive deaths at Ginnie, and for that, Bobbie Wray credits Wes.

With his common-sense smarts, passion, and diving skill, Wes was becoming a welcome fixture in springs country. At home, he was still surfing Jacksonville Beach and reluctantly attending high school.

"Until he took his scuba diving class, Wes was—and I say this lovingly—probably considered the lazy kid of the family," Wes's brother Jim says. "Wes always had a mechanical ingenuity and curiosity. We've got movies of him lying on his homemade skateboard, rolling underneath his bicycle like he was doing work on his chain. He was probably clipping playing cards on his tires with clothespins to make it sound like a motor. When he was younger, he took the box that a washing machine came in and he cut out holes in it and took a lamp and put a light through it to make it look like it was some type of Wizard of Oz machine. He created his own little magical world.

"Our sister Shirley was the academic. She was the top ten in her class. She was a scholarship college student. I was not as bright as Shirley, but more outgoing and social, involved athletically, and I participated in student government. I had to live up to Shirley's academic standards; Wes had to live up to Shirley's academic standards *and* my athletic and social skills. Wes didn't care a flip about either one of them. Before he found diving, Wes's routine was, come home from school, put the headphones on, listen to music and retreat to his own little world. He had to be encouraged to get his homework done. Wes's fire got lit when he took scuba, and all of a sudden he learned you need to know some math to figure out how to do decompression tables and dive times. Everything all of a sudden got tied into, in his mind, 'I need to know this stuff so I can dive, so I can do this and that.' He always had that mechanical interest, but he didn't apply it until he found the love of diving, and the pieces starting connecting. Then he learned everything he could about the sport."

Wes's childhood friend Allen Skinner remembers: "In his senior year, Wes is building dive lights in his garage. He felt like he could make the lights better. He may have been constructing enclosures for cameras, too. He's not even thinking about going to college."

Wes graduated from Englewood High School in 1976. His sister Shirley drove him home from the ceremony, and she asked him: "Well, what now, Wes?"

"He told me: 'I've just had enough school for a while,'" Shirley says. "Wes learned best by doing."

Diploma in hand, Wes came across an unusual opportunity far away from all he knew in Florida, and he took it. He headed off to work at a hotel in Haiti, where he helped lead people on diving and sailing trips.

"When Wes didn't go to college, I thought he'd be a typical blue-collar guy," Skinner says. "I had that real prejudice, you know, thinking: 'If you're not going to go to college, you won't be successful.' Of course, that wasn't true in Wes's case. It was more important for him to pursue his passion than it was for him to make money. He didn't have that worry of 'Who am I going to be when I grow up?' He figured it out as he went along and didn't worry about it."

After eighteen months in Haiti, Wes was plagued with both amoebic dysentery and dengue fever, and he came back to Florida to get well.

"I got to Haiti with forty dollars in my pocket and stayed for a year and a half exploring around, working at dive shops. It was a very worldly experience," Wes told the *Gainesville Sun* years later. "When I came back, I knew things that other twenty-year-olds didn't know, like, we're not the only society on Earth, and other cultures may see things differently than we do. I got leveled and humbled by the experience."

Back in Jacksonville, Wes went to work at Pro Dive Shop, and he fell back in with the group of elite cave divers who gathered there. Among his mentors was Sheck Exley, who was at the time one of the world-renowned pioneers of cave diving. In 1969 Exley had written the go-to book about the new sport, *The Dixie Cavern Kings Cave Diving Manual*. Like Skiles, Exley was a natural-born cave diver who started in his teens. By the time he was twenty-three, Exley held a world record for the most cave dives—more than a thousand.

To make that record, "Sheck had to average almost three cave dives a week," diver Robert Burgess writes in his 1999 book *The Cave Divers*. "All this during a period in which he graduated from high school, and later the University of Georgia at Athens, which is 600 miles round-trip from the north Florida spring caves he was diving so frequently."

On weekends in the late 1970s, Exley and his dive buddies were pushing the extreme limits of their new sport in the cobalt heart of Florida's springs country. The springs and sinkholes were an inner-planetary wilderness ripe for exploring. Wes was in one of the best places on the planet to do what he loved, and now he was exploring with a true master.

"Of course Sheck was older and Wes was a neophyte," remembers Wes's longtime friend Spencer Slate. "But we all knew Wes was capable, and we all looked up to him as a cave diver. If you do that for a living, you've got to be mature, and you've got to be calm and collected. He was a leader."

When Wes went cave diving, he was never without his camera. He continued working with underwater lighting, to see if he could improve the images that people were getting inside the caves.

"I was using flash-bulbs back then, taking actual flash-bulbs underwater and illuminating cave photographs," Wes told *SCUBA* magazine.

At the dive shop, where Slate taught open-water scuba classes in the evenings, Wes would set up a slide projector to show his cave diving photos. People who saw Wes's early cave images were impressed. Hardly anyone but divers had seen the landscape below the ground's surface. People hadn't imagined it was such an ornate place.

"There was no literature you could go to anywhere, there were no programs, nothing on how the aquifer system was created, what was there, how much water was there, where it was going, or what was the quality of the water," says Paul DeLoach, a cave explorer from Georgia who dove with Exley and Wes. "There was very little documentation, very little discussion of water science, particularly with schoolteachers and educators across the country, and most of the times, when they did bring in someone for an education program, they brought in a hydrologist or a geologist who had never been in those environments. They could talk about what somebody else had said, or something they had read in a well core sampling that a well driller found."

The only way to really know what was going on with the aquifer at the time was to physically go down inside it and swim through the subterranean rivers. One diver remembers swimming through a tunnel and feeling an earthquake start, then hearing a cacophonous rumble. It turned out they were swimming under train tracks. Sometimes, while he and his friends were cave diving, they would know that they were swimming under someone's house because they would suddenly come up on a well casing pipe sticking through the cave ceiling.

"We've banged on the well casings and giggled," Wes recalled, "like someone up above was listening and thinking, 'What the—?' I mean, I'm swimming in your drinking water! It's all such a great, grand mystery. Down there, it's a world of unknowns. You're diving into this cold flow of water. It's sort of an endless question mark as to what's around the next corner. Sometimes it's a tunnel, sometimes it is two tunnels. Sometimes, it's a room. For me, the fascination has always been—where is this water coming from? Could I solve the mystery?"

By this time both Exley and Wes shared the goal of improving the safety of the sport by creating official protocols for training and equipment. Years before, Exley had organized the Dixie Cavern Kings, a group of divers from southern states, and he worked with the National Speleological Society to create a special section of the club for cave diving. Exley was setting world records for longest and deepest cave dives. At the time, many cave divers were obsessed with how deep they could go, and that pursuit was particularly dangerous, says Wes's longtime dive buddy Woody Jasper:

In Europe, Jacques Cousteau had a rope underwater with pieces of slate on it—the idea was that you'd go as far down as you could go and write your name on the slate . . . you were experimenting with depth.

But looking at it now, in the cold gray light of dawn—in retrospect, basically you stopped when somebody died.

In France, a German diver set a record of 476 feet deep into the Fontaine de Vaucluse, 100 feet deeper than Exley's depth record at the time. Jasper didn't see the point.

"Here we have unexplored caves stretching for miles, and these guys are fixated on going deep," he says. "Somebody had planted a flag at 360 feet at the bottom of Diepolder Spring [near Crystal River, on Florida's west coast]. It was referred to as 'saluting the flag.' That meant you'd gone to 360 feet on compressed air and lived. It's a form of roulette."

Divers who go deep and don't spend time decompressing at progressively shallower levels on the way back up risk death. When a diver rises too quickly, it is like opening a soda bottle after you shake it up. The bubbles trapped in a diver's blood or tissues cause decompression sickness, or "the bends," a crippling pain that can kill a diver or cause temporary or permanent physical damage. Rising to the surface in stages allows the bubbles to escape gradually from the body. Another hazard with diving deep is that the oxygen in the compressed air in the scuba tank becomes toxic to a diver's body. Divers can get disoriented, delirious, and, in the worst case, pass out. As Exley writes in his 1994 book *Caverns Measureless to Man*, "The U.S. Navy Diving Manual states that few divers can work effectively below 200 feet."

During the early days of cave diving in springs country, Exley was unnerved to find one Florida spring posted with a huge sign notifying visitors that eight people had died there—which was more than any other cave diving site in the world at that time. "The most ominous thing about the sign," Exley writes, "was that the death toll was shown by an interchangeable number hanging on a nail."

While Exley would continue his efforts all over the world to dive deeper than anyone else, Wes went in a different direction.

"Wes got attracted to exploring caves in North Florida. He didn't get fixated on deep diving like a lot of them," Jasper says. "Wes was a showoff, so it made sense he'd be attracted to the deep diving records. But he didn't go that way. So he was either lucky or smart."

Eventually, deep diving grew safer because divers switched to different gas mixes in their tanks. Early deep diving began with compressed air, and then divers started adding helium to the gas mixture, which made it safer at deeper depths by curbing nitrogen narcosis. Deep divers now frequently take a bottle of oxygen with them, which helps them decompress at the upper levels in less time. Despite taking precautions, Wes got the bends several times in his diving career, with effects so painful that a doctor at a decompression chamber in a Gainesville hospital flat out told him to stop diving for good in 1984, when he was just twenty-six years old.

He didn't listen.

4

Cave Booty

IN 1983, DURING A DIVE with a friend in a spectacular underground North Florida cave system called Peacock Slough, Tom Morris was swimming around picking up trash when a diver they didn't know whizzed past and crashed onto the spring floor nearby. The man looked like he was in deep trouble.

"He's seizing there on the bottom, so I go over to him and he immediately rights himself and points at me and he mimes a belly laugh! He was faking the whole thing. He didn't even know me, but he was pulling a prank on me. Then he points to the trash bag I had and he mouths: 'Real good'! And then he swims off. Later, I was still around there when he came out of the spring after his dive, and we got to talking, and that's how I met Wes."

If Wes's creepy prank had offended Tom Morris that day, he and Wes probably would never have become dive buddies. But Morris got a kick out of the stunt, and the two made plans to dive together shortly thereafter.

Morris was thirty-six at the time, a broad-shouldered Florida biologist who was intrigued by the specialized creatures that dwelled in rivers, lakes, and caves. Like Wes, he grew up in Jacksonville. Morris was eleven years older than Wes, and the two shared certain essential qualities for cave diving—athleticism, an adventurous spirit, fearlessness, and extreme skill. Like Wes, Morris had been diving Florida caves since he was a teenager, starting with rudimentary equipment. He admits that when first trying the sport, he used a flashlight in a plastic bag to see what was inside the stony underwater caverns.

"So I'm lucky I'm alive, right?" Morris says, grinning, when I interview him at his Gainesville home, a place with diving equipment strewn about the backyard in various states of readiness for his next trip into dangerous caverns somewhere on the globe. "There were no pressure gauges back then. We were constantly guessing how much air there was. These old tanks had a little thing called a J-valve, and you pull a little rod and it gives you a couple extra minutes of air—that was your backup."

Once he started diving with Wes, Morris says, he was amazed by Wes's dive skills. He noticed that Wes didn't get winded, even on particularly strenuous dives when they fought strong currents flowing from massive spring caves. Wes didn't panic when equipment failed, or when a cave silted in, or when a tunnel to the next cave room looked too small to get through. He was an exceptional swimmer and was able to stay perfectly parallel in the water.

"His body style, his technique, his understanding, and his intellect allowed him to see water movement so much differently than all the other divers I was associated with," says Jeffrey Haupt, a cave diver who would later work with Wes for many years on film projects. "He was so like a sailor who can see the wind."

Wes also had a gift for seeing things spatially.

"I don't think I knew anybody who could remember a cave better than Wes," Morris says. "That son of a gun—I would never question him. When I did, I was always wrong. Wes had a steel trap memory for that stuff."

BY THE TIME he met Morris, Wes was no longer commuting back and forth between Jacksonville and springs country. He had become a local. Wes was now working at Branford Dive Center, a dive shop in the tiny dot on the map called Branford, an old-timey rural town on the banks of the Suwannee River. Branford had little in the way of culture, but it had what Wes and his friends wanted: plenty of nearby rivers and a vast unexplored karst landscape.

There was another major change in Wes's life—he was married. Wes had met Terri Ann Paulson in Jacksonville, where she was working in a camera shop.

"He had put a camera on layaway, and he wanted to pay it off," Terri Skiles says. "I sold him the camera. It was a Nikon FE. And then he asked me out on a date, and I told him no, because I thought he was weird. He seemed so full of himself—he had braggadocio."

Once Wes saw Terri, he set his sights on her, and his persistence paid off. She was twenty-five, two years older than he was, a petite brunette with a kind, open nature, a sense of humor, and a beautiful smile. Like Wes, she was an artist. She studied visual communication at Florida State University.

"He just kept coming back to the shop," Terri says. "And I finally realized that he wasn't that weird and he was kind of exciting. And I went out on a date with him and that was it. A year and a couple of months later, we were married."

Terri was the daughter of a naval officer (he later earned the rank of admiral), so they were married at the naval air station in Jacksonville on March 7, 1981, before a crowd of 150 friends and relatives. In Branford they rented a little wood-frame Florida "cracker" house for $75 a month. Two hundred years old, it was made of the sturdy southern wood known as heart pine. The house had no central air conditioning to ease the sweltering summers and only a modest kerosene heater for the North Florida winters.

"It was cold, cold, cold in the winter. The water in the toilet froze!" Terri says. "But we really loved that house. We met so many people through that dive shop. They all became our friends through the years and stayed with us and camped in our yard. We were just the host of hundreds of people, I would say. We had good, fun, innocent times."

"If you were part of the elite group of explorers, you knew where to go," says cave diver Jeffrey Haupt, who would make a sixteen-hour round trip from his home in New Orleans to Branford some weekends. "We all used to camp out in the yard and eat breakfast together and go out and have adventures. We used to call it Skiles Campground."

At night people would bring out instruments and tell stories while the sparks from the bonfire swirled into the star-packed sky. Wes and Terri's place in the country had so little artificial light that you could clearly see the Milky Way splashed overhead. In the region's deep woods, the stars reflected off the sinkholes and springs the divers had explored that day. Sometimes the divers loaded up their gear and headed out for night dives. When you are exploring underground, it doesn't matter if you are doing it in daylight or darkness.

The cave divers were young, hungry, and full of energy. Terri was game to learn how to cave dive, so Wes trained her. But she wasn't diving nearly as much as he was. She worked alongside Wes at the dive shop and started her own business designing and hand-screening T-shirts.

"He told me when we first got married that I could not tell him he couldn't go cave diving, because it was just a part of who he was. So I accepted it from the beginning," Terri says. She worried some, but didn't dwell.

"He was just a very, very safe diver. He was an instructor. He was all about diving the *right* way. He constantly was stopping people at different diving places if he saw them doing something that was dangerous."

Wes was meeting the important people who would become his closest dive buddies, the Mole Tribe. A few years before he met Morris, Wes was working in the dive shop in 1980 when he met Woody Jasper. Jasper was a local character with a heavy southern drawl and a wicked sense of humor. Eleven years older than Wes, he had extensive experience finding caves to dive in the region's rivers, woods, and swamps.

"Wes tells me about this cool place to go diving that I hadn't been to," recalls Jasper, whose drawl remains even-toned no matter what hair-raising adventure he's describing. "It was the Lower Orange Grove Sink, which was an interesting place. He drew me a little map."

Lower Orange Grove Sink, when you see it in underwater videos, is simply terrifying. At first it looks okay, a pretty blue sinkhole, going down. Then it's just walls of craggy limestone boulders piled on top of each other with small gaps between the rocks—creepy gaps that cave divers squeeze through.

Jasper remembers that he thought it was unusual for a cave diver like Wes to be so forthcoming about recommending a place to dive. At that time, with so many unexplored caves, so few divers in the area, and trespassing laws being ignored left and right, people kept information to themselves.

"We were competitive," Wes's dive buddy Tom Morris says. "At any one time, there were generally about a dozen cave divers out looking for new places."

"We had leads going, lots more back then than now," Jasper says. "You are exploring a cave, and you keep it a secret because you don't want anybody else to know you're exploring that cave because they may go and pick up where you are and take your cave away from you."

Meaning that they would dive into the cave, find the previous line left by explorers before them, and when they reached the end of that line, they'd tie their own line onto it and get the glory of exploring virgin passages. Cave booty.

"It's politically incorrect to do that," Jasper says. "People used to follow people to figure out where they're going diving. You show up at Branford Dive Shop with two or three of your buddies and a load of cave diving gear, and it wouldn't be unreasonable for somebody else to try to follow you without you knowing it, so they could figure out where you went so they could go explore the cave that you'd found. You might have found this cave by spending ten hours looking at topographical maps, hanging out in a bar for three days to befriend the locals, buying them beer, so they'll start telling you where the stuff is, which was one of my better tricks."

All the cave divers were hoping they'd be the first ever to see a place, just like wilderness and space explorers throughout time. Nowhere was that more possible than in the water-filled cave passages beneath Florida, where they were venturing farther than anyone had before in history. These were the days before GPS; the cave divers all carried crumpled rural road maps and had their diving gear ready to go in pickup beds and car trunks. Once underground, they drew their own maps of places once unknown.

"It's really fun to be in a cave with that reel of line in your hands," Morris says. "You're looking ahead, and nobody's ever been out there before. Cave diving is the ultimate 'What's around the next corner?' And to be the one that discovers what's around the next corner is the best. Once you've heard it from somebody else, it's not new anymore."

"You're exploring," Jasper says, "and you're in flowing water, then suddenly you don't have a flow. Oops, where did the flow go? If the visibility is not good, then it gets harder and harder, so you end up with these real wonderful route-finding challenges. Where the hell did it go? Let's see, if I was a cave what would I do? And suddenly, fifteen feet up this wall that you thought was just the side of the tunnel, is a fifteen-foot-shallower flow coming up from there that you've got to spend some time figuring out where it went."

After Jasper met Wes in the dive shop and Wes provided the lead to the Orange Grove sinkhole, Jasper asked Wes to go with him to an unknown cave system he'd been exploring by the Withlacoochee River, a wild waterway that flows from Georgia south into the Suwannee.

"We go down this little tunnel, and the line stops, and we keep on going," Jasper says.

In a tunnel that's about two and a half feet tall and six to eight feet wide, they reach a mound of silt that blocks their way.

"So when we go through that, it is a complete silt whiteout. Wes keeps going, and I keep following. We're not going to be able to see when we are coming back out, there's no doubt about that. We go through a couple of these little [cave] rooms and finally we get to the third one. It's kind of a dead end, and Wes stops. Surprisingly, to him, I'm still behind him. He's figured that I would have stopped back there, which probably would have been a better thing to do. Wes finds a place to turn around, and we bang around this room a little bit and head out. We probably had fifteen minutes with no visibility at all, whatsoever. I mean, not six inches. That's kind of a bonding experience. Since that worked out all right, we said, 'Let's do some more diving.'"

Jasper was a wry companion, a good cave diver, and he had an important skill: a knack for inventing things. In 1983 he came up with an innovation that changed the way they dove the caves, and it is still in use today. Cave divers who wanted to make it through tight spaces had a recurring logistical problem. They might be crawling through water-filled parallel plates of the earth with only a few feet between the floor and the ceiling and with heavy tanks sticking up on their backs. Or they might need to get through restrictions that were wide enough for their bodies but not wide enough for their bodies and the tanks.

Jasper configured a streamlined way to put the tanks on either side of the diver's body. Called "sidemount," it was based on a similar method British divers were using. With tanks mounted between the shoulder and the hip, there's less resistance, it's easier to change them out for fresh tanks, and it's easier to check the regulators and valves. Sidemounts made cave divers more nimble in the water.

The divers still ended up occasionally doing a death-defying maneuver: sometimes, far back in a cave, they'd reach a hole so small that they had to take the tanks off, push them through, wriggle their bodies through, and grab the tanks on the other side. They had already been doing this with tanks on their backs, but having the tanks on their sides made the maneuver easier and faster.

Another member of the local cave diving community, Mark Leonard, started a company to make dive equipment. Called Dive Rite, it began manufacturing sidemount systems in the 1990s. Wes, Jasper, Lamar Hires,

Mark Long, Ron Simmons, Tom Morris, and other divers would tinker with equipment and dive constantly in the uncharted underwater wilderness.

The cave diver who would become Wes's loyal right-hand man, close friend, and longtime business partner, Pete Butt, moved to High Springs during those days. Butt was a quirky young scientist from "up north" who ran a dive shop and taught diving in Wisconsin. Like Wes, he was singularly focused on diving.

"In Wisconsin," Butt says, "we were diving in iron mining pits. At that time, we realized: we are going to die doing this—we need to get training."

Butt started traveling to North Florida's springs country to take cave diving courses.

"Me and three friends, we'd come down in my van. We'd saved up some money. Back in those days you could take a cavern diving course for fifty bucks. We took a cavern course from Wes. Here I've been a dive instructor up north for years, and I learned more from Wes in those two days. I mean, it just blew me away. I learned a different way of looking at how you dive— that was the big thing. How you rigged your gear, what you needed, what you didn't need, what was practical, what was superfluous," Butt says. "The stuff I was using, I quickly realized, was junk. These cave divers had it going on, they were on the cutting edge of what you call technical diving. It was beyond what any of these wreck divers up north were doing."

As they grew better known in the area for their competence, gregariousness, and energy, Wes and Terri were soon offered jobs at the dive shop at Ginnie Springs, and they quit working at the dive shop in Branford. Butt came to work at Ginnie Springs, too.

"In '83 I show up with my old Dodge van loaded up with whatever I could haul," Butt says. "Then I was living in a trailer and punching the clock at Ginnie Springs."

Butt managed the Ginnie Springs store. It had become a bustling place that rented snorkeling and dive equipment and sold tourist trinkets, outdoor supplies, dive equipment, outdoor books, snacks, and camping supplies. Wes was director of operations. Ginnie Springs' owners now relied on Wes to promote their dive resort and drum up business. Terri worked at the store's counter. Butt was soon a certified cave-diving instructor. He was, however, less interested in the extreme adrenaline-junkie exploration that the Moles were obsessed with.

Wes made dive journal notes on a lot of his explorations throughout his life, and they endure in a stack of weathered notebooks he left behind. Some are bound composition books and some are spiral notebooks, stacked on an office shelf behind his desk. They provide a rare window into those early days underground, as well as ocean dive trips he took. The entries start when he was just twenty-one years old.

3/29/79

Alachua Sink

No narcosis. I guess I got rid of that problem in Haiti.

6/27/79

Dove left prong of main tunnel, approximately 400 feet past half hitch, added 170 feet of line in body-sized tunnel. Lots of clay. Had a few problems getting turned around and finding reel. Solo'ed small section where Sheck couldn't get through.

7/29/79

Peacock Slough

Test scooters. Scooters crap out within 10 minutes of use.

9/23/79

Drift dive, Breakers Reef, almost got ran over by a schooner on the surface.

11/24/79

Lucayan Caverns, Freeport, Bahamas

Love crystalline formations in rooms. Lots of bats in Lucayan Cavern. Orange jello on floors—weird. Neat color changes in strata.

12/29 & 30/79

Morgan Spring

Sneak dive.

Clark got CO2 from poor regulator and I towed Clark, who hung onto my tanks for 250 feet before he regained consciousness. Scary, huh?!

3/15/80

Vortex Spring

Scared a few divers when we came up on them without our lights on.

3/16/80

Vortex Spring

Fantastic wall fossils.

Got into playing with eels during this venture.

3/8/80

West Palm Beach

Played with a moray.

4/13/80

Scott found restriction that I'm sure will lead to something fun.

4/20/80

Dove two singles with new harness strapped to my side, enabled me to pass through really little stuff.

Counted 10 or more turtle shells in this pass, called tunnel 'Turtle Heaven.'

5/30/80

Offshore Day, Florida Keys

Got a big flounder, played 'Chase Shark Away.'

2/13/82

The Jon II

Explored an unusual diagonal fault, ran almost 100 feet before pinching out. Climbing in and out was quite a feat. Also being that it was 50 feet to the water.

6/11/83

Royal Spring

Body recovery, three divers, see accident file for details.

10/28/83

Blue Spring, Madison

I pulled out bone, what appears to be a mastodon, will know later.

2/4/84

Devil's Eye

Found another bone in the capybara room. Seems to be same approximate age of capybara. Took new routes out and identified all tunnels on right after main split.

2/13/84

Indian Spring

Dove downstream to the deep siphon. A very beautiful high-current siphon at 55 feet seems to be accepting all the downstream water. Floor was siltless and walls were beautiful white.

3/6/84

Azure

Found a goat head and a large liquor bottle.

4/26/84

Jail Sink

I just slipped through with side mount. What a sensation, diving with a side mount rig that actually works.

9/27/84

Climax Cave

Woody Jasper and Pete Butt explored the south passage looking for the right way. We did several nifty circuits up to solution domes—going up both passages, looped back out to the main south passage. When we did finally select the passage we thought was it, my hero Woody pushed through feet first, nose up, through an almost completely filled water passage to discover the south passage. What a moment. Pete and I followed. That was really neat, but the rooms we were to discover with diveable sumps even topped that—can't wait to go back.

11/9/84

Bicentennial Cave [a dry cave in Tennessee]

Eight and a half hour trip . . . The lower level rated high amongst the prettiest and most exciting tunnels I have ever entered—also good for climbing and bridge walking. As usual I learned many things, some are: watch wet rope if you know drops are short, take figure 8 and knots when there's lots of caving to do, take more food, spare bulb, buy a little pair of pliers, put knife somewhere else, make a lanyard system for flash camera and bulbs.

12/02/84

Skiles Sink, Green Sink System

Got stuck fairly good at maximum penetration. During attempt to free myself ceiling began to pour rocks and clay—made me a little nervous until I freed myself.

12/14/84

Mystery Cave

Well, I didn't fit, but I tried.

12/16/84

Ellison's Cave [an extensive dry cave in Georgia]

Eight hours. Did the awesome 510 feet off the balcony—what a gas! Did a little flying, couldn't resist. Went slow the rest of the way. Rope acted different with the greater length. Went downstream to

a massive breakdown wall—I climbed through it at three different
levels. All made me stop . . . The climb up took me 30 minutes, I was
taking about 45 steps average before having to rest. What a cave!
Nice pit!
  1984: Ended year with 168 logged dives.

EVEN THOUGH THEIR BACKYARD around the Suwannee, Santa Fe, Ichetucknee, and Withlacoochee Rivers was a cave-diving paradise, the Moles
knew that important exploration opportunities were to be had just south
of Tallahassee, a two-hour drive away, in a landscape called the Woodville
Karst Plain. This plain of ancient limestone had miles of underground caves,
springs, and sinkholes to explore, and they wanted that booty.

"Wes had the fever," Morris says. "Woody had the fever. I had the fever.
After work, we were heading to the springs around Tallahassee, going diving, and coming back and going to work the next morning. We were young
and could do that."

"We're an elite circle," Wes told a South Florida reporter, knowing that
his hubris was earned. "I'd say that ninety-five percent of all virgin passageways in Florida are penetrated by about ten explorers, and we all try to
scoop each other by penetrating a cave that someone else is just starting to
map. It's like we're following each other's scent."

One North Florida spring in particular had always captivated cave divers: Wakulla Spring, about fifteen miles south of the capital. One of the
largest springs in the world, it had been privately owned since the 1930s
by the development and timber baron Edward Ball, who had married into
the DuPont family. In 1937 Ball built an impressive Mediterranean Re-
vival–style lodge on its shoreline. The lodge was used as a private retreat,
but Ball also opened it—and a swimming beach he constructed along the
spring—to day visitors who ate in the restaurant, rode in glass-bottomed
boats, and swam in the cool waters. Access to diving was strictly con-
trolled for decades.

Legendary global cave explorer Bill Stone writes that Wakulla at that
time was "part of a dwindling, finite domain of places on earth never before
seen by man. But even in this niche it is special. The allure of Wakulla is
perhaps best captured in Sheck Exley's 1981 article, entitled 'The Search for
Wakulla.'" Stone quotes:

It might as well be the search for Valhalla. Ask any Florida cave diver what the world's best cave dive is and invariably he will get a faraway look in his eyes and pronounce the name Wakulla Spring with tones of reverence and awe. Its sister-spring, Sally Ward, is so well thought of that cave divers have renamed it Numero Uno. Why all the fuss? Imagine yourself suspended weightlessly in warm, air-clear water with powerful aircraft landing lights, able to fly through giant, apparently endless, 60-meter diameter bore-hole, honed from the purest bone-white limestone, with a prehistoric bone-strewn floor of silvery sand and you get the general idea.

When Ball died in 1981, he left his estate to the DuPonts' charitable Nemours Foundation. The foundation then sold Wakulla Springs, complete with the lodge, to the state of Florida in 1986. The mammoth spring, which cave divers had the chance to legally explore only a handful of times in the 1950s and briefly in 1981, would now become a state park.

If the ancient Roman philosopher Seneca was right that "luck is what happens when preparation meets opportunity," then Wes was about to get very lucky.

Shortly after the state took ownership of Wakulla, Bill Stone applied for, and won, approval for a major exploration mission there. Stone's 1987 United States Deep Caving Team expedition set out to test cave diving's limits at Wakulla Spring and at the adjacent, and possibly connected, Sally Ward Spring. For the expedition, Wes landed his best assignment yet: documenting the groundbreaking Wakulla deep-diving expedition for *National Geographic*.

5

Expedition Wakulla Springs

ON ANY SUNNY SUMMER SATURDAY at Edward Ball Wakulla Springs State Park, the narrow white sand beach is filled with kids splashing in the cold water and college kids sprawled on the grassy lawn. There's a roped-off area for swimming, and lifeguards keep a constant eye out for any alligator that looks like it might cross the line of buoys toward swimmers. A small boat sits at the ready to zoom out from the dock and back off the gators if the reptiles move too close to the swimming area. They keep the gator-scaring boat over at the dock by the spring's edge where canopied, flat-bottomed, open-air boats take groups on slow "jungle" rides all day through the lush Wakulla River swamps.

You can see snorkelers paddling around a large raft in the swimming area and watch people climb up the tall dive tower to plummet down, down, down into the fathomless spring bowl.

Inside the impressive lodge are guest rooms, banquet rooms, a snack bar, and a restaurant. Marble covers the floor and the snack bar counter. The walls in the sixteen-foot-high great room, facing the spring, are made of cypress that is painted with Florida nature scenes. Black metal silhouettes of Florida birds decorate the banister of the curving marble staircase. Edward Ball, who helped build a Florida timber empire, supervised the design and construction of this grand building. The state runs the restaurant and snack bar now, and people come from all over the world to get an eyeful of the industrialist's treasure.

It's safe to say that most visitors don't have a clue about what lies beneath them. Under that lodge, there's a yawning cave room called the Grand Canyon that's big enough to park a Boeing 747 airliner in. And that's just the beginning.

In the fall of 1987, Wakulla was about to give up some of its deepest secrets. Bill Stone's team of twenty explorers and scientists from the United States, Great Britain, and Mexico gathered for a groundbreaking ten-week expedition to explore an underwater landscape that no modern humans had ever seen. Wes, age twenty-nine, was a key player in the adventure. The stakes for him personally had jumped higher than ever before. He was still a risk-seeking cave explorer, but now he was a dad, too. Two months before the Wakulla expedition, thirty-one-year-old Terri had given birth to their first child, Nathan.

By this time Wes had left his regular gig at Ginnie Springs (he still worked for the dive resort as a consultant) and was trying to make it as a photographer, filmmaker, and adventure personality. Cave diving brings glory to the adventurer, but it doesn't necessarily bring cash. He had given up most of his cave diving teaching gigs, because a diver who has suffered a serious case of the bends, like Wes, has to limit his deep-diving exposure or face a lot of pain. Since he was stubborn and refused to heed the doctor's orders to quit diving, Wes still had throbbing pain in his back and shoulder when he ventured deep. He made the hard decision to reserve his deep diving time for the pursuit that was most important to him: exploration. He still earned some money teaching underwater filmmaking classes, because those could happen on relatively shallow dives. Wes was always hustling to earn money, traveling to network with people at dive trade shows and chatting up magazine and television editors.

Having a baby at home motivated him even more to get professional recognition and higher-paying jobs. He knew this Wakulla expedition was key to his *National Geographic* trajectory. If Terri was worried about her husband venturing into this dangerous subterranean experiment while they now had an infant, she didn't let on—she continued to respect Wes's rule. For a few days, Terri visited the expedition. She packed Nathan up in the car in High Springs and traveled two hours north to Wakulla. Wes carried their baby boy around, showing Nathan off to his diver friends, before he went back to work inside the spring.

The expedition had the latest in technology, much of it being used for the first time: a new computer-controlled life support system custom-built by Stone, battery-powered scooters to propel divers through caves faster than they could swim, and personal buoyancy systems to keep divers from shooting up to the cave ceiling or dropping precipitately to its floor. Perhaps the most mind-blowing piece of specialized equipment for the 1987 Wakulla expedition was a giant underwater habitat they built and installed inside the spring bowl. Shaped like a hot-air balloon and filled with pressurized air, the habitat could hold six divers. A system of winches and weights, including a staggering twelve tons of lead ballast, allowed the divers to raise and lower the habitat inside the spring's fast-flowing entrance.

Besides his assignment as *National Geographic* photographer and filmmaker, Wes played several key roles for the expedition, including researcher, logistician, surveyor, and lead exploration diver.

There had been inklings over the years about the treasures that lay inside Wakulla. For one thing, mastodon bones were long visible on the spring's bottom, and efforts to get them out were first documented in the 1800s. The story goes that some of the bones were indeed raised from the depths but were later lost in a shipwreck off North Carolina on their way to a Philadelphia museum. In 1930 a team using a helmeted diver, a raft, a pump, and grappling hooks excavated another full mastodon skeleton, including leg bones weighing fifty pounds apiece. The impressive find is now on exhibit at the Florida Museum of Natural History. Six Florida State University students were able to get permission from Ball in 1955 to go deep diving in the spring. Over four years, they did more than two hundred dives and identified more mastodon bones, as well as bones of an ancient horse, a giant ground sloth, a giant armadillo, a camel, a giant bison, and a tapir. They also recovered more than six hundred bone spear points from the spring—exciting evidence of its long human habitation. Cave divers snuck into Wakulla over the ensuing years, leaving exploration lines tethered inside dark tunnels.

The next officially sanctioned dive attempt happened in 1981, when two divers ventured into the cave system to test new equipment. Riding on new-fangled dive scooters, they were able to enter the vast subterranean chambers and explore nearly a quarter of a mile through the stony wilderness. As Stone wrote in *The Wakulla Springs Project*, "the passage was so large that the walls remained in darkness, even with modern high intensity dive lights."

He also noted that the divers were "equally quick to point out that they were heavily impaired by narcosis."

In 1987 Stone carefully chose the divers who would be part of his cutting-edge *National Geographic* expedition.

"Given the limited number of positions available on the diving team, it was inevitable that personnel selection would be somewhat controversial," Stone wrote. "The criteria, however, were simple and were applied uniformly; all individuals had to be extremely competent cave divers, respected by their peers, able to adapt rapidly to unusual problems and new environments, and be very level-headed—more importantly, they all had to be team players. In the end, these proved to be the correct criteria."

As for Wes, Stone described him with three words: "unstoppable, pure enthusiasm."

"When we got to Wakulla," Stone says, "it was clear that Wes was the best prepared, and that he had put a lot of thought into this."

Dive technology had improved since the last forays into the Wakulla cave system, and Stone would use the best. That included his own invention called the MK1 Cis-Lunar Rebreather, a closed-circuit life support pack about the size of a small desk. To test it, Stone set a record by spending a full twenty-four hours underwater in Wakulla, reading paperback books and dozing while breathing his own exhalations, recycled and scrubbed of carbon dioxide.

"Redundancy, the cave diver's favorite word, was the challenge," Wes explained in an article he wrote about the expedition. "So Bill and Cis-Lunar Labs combined two mixed-gas rebreathers into one. These multiple components included gas supplies, scrubbers, and controls, and they were cross-connected within the system. Finally, computers analyzed and displayed system status, identified problems, and offered solutions. The MK1 weighed 165 pounds fully charged and was substantially larger than a set of standard double tanks, yet a strong diver could still get in and out of the water unassisted. It was an experimental platform, so bulk wasn't a concern, and the MK1 showed the potential for a 50:1 increase over the range of our present systems!"

With cutting-edge technology like Aquazepp scooters, everyone on the expedition knew they would be able to go deeper into Wakulla's cave system than anyone in history.

"When Wes showed up, he said, 'I want to show you something,'" Stone says. "He pulled out these two aluminum, strange-looking gadgets, and everybody says, 'What's that?' and he says, 'Well, you put a stage bottle on either side of this thing, and you strap it to an Aquazepp.'

"I'll never forget the day Tom Morris drove up in a Volkswagen Bug with two Aquazepps—each of which was worth more than the vehicle—strapped on the roof rack."

A major challenge was to prevent the problem that deep divers had experienced in the past: disorientation from nitrogen narcosis. This was a big issue at Wakulla, since the tunnels they wanted to explore were some 300 feet down under the spring—a football field away from Ed Ball's fancy lodge above. Nitrogen narcosis, long nicknamed "the rapture of the deep," could start to make divers feel fuzzy and drunk at a depth of about 100 feet.

"Let's just say that thinking your way out of situations becomes harder to do," says Morris, who was among the divers Stone chose for Wakulla.

By 1987, special breathing gas mixes were available that allowed divers to go deeper and still retain clear thinking. They decided to use heliox—a mixture of helium and oxygen—which Stone recalls as a radical idea at the time. Decompression from heliox was tricky. Divers around the world had long relied on breathing pure oxygen during decompression because it helped to clear any lurking nitrogen bubbles out of their bodies. Until the Wakulla project, the only known method for decompressing on heliox was for divers to use oxygen starting at 50 feet. But this had already led to at least one fatality within the Florida cave diving community, because breathing pure oxygen below 20 feet can cause convulsions. During the Wakulla project a hyperbaric physiologist, Dr. Bill Hamilton, developed the first decompression tables specifically for cave divers using heliox.

For the Wakulla expedition divers, a two-hour dive at a depth of 300 feet would require a whopping fifteen to twenty hours of decompression underwater before they could go back to the surface safely. But that posed another problem. At 69 degrees, Wakulla's deep water was cold enough that divers could get hypothermia after about six hours, even using the best available cold-water diving gear.

What to do? They could send superlong hoses down inside the spring and pump warmer water into special diver's wetsuits, perhaps. Or they could build a warmer decompression facility underwater. That's when the idea of the habitat took shape, a bubble filled with pressurized air, anchored to the bottom, which could be raised and lowered. Before they reached the habitat, a returning exploration party would hang in the water, decompressing as usual, for their first several progressively higher stops. Then, at 60 feet, they would reach the suspended habitat. They could hop on its outer decking, remove their heavy equipment, and finish their final decompression stops in comfort, raising the habitat in stages to the surface. Stone set his sights on building the habitat, with design options debated during an American Academy of Underwater Sciences conference at Florida State University.

"Financing of this expensive experiment had to be arranged," Stone wrote. "The habitat was on the verge of extinction on several occasions. Then, on July 6th, 1987, Roland Puton, President of Rolex USA, sent the following message: 'We have been keenly interested in the Wakulla Springs project from its inception. The dual-purposes of exploration and systems development are both laudable goals and we are delighted to provide funding.' With that single decision, the habitat became reality."

Because Wakulla Springs was a sensitive, treasured ecosystem, state park managers prohibited the expedition from building any permanent equipment on shore. That's why they had to design the habitat to operate independently. They also had to do extensive tinkering to keep the habitat from getting tippy when divers and their heavy equipment climbed aboard. The frame was aluminum tubing and the outside shell a super-tough rubberized nylon similar to the material used for military pontoon bridges. The habitat weighed more than twelve tons. They floated its parts in pieces, using an onshore crane and six-by-ten-foot inflatable bags, then divers assembled the structure inside the spring. They transported the parts across Wakulla's 300-foot basin to a limestone shelf along the spring boil that was about 30 feet underwater. This shelf had been a logistics point for filmmaking at Wakulla in the past, including the classic *Tarzan* movies, *The Creature from the Black Lagoon*, and *Airport '77*.

Right away there was a problem. Two of the 1.3-ton ballast cylinders rolled off the shelf and plummeted 120 feet into Wakulla Spring. They were able to fish one out, using an inflatable lift bag, the next day. The second had sunk deep into the silt and required four days of searching before they found it with a probe rod, 30 feet inside the entrance tunnel. When they tried to raise it, the inflatable bag caught on a jagged rock and ripped open, and the ballast plummeted again. With new bags and more tinkering, they finally recovered the ballast and went back to assembling the habitat. It then became clear that the expedition's electrical needs, to run the compressor systems that filled the many scuba tanks and also pumped air into the habitat, were more than the state park could handle. The expedition paid the power company to install more utility lines, power poles, and transformers—tripling the park's electrical capacity. The habitat was fitted with phone lines so that decompressing divers could call people on the surface. In fact, they could call anyone in the world from in there. That was quite a perk in those days, when long distance was pricey and cell phones weren't yet available. It was very James Bond to call someone across the world while sitting inside a Florida spring. Once they finished building it, they pumped compressed air into the habitat. Nine tons of lead were affixed to its bottom—the equivalent of strapping on six Toyota Camrys—to keep it stable in the fast-flowing spring.

The habitat had a system of dry tubes going down into it so that support people on the surface could send things down to the exploration divers, including takeout food from local restaurants. Inside the habitat, the cave explorers had beach chairs to sit in. They could warm up, eat fried mullet and French fries, doze, play cards, and compare exploration notes. Bottles of pure oxygen were provided to help divers decompress once they got within 30 feet of the spring's surface. To deal with the buildup of carbon dioxide that the divers were exhaling inside the habitat, the expedition created a system to purge it with a clean flow of compressed air.

Wrangling all the moving parts of the dangerous and complex expedition was a challenge, but one Stone was certainly up to. By 1987 he was well known for having led numerous death-defying deep expeditions into Mexico's vast subterranean cave systems. But financing continued to be a concern. In Stone's words:

> We had set up our headquarters in the small concession stand building left over from when Wakulla was a private resort. The expedition was short on cash and we had let this fact be known to our sponsors at *National Geographic*. At that time, the best known underwater photographer at *National Geographic* was Emory Kristof. Not long after sending the emergency note to *National Geographic*, Wes and I were working on gear together in the concession stand when comes a knock on the door.
>
> Wes goes and answers it and there, in a trench coat in the rain, is

Emory Kristof. He walks in, and, doing his best James Cagney imper-sonation, says, "Da boys in DC heard yer message, so dey sent me to deliver de money." Whereupon he opens the trench coat and slaps a $3,000 wad of cash on the table. Then he turns to Wes and says, "Hey kid, I hear you knows how to run a camera underwater?" And Wes is stumbling for words. So Kristof continues, "Well, de boys in the de basement at 17th and M sent me with another present for yuz." And he has his assistant outside bring in several boxes with $20,000 worth of Benthos deep submersible camera gear. He and Wes then disap-peared for some time together, and the next thing we saw was this tank sled that bolted under an Aquazepp carrying all this camera gear. With Emory's encouragement, Wes set off on a mission—one that would become his life's mantra—to get a series of powerful images that would turn heads at *National Geographic*.

Looking back on it, Stone says, "All along that trip I began to see the mak-ings of a superstar. His ability to orchestrate people to be in the right place at the right time and have himself in the right place with the right camera was mesmerizing to watch. It was almost like a choreographed dance. He had it all in his mind, what he wanted, and he knew how to, with a flick of his hand, signal what he wanted somebody to do, and they would understand it—the whole thing would come together."

If the photograph didn't work the way Wes envisioned it, "he'd pull all those people together and say, 'Okay, remember what you did here? We're going to go back and we're going to do it again.' And he did."

It's important to remember that Wes was doing all his photography work in the era before digital imagery. And he was trying to make his name as a photographer by taking pictures in a place with zero available light. He had to carefully plan each shot, because film was expensive to buy and to develop. Each pricey camera he took underwater, inside a waterproof enclo-sure, had a roll of just thirty-six exposures. He couldn't instantly review his photos to see what he had, the way you can today. He would start by scout-ing the cave and identifying cool-looking features and figuring out how he could light them up. By trial and error, Wes learned how the camera sees images.

To create imagery in the pitch black, Wes custom-built his own remote flash sensors and mounted them on backpacks that the divers carried as they swam along. Wes would open the camera shutter, hold himself steady while suspended in the water, and then push a button in his hand to trigger the remote strobe as the divers pointed the lights away from the camera and toward whatever cave feature Wes wanted to illuminate. He'd also have divers positioned behind formations, holding huge powerful movie lights. He used other types of flash technology to freeze movement so divers wouldn't look blurry as they swam through the dark.

Since detailed communication between divers was difficult, Wes would draw the photo's composition beforehand, choreograph each diver's role, and hold rehearsals with the divers before they went underground.

"He could actually kind of scream and talk underwater, so you definitely knew when you were doing something he didn't like," says Kenny Broad, a longtime friend and fellow cave explorer who worked on many of Wes's cave films and photography sessions.

Although the expedition at Wakulla was a major international event in the realm of inner-planetary exploration, very few people living in the surrounding Spanish-moss-draped landscape of sand roads, rusty house trailers, country churches, and barbecue joints even knew what was happening there until much later.

"Never before had I been part of an expedition as equipment intensive," Wes would write in a 1990 article for *Ocean Realm* magazine. "Through the generous support of many sponsors, including ITV-4 of Great Britain and the National Geographic Society, we had the latest in technology that we needed to pull this off. We would be going deep, and this meant a trailer full of premixed heliox, filling systems, and lots of cylinders. . . . Capturing the expedition on film was a priority. Rooms were filled with still cameras, strobes, movie and video cameras, their lights, and endless arrays of batteries and chargers."

The plan was for divers to drop little piles of air tanks at intervals in Wakulla's tunnels, creating "safety stations" where they could get more air along the way during exploration. Wes went further, designing those special sleds to carry spare air tanks behind some of the Aquazepp scooters. In keeping with their *Star Trek*–like mission to "boldly go where no one has gone before," the Wakulla sleds were named *Enterprise I* and *Enterprise II*, after *Trek*'s starship *Enterprise*.

The amazing Aquazepp dive scooters could take divers much farther into the tunnels than they could go on their own. The flip side was that if a scooter failed, a diver might get stuck too far back to swim out safely. This is where the buddy system was critical: if someone's scooter failed—and diver Sheck Exley's did—the buddy could use his or her scooter to tow the disabled rig and its diver to safety. The scooters turned out to be powerful beasts that were difficult to control. Wes made extensive modifications to his, adding a pair of skis to make it easier to land without causing a silt whiteout, and eventually creating special holders for his cameras, lights, and dive gear.

"It was raining hard the first day I ever dived Wakulla Springs; the granddaddy of all Florida springs," Wes wrote. "Its size humbles. It contains a history as rich as the creation of earth itself and perhaps a significant message for our future. . . . I descended from the bank of the spring and drifted effortlessly toward its large gaping entrance. . . . Trying to keep calm as I shot some film, I moved toward the bottom. Looking down, I felt chills run through me as I saw directly in front of me the remains of a great mastodon scattered on the floor."

The divers imagined that one main tunnel would lead away from Wakulla's main spring, but they soon reached a second tunnel, and the divers split up. Some mapped the A tunnel, and some mapped the B tunnel. As they moved deeper into the cave system, more and more tunnels led off into the cold dark. Soon they were up to the letter G.

Exploring the B tunnel, Skiles and his dive buddies were following a passage that was rising, as if on a hill. Then they were in a giant room, at least a football field wide and nearly as tall. In its center stood a pile of rocks, with a rectangular white stone standing on its edge on the top. It was natural rock accumulation, but it looked intentional.

"There it was," Wes told author Robert Burgess for his book *The Cave Divers*. "The rock slab similar to the monolith in the movie *2001: A Space Odyssey*. It flashed through my mind that here we were exploring an alien landscape, in one sense, using advanced technology to visit and explore an unknown world, while in another sense we were the most primitive of beings. The irony of it struck me. There was the monolith sitting there. It was seven feet tall, three feet wide and pure white. We all felt it. It gave us chills!"

"Inside the habitat, we were ecstatic about our discovery," Wes wrote in *Ocean Realm*. "We all agreed to dub it the Monolith Chamber, considering the setting and the circumstance. Rob asked, 'What if it's not there when we go back on the next dive?' With vocal cords still under the effect of pressure, I hummed the *Twilight Zone* theme in a Donald Duck voice."

Wes not only had to help plan dives, explore and map the caves, and coordinate research, he was also documenting it all for *National Geographic* on film and in photographs. He used still cameras and a 16 mm film camera—*National Geographic*'s Arriflex, fitted with a waterproof housing that measured about 12 by 18 inches. Inside the underwater tunnels and caverns, he had to perform an awkward maneuver, holding the large camera in one hand and carrying a bulky filming light in the other, which left him no hands for steering his scooter. His solution was to grip the scooter tightly with his legs like a rodeo trick rider and steer the best he could.

"That's how I went through the cave filming," Wes told Burgess for *The Cave Divers*. "The others were getting to lay the line and I filmed it. I would scooter ahead, stop, get off the vehicle in 350 feet of water and film them go by, then get on my vehicle, race ahead, get off, and film again. It took incredible concentration."

"After all those grueling trips filming the team's progress with the large movie camera," Burgess recounts, "Skiles came up only to be told that the rear lens element of the Arriflex had fallen off. Everything he had filmed for the *National Geographic* and television was out of focus!"

"At first I just sat inside the habitat in shocked disbelief," Wes told Burgess. "I had put so much effort into it. You see, I thought the filming was over. I had put it behind me. I was savoring the fact that I was going to get to go exploring the cave after my filming objective. The next time, *I* was going to be the one pushing the unknown with the reel in my hand. There were only a couple of days left on the expedition, and it set me back right to the beginning again."

Burgess picks up the tale:

Skiles' next reaction was to say "No. Too bad. That's the end of it." But after he slept on it, he realized that the filming was more important to him. Throughout the dive, he had been shooting video as well as film. The small video camera was mounted in an unobtrusive way so that it shot everything that occurred. Now, Skiles determined to rig an upright pole behind him so that the movie camera would shoot over his shoulder and get a bird's eye view of everything they did. At the same time he would continue shooting video. This was it. He had maybe only three dives left before the whole thing would be over. As soon as he tried out his idea, he realized the Aquazepp was almost impossible to drive with its unfamiliar load. Skiles had to move the vehicle's balancing weights to counter the backward pull of the big camera. He admits now the idea was impractical, but in his fascination of the moment it seemed the only logical solution.

"It was like attaching a year's harvest of watermelons onto an airplane wing and expecting the airplane to fly," he said. "But I went scootering off into the cave, mad and determined to film and videotape. I got down to this critical point where we were diving at a 45-degree angle down into this pit with this tremendous flow then you have to level back and head up into the Monolith. Suddenly, I misjudged where I was going and the line caught the camera. Instantly the vehicle swung up uncontrollably, dropping its 26-pound ballast weight. My vehicle is now close to 30 pounds positive and instead of calling the dive I was just so absolutely determined to ride it out, that I twisted into a line entanglement that I almost didn't come out of. I landed on the floor and signaled everybody that I was in trouble. They stopped. The current was ferocious. The coming together of these vehicles was almost suicidal. You can't very well let go of them and you can't get off of them in this kind of difficult place. One of the divers, Rob Parker, bailed out and helped extricate me from a very dangerous entanglement at 321 feet. A tank of gas lasts 30 breaths at that depth. Thirty breaths and it's gone. We had eight tanks collectively on us. But this was a one-tank solution and we were already three tanks into the dive. So suddenly I just . . . this was where I momentarily lost sight of my objectives as far as safety was concerned. The vehicle started getting even more buoyant. Also, my dry suit was now inflating. I had to get the expanding gas out of my dry suit. I started rising faster, being pulled up at a blood-boiling rate of ascent toward the ceiling. If I hit the ceiling, I would be dead. The bends would take me so fast from the fast-forming bubbles in my blood, it would be almost instantaneous. . . . So there I was—feet down, head up—holding onto a vehicle that was ballooning me to the ceiling. I thought, let go of the vehicle and all three of us are going to die. Continue on this ascent, and I'm going to die. I managed to let go of many thousands of dollars worth of camera equipment at that point, that being a very low priority. I managed to hook my arm and deflate my drysuit at the same time. Then I made one major effort to get me and the vehicle back down to depth, down to the Monolith. I managed to get down and grab hold of rocks and Rob came in and tried to hold me down for a minute. I was at that point . . . It was like someone saying goodbyes, but really not . . . The whole world was there, all existence being that moment, and saying to yourself . . . I can't believe I've done this, I can't believe I'm in this situation. I felt awful. It was like a combination of wanting to throw up and pass out.

"Getting out of the cave was the only choice I had. I got on the vehicle and forced its nose down. It was the only way to make it go. Force it down and push it forward. I had 2,600 feet to go like that with less than half my gas I needed to get out. But we had some safety stations along the way. We made it to the safety stations and by then my attitude had vastly improved. Rob carried out the camera and we got to decompression. I cut the vehicle loose, tied a line to it, and it went kiting to the surface. There was no way to hold onto it anymore; I was exhausted. The vehicle hit the surface like a jet crash-landing on an airstrip. The topside team knew at once that something had gone wrong down below. The decompression chamber was ready, the people were ready for a bad outcome. But as it turned out everything was all right."

The irony of it all was that Skiles still hadn't filmed. Some footage was shot but it wasn't enough. So, with only two dives left to go in the project, back the camera team went again with the camera where it belonged and the weights on the vehicle realigned.

This time everything clicked. They shot a stunning 400 feet of film, most of which was used virtually unedited in the *National Geographic* special on the exploration. It was a total team effort, a collective victory.

By December 2 the expedition was winding down. A British film team that had also been documenting the expedition left for home. A small group, including Wes, stayed to help dismantle the habitat and wrap things up. They embarked on one of their last Wakulla dives. "Equipped with a *National Geographic* Benthos camera (the same type used to photograph the

Titanic) I began to expose the first frames of a 400-frame load," Wes wrote in *Ocean Realm*. "Two frames later, at 280 feet, the camera stopped working. I peered into the power pack to see a mixture of smoke and water through the lens. I clearly remember clipping off the camera to the line fearing it may blow up. I shrugged, said 'whoops' to myself, then scootered off to catch up with the guys."

His dive buddies, Paul Heinerth and Morris, then saw a rare sight: Wes speeding by them, without his camera in hand. Suddenly freed from the burdens of photography and filmmaking, Wes was now going to be able to indulge in pure exploration in one of the most wondrous virgin underground cave systems in the world. He described the day in *Ocean Realm*:

> We felt confident, had the perfect mindset, and an almost magical feeling about what was ahead of us. At the end of the "B" tunnel line, 2,500 feet in, we tied off. Soon this tunnel gave way to a very straight section and 800 feet of line had spilled off my reel before I knew it. As I stopped to tie off, Tom landed nearby and collected one of the largest crayfish specimens we had yet seen.
>
> Another 600 feet of line was soon being released through our increasingly complex tunnel, with runs and offshoots appearing before us. Tied off, with gauges checked, the third reel was now out in front, and we entered a "sneaky" tunnel, littered with bones and decorated with "goethite" cave mineral formations. We reached a room with a deep lead dropping down to lay the last of our line. We had been successful so far in our push with survey work ahead of us, it was time to scramble.

"Wes did most of the laying of the new line," Heinerth recalls. "At the last reel, he motioned for me to lay it. I said no, he should lay it, as he was so good at it. He insisted. We had this verbal exchange at 300 feet deep, almost 4,000 feet in. With Wes's approving nod, I went for it."

Heinerth, Morris, and Wes ended up making history that day for the farthest-ever exploration inside Wakulla: 4,176 feet, a record that stood for at least seven years.

"The last thing that had to be done was to survey," Wes told Burgess. "My pet peeve for years has been: Don't explore unless you survey. Exploration does no one any good unless you bring out the data. I hate being a purist, but it's true. Without a map, the benefits of the entire project would be erased."

Burgess in *The Cave Divers* describes what happened next:

Skiles began mapping his way back. It entailed counting the knots on the survey line they had laid coming in, a knot every ten feet. At each knot he put a depth gauge on that station and recorded the depth. Then he shot an azimuth, or compass bearing. After that, he went on to the next knot and repeated the procedure. As he progressed along the passageway he looked left and right, then at the ceiling and the floor, noting on his slate any side tunnels, type of floor sediments, any unusual geological features while also jotting down the dimensions of the passageway. At each new depth, each new azimuth or change in cross section, he repeated the process, then started counting knots again. The whole thing involves extreme mental discipline. Skiles mapped his way out of the extreme penetration, highly elated by the experience. As he later described it: "It was an incredible ending to be passing through all those chambers and tunnels and rising up into the Monolith and saying goodbye to it in solitude, journeying back down to the deepest point in the cave."

They had explored nearly a mile from the spring's entrance at 300 feet deep—a new world record. Skiles wrote:

Fourteen hours later, at 2 a.m., we surfaced to 22 degrees Fahrenheit surface temperatures. The celebration of our achievement was shared with Jim Taylor, a close friend of mine, and the only person crazy enough to stand on a dock in 20 degrees Fahrenheit weather watching us decompress inside a giant beach ball. (Jim later commented that cave diving certainly doesn't rate very high as a spectator sport.)

It had been an incredible three months for me. Through the efforts and judgment of the more than 20 people that made up the team, things went smoothly and safely; no one was injured during the entire operation. Scientific projects were productive, and a television documentary has since been produced from the film shot. We saw a taste of things to come in the MK1 rebreather. Most importantly, exploration cave divers, state agencies, and scientists from multiple disciplines cooperated to reveal secrets long held by the famous and little-understood Wakulla Springs. Plans are underway for our return to Wakulla in 1992.

Unfortunately for Wes, the dynamic still photographs he worked so hard to get in the lightless tunnels of the Wakulla cave system never ended up in *National Geographic* magazine. The story was laid out, ready to go, with Wes's photos in it, and editors cut it to make room for stories about the magazine's centennial instead.

"Basically, we had the bad timing to show up right when they decided to do their centennial series of issues," Stone says. "The article never got published."

Wes's video became a documentary that British television bought, and later *National Geographic* bought the rights and it aired in some American markets.

"His shot 'Phantoms of the Cube Room' in Sally Ward Spring, and others of divers riding Aquazepps into the Grand Canyon of Wakulla—suspended in blackness as if flying in space—became the centerpieces of the book that was written about the project," Stone writes, in a tribute he penned after Wes's death. "That book, propelled by Wes' stunning photos, was one of the principal catalysts of what later became known as the Technical Diving revolution."

Climbing out of Wakulla Spring that freezing December night, helping set a new world cave diving record, finally getting hired by *National Geographic*, father to a newborn son, Wes was at the top of his game.

Just ten months later, Wes and Terri would leave their toddler son Nathan in the care of his grandparents in Jacksonville while they traveled across the globe to their new assignment—a two-month expedition into a cave system in the remote Australian desert. And Wes would be the subject of this screaming headline in an Australian newspaper:

13 BURIED ALIVE!

6

Buried Alive

LET'S HEAR HOW WES BEGINS this story for the *National Speleological Society News*:

The Nullarbor Plain is a large, treeless expanse above the southern coast of south and western Australia. Hot, dry, dusty and uninviting overall, it fits the classic image that most envision when the word "Outback" is mentioned, but the Nullarbor also is one of the largest masses of limestone in the world, and contains caves of incredible beauty and challenge—many as yet unexplored. Woven deeply into the local Aborigine "dream time" folklore, these caves have now drawn modern men into their power; many of them friends of mine who now keep returning to this hostile place.

That's the reason my wife, Terri, and I were on a plane in late October 1988 heading for Sydney. I had been hired as a cameraman and director of underground filming for production of a one-hour-long documentary on the next phase of exploration in the Nullarbor—a place called Pannikin Plain Cave. This cave, like most in the area, is water-filled to varying degrees. This meant cave diving; the focus of the expedition was to put a team of divers farther back than anyone had previously penetrated. I was to film it all above and below the water....

The idea of travelling to a strange continent, going to the middle of a desert, then to go underground and underwater was very appealing.

On November 12, Wes and Terri arrived in a Western Australian landscape that looked like the surface of the Moon. Their destination was a gash in the ground that led to the extensive Pannikin Plain cave system. Below that gnarly hole in the pale brown desert, there was a chamber the size of a football stadium. Wes and Terri and the rest of the international explorers set up the expedition's main camp topside, next to the cave hole.

Their Outback camp had generators for electricity, a field kitchen to cook the high-calorie meals that divers needed, a reverse osmosis desalination system to make clean drinking water, and air compressors to fill scuba tanks. The team began the laborious task of climbing through dry caves to get to the beginning of the water-filled cave system 300 feet below. They had to navigate sheer 50- and 60-foot drops and piles of treacherous boulders, ferrying massive loads of equipment to the Lake Room, the subterranean shoreline where they would begin their daily dives. They laid 600 feet of copper pipe to send compressed air to fill their tanks below ground, and strung nearly 200 feet of steel wire to make a trolley system to ferry equipment up and down.

"After five days," Wes writes, "we had nearly five tons of equipment in place at the beach and were on schedule. The next phase was soon to begin. Minds, bodies, and equipment were primed and ready."

Once suited up and cave diving, video camera in hand, Wes reached his happy place.

> I felt as though I were filming a hallucination of sorts, the divers' multi-colored exposure suits, helmet lights, and quadruple tanks making them appear as men from space riding into the unknown, on rigs that looked like robotic dogsleds. As our lights cut through the darkness ahead, guide-lines spooled off automatically behind us. The stillness and quiet of the cave revealed beautiful geologic formations, the cave becoming so large at times that the feel of water rushing past us was the only way to tell we were moving.

More than 3,000 feet back inside the system, they reached a room they named the Concorde Chamber, because it had a sleek subterranean rock that looked like the international supersonic jetliner. The room was spectacular—1,000 feet long, 200 feet wide, and 100 feet tall—and it became an expedition staging area. The air sealed in the chamber had low oxygen and elevated carbon dioxide, making physical tasks especially exhausting. Wes's story continues:

Sleeping bags, food, stoves, cinema lights, tripods, and a wide variety of other support gear were unloaded from the sleds. Supplies were cached here, a cave radio was set up for communications with the surface team, and equipment was moved over the rock pile for the dives ahead. This would be a place to rest, to eat, and to vent out the excess nitrogen in our bodies between the forays in and out.

. . . Beyond this chamber, the second lake beckoned, and here I saw one of the largest underwater chambers imaginable. Again, speed of travel became a relative sensation as the distant walls and bottom made me feel as though I were in a plane high above the ground. I had never felt so small in my life.

The divers spent fifty-four hours underground and traveled 1.4 miles from the Earth's surface. For the next three weeks they continued surveying the cave system, spending hours decompressing, and taking breaks at the topside camp to purge nitrogen from their bodies. Wes was the guy bustling around everyone, moving lights and cameras into position.

The last day of the expedition, December 2nd, saw the last three divers and the support gear leaving the Concorde Chamber heading out. I was setting up cinema gear at the midway point to film the transport of equipment from the cave. Excited voices suddenly came echoing down from the entrance. Three team members, now on the surface, had seen a menacing storm cloud rapidly heading in our direction. Terri yelled this information down to the two people above me, who relayed it down to us. Knowing this cave, like any other, is basically a natural drain, I didn't like what I was hearing. The next sound to fill my ears was that of rushing water. "I don't like this!" I yelled. "Pick up your gear and head to the lake!"

Water roared into the cave above them.

The air around me quickly changed, its stillness whipping into a wind, and now charged with the fresh smell of negative ions that filled my nose and lungs. Sixty feet above me at the vertical drop, a wall of brown water filled with small rocks poured over the top. It cascaded down, ungluing the boulders and rocks that made up the passage—an already unstable place. Adrenaline pumped through my system as

I turned and rushed back down into the cave, the specter of being crushed and drowned simultaneously—a very real threat.

At the midpoint, eight people and equipment were waiting. "Get down, and quick!" I yelled. "Leave everything where it is—the equipment is not worth our lives." I was not about to predict when the boulders above us would let loose. Everyone hustled down the slope into the Lake Room. Behind us, over $80,000 worth of equipment, lights, cameras, film, SCUBA cylinders, left behind. . . . With thunder and crashing boulders at our heels, we all made it to our refuge, and then watched the cave passage disappear above us.

Three submerged divers who had been exploring underwater now surfaced in the cave room to the frenetic sight of their expedition team members running for their lives.

We'd all made it this far, but we feared the worst for Andrew Wight and Vicki Bonwick—the two that had relayed the warning and probably saved our lives. For the next hour and a half, rockslides continued, and water poured past us into the Lake Room. I kept thinking that we would still have a chance to find an exit out. . . . Above us, the "guts" of the cave entrance passage let loose, the noise filling us with instant terror. Now tons of rock exploded over the top of the Lake Room slope, throwing pieces of our abandoned gear ahead of it. If I was to die in this cave, it would be now. . . .

Minutes passed, the ceiling held, and the air was not compressed to a lethal blast. After the big crash, the continuing cascade of muddy water would loosen and bring down a few tons of rock every 15 minutes or so. We sat tight, waiting with the feeling that we were almost certainly entombed, and that two of our friends had not survived the initial collapses. I also had my own deep fears and concern for Terri's condition.

Topside, Terri and the rest of the crew had taken refuge in a big heavy trailer when the freak storm blew in.

"I just sat there and prayed that we would live though it," Terri says. "It lasted maybe fifteen minutes. And when the storm was through, we get out of the trailer and our camp is gone. All the tents are sucked up in the air, we can see them way out. The cars are moved. There's so much water it topped our rain gauge—our rain gauge was eight inches.

"And we were just going, 'WOW! No one will believe this story!' So we walk over to the edge of the cave. What we didn't realize was, this water that was massively dumped where we were, all that water was flowing into the cave. We get to the edge, and we couldn't believe it. The tanks we had been pulling out were flowing back into the cave and hitting and exploding. We knew that these guys were going to be in major trouble. And then we were hearing tremendous rocks move underground, you could just feel the ground was shaking as the water poured in."

Below ground, it took three and a half hours for the crashing sounds to stop. Two expedition members started to carefully climb the rock pile that entombed them, looking for a possible route out. Shortly after they climbed away, the team members in the Lake Room heard a huge crash, and they feared their friends had been crushed. "It was a great relief," Wes wrote, "to see them dashing back in our direction."

Luckily, the trapped cave divers still had some food, some warm sleeping gear, and the ground-penetrating cave radio. "As the radio was quickly set up, we inventoried our water supply," Wes recounted. "We began to supplement it by skimming the muddy fresh water off the top of the salty cave water and letting the mud settle out. The radio clicked to life and we were in communication with the surface team. We told them that 13 of us were alive and well in the Lake Room."

They heard good news from above ground, too—no one was injured. The twenty-five-minute superstorm packed 200-mile-an-hour winds and dumped twice the amount of rain the area normally got in a year. The expedition members later found some of their heavy diving gear lying on the desert more than a mile away. Down below, trapped by the cave-in, the team inventoried water, food, and battery power. In the wet cave, the team members were starting to get seriously chilled. Wes and another team member, Rob Palmer, decided to try to climb to the midpoint—the spot where Wes was when the cave-in started—to see if they could salvage any supplies, especially wetsuits. Wes's account resumes:

I'll never forget the mixed emotions I experienced at that moment. I felt like I was playing a role in a horror movie. There I was, walking towards a force and condition which could crush me at any second. Logically, one should scream and run away. Instead I pursued Rob's path toward the ominous wall of freshly fallen rock. As we approached the base of the rock pile, I could see the route that we had used to trek in was now gone. What was once an archway at the top of the rock pile was completely filled in, floor to ceiling. The cable of our flying fox [trolley system] hung limply out from the tons of fallen boulders. Several tanks poked part way out from the rocks, but most of the cylinders were buried and would never be seen again.

My heart raced as we climbed around, and past, our first obstacles. Rob had located a route that would take us around the first collapse zone. After several minutes of very delicate climbing on a near-vertical face, we had made it to the room I had been filming earlier. I stood on a slippery, mud-coated rock, and stared down in disbelief at this room. Everything I had left there was gone. Worse, I didn't even recognize where I was. Hundreds of tons of new rock had filled in all the room and buried almost all of our gear.

Amazingly, they found two of Wes's camera cases, intact, with cameras unharmed. They also found a few bags with clothes, a wetsuit, and a piece of carpet—a warming barrier from the cold rocks they huddled on.

Back with the team, these items were divvied up and gulps of precious water were passed around. The scheduled radio transmission with the surface told us we were making headlines. State emergency services teams, police, and military units were on the way.

The U.S. Cave Rescue Team was on alert, and there was talk of bringing in the U.S. military with a special rock drill. Even so, Wes wrote:

As I tried to shiver off to sleep, I knew that we could not count on outside help. Our best hopes for rescue were with ourselves and the other team members on the surface.

Around 7:00 the following morning, our team of 13 began to stir. As I awoke, I realized that my head had rolled off my wetsuit "pillow" and I had been sleeping for some time with my face in bat guano. I started shooting some video and we made plans. Perishable food had to be eaten first, and my breakfast ration was a gooey wad that Rob smeared into my hand—it was a bite of three-day-old bologna sandwich and I shut my eyes as I gulped it down. Good morning campers!

Rob and I again headed up, getting 40 feet further up than before and seeing potential ways to continue. At about 2:00 p.m. on the surface, Vicki Bonwick put her 25 years of experience to the test, rappelling down through a body-sized tube into an extremely unstable area of the cave. Reaching a ledge she hoped would still be there, she began to search for routes through the breakdown. Some routes didn't "go," others had rocks so precariously perched that to touch them could mean death. Finally, a sloping squeeze with a 50-foot drop below it allowed Vicki, feet first, to rappel to a ledge that looked vaguely familiar. There she found a piece of our hand-line. She was on the way to us.

Wes and two other men were trying to climb out, stringing a line to help others past unstable areas. "Fifty feet beyond our last climb," he wrote, "we met Vicki, who looked to us like a goddess in a white helmet."

They wanted to shout with relief, but knew that whispering was the better option in a place filled with teetering rocks. They whispered a plan, and Wes and another team member went back to bring up the others, two at a time. Rescuers above dropped a cable ladder into the cave, and one by one, all thirteen buried team members made it out unharmed. In Wes's words:

> After many dicey moments within the past 29 hours, it felt good to be alive and on the surface. In all my years of diving and exploring, this was the closest I came to the "envelope of death." Only on its edges before, this was the first time I felt myself being drawn into it.

The freak desert storm got them all thinking, and Wes found himself focusing on the spiritual aspects of the near-death adventure.

> To us, caves are simply fascinating, natural places to explore. To Aborigines, these caves have deep sacred meaning. Curious as to our motives and methods, local Aborigines would visit us regularly telling us incredible stories, especially about spirits that even now inhabited the caves. They would never enter the caves lest they disturb them. Inside the cave, I'm sure that more than one member looked over their shoulder to see if a "woodaagie" was there; these were playful and mischievous spirits we were told that inhabited the caves. They would tug at your hair and then disappear, and otherwise taunt and tease. They could also scare a person to death. I have no doubt of that latter ability after our final ordeal with the storm and avalanche.
>
> Another type of spirit who also lived in and around the caves, the "Wajanaa," protected this cave and, within it, the sacred story

of human creation. These were good spirits, we were told, and they inhabited the bodies of snakes. All snakes in the area, poisonous or not, eventually gained an additional level of respect from us.

As our stay wore on, isolated from the main body of our modern culture in a strange and timeless landscape, these stories would more and more occupy our minds. . . . Three days before the avalanche, team members spotted a six-foot-long brown snake—a poisonous species—near the entrance. Later in the day, I saw it 80 feet down in the cave.

For the next three days, it kept appearing to us on the path down to the cave. Repeated efforts to scare off the snake were futile. After our escape from the cave following the disaster, expedition members went over to the ocean for a swim. As they were swimming, dolphins swam around them in a figure eight pattern, then vanished. The team returned to the cave [camp] to watch the sunset. As they sat enjoying the spectacular visuals of the dying sun, the snake that had been on the trail reappeared. As if possessed by the Wajanaa spirits, the snake rose proudly to face the team. Seconds later it collapsed, falling and vanishing from sight.

Rising and walking away from the cave for the last time, they were all aware of the freaky nature of this place. Events such as these no longer went unnoticed as they might have when we first arrived. It was easier now—and more tempting—to look for meanings and interpretations in them. Perhaps the Wajanaa spirit, having seen us through our ordeal, was now free to leave the snake as we were now free to leave this sacred place.

7

How to Succeed in Business

FACING DEATH IN THE AUSTRALIAN DESERT might make some couples reevaluate their life choices. Terri and Wes really didn't miss a beat. They continued the odd juxtaposition of their lives, a mixture of bucolic homespun routines in Florida interspersed with episodes of exotic danger abroad.

It was the late 1980s in Florida, and the state had a new, business-friendly Republican governor and a development boom going on. A prodigious amount of cash from the state's biggest business lobbyists had helped Tampa politico Bob Martinez to make it into the governor's mansion in Tallahassee. The whiff of business opportunity was in the air, even in tiny High Springs. A man came into town with big plans. He wanted to make Ginnie Springs famous for more than just cave diving, camping, and swimming. He wanted to bottle the spring water and sell it.

The prospect of outsiders coming in and bottling Florida spring water wasn't on environmentalists' radar then. It would become an issue years later, when many environmentally minded people argued that there was no way to know if pumping so much water for the bottling plant would screw up the balance of the natural system that had been humming along in the Santa Fe basin for thousands of years. They would also chafe at the idea of outsiders coming to poach local water and make a profit off it. It's hard to believe, but the state of Florida—even today—requires little of corporations, even international ones, to get a permit to sell the public's water.

In 1988, Wes and Terri and the Wrays were pro water bottling, and they believed their position was a practical one. Local leaders in the rural counties around the Santa Fe, Suwannee, Withlacoochee, and Ichetucknee Rivers were constantly searching for economic growth, and the state offered incentives to lure any kind of industry to rural parts of Florida.

If an industry was going to come into this part of paradise, they reasoned, what could be better than one with a vested interest in clean water?

"Wes would say, 'If people are stupid enough to pay a thousand times more than the cost of the water that they pay their taxes for—clean, public water—then that's the way the world is,'" says Wes's longtime friend and collaborator, cave diver Kenny Broad.

Wes knew that the main industry in the area—agriculture—was among the worst land uses to locate on top of a delicate clear-water cave system. Not only is agriculture a huge groundwater hog, but the fertilizer used on crops and the manure from cattle operations run off the fields and soak directly into the ground, where the pollution fuels noxious algae explosions in springs, rivers, and lakes. The bacteria that feed on the algae rob the water of oxygen, and that can kill fish and other aquatic animals.

Wes and some of the other cave divers knew that a bottling company would be constantly testing local waters and could be a critical ally in chasing away the huge factory farms that were headed their way. The dairies were proving disastrous in South Florida, badly polluting Lake Okeechobee— a public water supply. The agricultural pollution fouls pricey neighborhoods along the Gulf of Mexico and the Atlantic Ocean because the government periodically opens floodgates at either side of the big lake, sending industrial farm waste down rivers to the state's southeast and southwest coasts.

Maybe, Wes and some of his cave diver friends argued, water bottlers were a better fit for springs country than corporate farms.

The Wrays would earn a percentage on every gallon pumped out of Ginnie, and they were game to do it. Their main issue was that they didn't want people to see pipes sticking out of the campground springs where they hosted divers and swimmers, so they consulted with Wes and decided that the best approach was to tap into the cave system further back. That way, they would be able to meet U.S. Department of Agriculture labeling rules by bottling the same water that was bubbling to the surface at the spring.

They believed that Ginnie's massive flow would make it possible for the bottling plant to take a share and still leave the springs and the Santa Fe

River unaffected. To get a permit, they needed underground surveys, discharge measurements, and water sampling. Wes was perfectly positioned for these tasks, and he wanted to get involved.

Wes's work flow at the time was a patchwork of vocations. He'd take periodic filming jobs for expeditions, sell his still photographs to publications, and work occasional gigs as cave-diver-for-hire for anyone who needed to know specifics about groundwater flow and quality. He was also teaching underwater filming courses—this was the advent of smaller, popular video cameras that were more widely available to amateurs.

In 1989, with work for the newly formed Ginnie Springs Water Company in their sights, Wes and his buddy Pete Butt took a big step. They decided to go into business together and incorporated two new companies: Karst Environmental Services and Karst Productions.

Karst Environmental Services would chase contracts for underground investigation work. Butt would head up Karst Environmental. He had a college degree (something Wes lacked) in water science from the University of Wisconsin. Since their diving buddy Tom Morris was a biologist, he would serve as a member of the firm's scientific team. Anyone who needed environmental information about the aquifer—including governmental agencies—now had a one-stop shop to hire in High Springs.

"It's the right time for Florida to get a bigger and better picture of what's happening with our groundwater, and we're right in the middle of that path," Wes told a reporter. "Anyone that tries to explore the groundwater is going to run right smack into us."

Karst Productions would be the home for Wes's growing film and still photography work. As it turned out, the companies would end up helping one another along. When the filmmaking business was going well, it could carry Karst Environmental. When the environmental contracts were pouring in, Karst Environmental could prop up Karst Productions during fallow times between film projects.

"I remember asking Wes one time, 'Wes, what does it take to take the kinds of pictures you take?' He says, 'Get out your wallet and spend the money.' And boy, is he right about that," says Tom Morris. "That camera gear is expensive, and every time it goes in the water, it is one dive closer to being in the repair shop or the garbage can. These film cameras are not point-and-shoot. You've got to be working dials and constantly changing things. We used to call it the 'big baby.' You're always changing its diapers. Wes had a filming crew. He couldn't have done it by himself. He needed guys to hold lights and stuff. And there wasn't a lot of money."

"We were instrumental in developing lighting techniques and trying different things," says Woody Jasper. "You can make a terribly boring cave video, you know. I always refer to these as the 'butt shot' videos, where you have one guy swimming along with a light and another guy behind him with a camera and off they go."

"Wes worked hard to make these things not boring," Morris says. "He had one little trick to speed up the action. A lot of [camera] people would just sit still with the camera and let us swim slowly by. Wes would say, 'Swim fast and I'm going to swim towards you.' So that just doubled the speed of everything. You put some action into the whole thing.

"Wes always wanted a hook, a goal, something to keep the audience wondering: Are they gonna make it? Are they not gonna make it? Are they gonna die trying?"

ALTHOUGH HE HAD JUST STARTED his business, Wes was already way ahead of the game in terms of publicity and name recognition—"a glory hound," says Jasper. Reporters could see a good story wherever Wes went, and they often called to write about his adventures.

Wes and Butt were even quoted in a national article about the trend of cave diving in *Newsweek* magazine during the summer of 1988:

> Every New Year's Eve at Ginnie Springs, Florida, divers enter a cool freshwater spring, descend 30 feet to its sandy bottom, slip through a crevice and drift into a huge open space that cave divers call a "ballroom." Just before midnight they turn off their lights and squeeze gobs of non-toxic fluorescent chemicals into a spring outflow creating thousands of tiny, greenish sparks in the current.
>
> "It's like being in the stars," Dive Instructor Pete Butt says. "Guys are standing on the ceiling shaking hands and kissing their girlfriends and wives—now, that's a rush!" . . . [Cave diving] training is neither quick (eight days) or cheap ($500). Equipment is expensive, too— about $1,000 on top of the $500 or so it costs to outfit an open water diver. The well-dressed cave diver carries two air tanks, two air regulators, five lights, a compass, an inflatable buoyancy-compensator vest,

a dry suit and two reels of guideline—one to lay down on the way in and then follow on the way back out again, plus an extra. The whole outfit can weigh 200 pounds. . . . But all the money and trouble are worth it considering the potential danger. "You don't rescue people from caves," says Wes Skiles of High Springs, Florida, "you do body recovery." Skiles, 30, has been cave diving since he was 15. One of the first people to chart local underwater systems, he is also frequently the one chosen by police to go in for divers who die in northern Florida caves. "If you get lost, silted up, or run out of air," he says, "there's no place to hide. Panic sets in and you go quick."

Local newspapers were also following Wes's career. In a 1988 profile about Wes in the *Gainesville Sun*, reporter Mitch Stacey wrote:

He says he rarely ever takes a vacation or goes scuba diving for recreation because his work is so much fun. He filmed a four-minute piece on the exploration of Wakulla Springs for the CBS Evening News, which aired last October, and also supplied footage to Cable News Network on the same project. Last January, ABC flew him to New York so he could talk about cave diving with David Hartman on *Good Morning America*. Skiles likes to talk about what he's done and what he hopes to do, but it seems to be more genuine excitement about his work and confidence in his abilities than arrogance or an inflated sense of self-worth.

Since many cave divers preferred to keep their pursuits out of the public eye, some grumbled about Wes's self-promotion. The Mole Tribe supported him.

"I didn't have any problem with it," says Morris. "He was trying to do this for a living. If he wasn't going to promote himself, who would?"

Wes told a local reporter:

I've gone from a sport cave diver to a person who is deeply committed to understanding what's underground in Florida. Ideally we'd like to have the right people come out of the woodwork and say: "We want to use your data to protect Florida's groundwater."

Florida Environments was a brand-new statewide newspaper that circulated among the growing ranks of environmental regulators, consultants, and environmental reporters in Florida. The editor was based in High Springs, which gave Wes an inside track to *Florida Environments'* pages, and that meant valuable exposure to the very sorts of people who might be interested in hiring Karst Environmental Services and Karst Productions. It was, basically, free targeted advertising, but in the news pages.

Wes got prime front-page real estate in the February 1987 premier issue: one of his photos is printed above the fold, showing an explorer venturing into a Puerto Rican cave where a river flows beneath stalactites hanging from its ceiling. "Travel the 'World's Longest Underground River,'" the headline says, and it teases to an article Wes wrote about his adventures tracking the "Enchanted River" in Puerto Rico.

> For hours we travelled downstream, swimming much of the time in water over our heads. At times, the air space above the water decreased to inches. Here, we were forced to remove our helmets and turn our noses up to the ceiling so that we could breathe from the inch or two of available air space. All the time, cold currents of the river carried us further into the cave.

Wes and his colleagues broke a world record for exploration in the Puerto Rican cave system, and, he writes,

> more importantly, our group had made a major new discovery about Karst conduit flow. We realized that in certain Karst conditions (like found here in Florida,) major underground conduits carrying water (conduit aquifers) can, and do, exist—even while defying . . . surface data. Accepting this means that room has to be made alongside the predominant and ever-popular theory of diffuse groundwater movement. In this author's opinion, major conduit aquifers do exist throughout the north and north-central Florida area. So, perhaps we should look at groundwater movement in Florida a little differently.

Wes's adventures had to be great reading for the many environmental scientists who spent their days studying the aquifer from above ground using well sampling, the limited ground-penetrating radar available at the time, and geologic core sampling. They sure weren't seeing it up close and personal, like Wes.

And the little author write-up at the end of the article? Business promotion gold:

Wes Skiles is the President of Karst Environmental Consulting Inc. and the Training Director of the National Speleological Society's Cave Diving Section. Wes has made over 3,000 cave dives to perform surveying, biological testing, dye tracing, and paleontological and geological testing. Recently, he was on *Good Morning America*, January 21st, discussing his cave diving experiences.

The second issue of *Florida Environments*, in March 1987, has a full-color photo by Wes that is half underwater. It shows the swimming-pool blue Ginnie Springs with divers below and canoers above. The caption reads like a paid advertisement for Ginnie Springs: "Florida's quality of life and abundant natural resources—the driving forces behind Florida's growth—are aptly typified by this stunning shot of Ginnie Springs, just outside High Springs in North Central Florida."

With that photo, Wes got a twofer—exposure for his consulting client, Ginnie Springs, and for his own business.

"It was a very good relationship, because he promoted Ginnie Springs, but at the same time Ginnie Springs promoted him," Ginnie Springs owner Bobbie Wray says. "It worked very well for both of us."

Wes kept up a *Florida Environments* column, showcasing his photography, describing the aquifer and his adventures in it, and gaining exposure and new clients.

Meanwhile, the man who proposed the bottling plant at Ginnie wanted Wes to produce promotional videos and commercials to advertise Ginnie Springs bottled water. He purchased top-of-the-line filming and editing equipment so that Wes could make the videos and commercials for Ginnie Springs water. He also needed dye testing and underground surveys of the springs network. Wes and Pete Butt hired people to work on the venture, growing their business.

But then the man surprised everyone by suddenly skipping town, and folks say that he left many—including the Wrays, Karst Environmental, and Karst Productions—unpaid. Wes and Butt's fledgling business venture was especially hard hit.

(A bottling plant would eventually make its way to Ginnie Springs, but not for several years. As of 2018, Ginnie Springs water is being bottled by a Canadian firm, which sells it to the Publix supermarket chain.)

Wes was building contacts by traveling to dive trade shows and giving speeches to any group that asked him, including government agencies. His shoe-leather approach to business development started paying off. Wes was finding a way to make an independent living as a cave diver.

"We were at the Diving Equipment Manufacturers Association convention," recalls Jeffrey Haupt, the New Orleans cave diver who did writing, editing, sound, and camera work on many of Wes's film projects, "and Wes was showing pictures in one of the booths for tourists, and I remember these fellows from Sony walked up and said: 'Let me see your pictures. We've got this new housing for a little underwater video camera that we may call a Capsule 8.' And they said: 'We'd like you to take this video camera on one of your dives. And so they gave Wes a couple of these housings and a couple of underwater lights.'"

In 1989, Wes gained more professional exposure when he was awarded the Lifetime Achievement Award from the National Speleological Society's Cave Diving Section for his contributions to underwater exploration. He was just thirty-one years old.

Not long after the debacle with the Ginnie Springs bottler, a big new client came calling. It was Vulcan Industrial & Mining, a major international corporation based in the Philippines. Vulcan hired Karst Environmental to do a scientific investigation into how its mining operations were affecting a reef off the coast of Mexico. Wes and his fellow Mole Tom Morris flew to Mexico, where they ended up with a lot more than just a paycheck—they ended up on the *CBS Evening News*.

Wes and Morris were diving off the Mexican resort town of Playa del Carmen when, as Skiles would write in an article in *SCUBA Times*,

> the sea began to reach down to us with a long and powerful surge. As the swells continued to grow in strength, a sense of foreboding hit me. We were being given an advanced warning of Hurricane Gilbert's arrival. . . . On the surface, the boat captain could see the first sets of swells racing toward their final destination. Even without radio communication, he also knew the hurricane was on the way. What he didn't know was that in less than 24 hours, his sleek diving craft would be scattered in pieces along the Yucatán coastline.

Once back on shore, Wes and Morris scurried to their hotel room to wait out the storm. At dawn the storm's force was now so great that the building began to quiver under the relentless blasts. Inside the room, pressure changes flexed the glass in the windows to their maximum tolerance. Pinching my nose and blowing, I kept myself equalized with the quickly dropping pressure. Peering outside, I began to wonder how any structure could withstand such an attack.

Wes opened the windows in the hotel bathroom a crack, hoping to relieve pressure on the front-facing windows.

Seconds later, the windows imploded under the storm's rising strength. The storm that was outside of my little world now blasted the interior of my room. I scrambled to collect camera gear, clothes, and all of my other possessions. Within seconds, the room was soaked.

They were on the second floor of a concrete structure. But Wes "began to have serious doubts—even about concrete—as one concrete structure after the other was crumbling under Gilbert's fury." It was turning out to be the work trip from hell.

At 8:30 a.m. on Wednesday, September 14th, Gilbert suddenly released its grasp on Playa Del Carmen. We entered the eye. For fifteen minutes, we experienced what few have ever seen—the calm, blue eye of a class-5 hurricane. Outside, many of the local Mayans and Mexicans began to move about as if the storm was over. Like a two-minute warning before a show, one spine-tingling gust, around 80 mph, let everyone know there was more to come. Seconds later, I scrambled against 100 mph winds and lashing rain to return to my refuge. Without windows, I now had the opportunity to document, on film and video, the storm's full force. To my surprise, the hurricane was even stronger after the passing of the eye. For the next six hours, Gilbert would blow with winds of up to 200 mph, wreaking havoc beyond comprehension on the entire Yucatán Peninsula.

Even though their room was soaked and lacking windows, Morris and Wes were unhurt and walked to the beach to see the surf still hammering the coast.

Jumping in the rental car, we weaved our way over towards the harbor. All along the way, trees lay shredded, telephone poles were twisted and broken, and home after home was virtually destroyed. Riding out the storm were the silent Mayan ruins; they still looked as they did the day before Gilbert's visit—just another small episode in their slow weathering process and a testament to their creators' skills.

All the boats, with the exception of the freighter, were gone. The 500-foot freighter's only excuse for surviving the storm was that it had been picked up and dropped onto a shallow shoal within the harbor. What part of the huge ship was still in the water was being mercilessly hammered by 25-foot waves.

By the evening, the immediate consequences of the storm began to set in. The three most apparent problems were lack of food, fresh water, and power. Like squirrels hoarding before the winter, my diving partner Tom Morris and I had prepared for this the night before. We each had our own avocado and two mangoes apiece. I also had saved a bag of peanuts and a mediocre apple from my airline flight several days earlier. We ate by candlelight and discussed the day's events and past hurricanes we had experienced. Both Tom and I swapped stories about Hurricane Donna and Dora that had visited Florida's coast.

Walking the coast and filming the next day, they found calmer seas. But the reef they had come to document for the mining company had blown apart.

What Mother Nature forms over hundreds, even thousands, of years, she could virtually destroy by her own hand overnight. For miles, the beaches were filled with corals, sea fans, sponges, and fish. One of the earth's natural phenomena had severely damaged the very coastline that environmentalists were concerned would be destroyed by mining operations. This one hurricane probably did more damage to the Yucatán coastal zone in 12 hours than ten mines could do in 20 years. . . . Now our thoughts turned to the realities of our immediate survival, and to a quick escape from whatever post-disaster scenario lay ahead.

At 10:45 p.m., the day after the hurricane, Tom and I were sitting inside the Miami production studio of CBS drinking long overdue cold beers and watching my hurricane footage. By nothing more than sheer luck, we had caught the first private jet out of Cancun—one sent to rescue some associates of ours. We had left behind an isolated, shambled world with no power and communications to the outside, and full of desperate tourists still standing in soup lines for food. For us, as journalists, it had been a tale of right time and right place. Unfortunately, the opposite was true for many others.

The mining company had sent the jet. They asked if Wes and Morris wanted to fly home to Gainesville, but Wes asked if they could go to Miami. Seizing opportunity, he went straight to the news station to sell his extremely fresh footage from Hurricane Gilbert. Other American journalists were still trying to get into Mexico to report the story; Wes was already out, and had the best film of all.

For seventeen years Gilbert would hold top ranking as the most intense hurricane ever to hit the Atlantic Basin, until Hurricane Wilma took the record. In the hair-raising video that Wes shot in the middle of the storm, you see him in his hotel room, where the window is blown out and wind and rain are roaring in. From behind the camera, you hear Wes shouting: "The building I'm in now has been shaking periodically, and it's enough force to give any man religion. There goes an entire brick wall, folks!"

The striking thing about the video is that, over the sound of the ferocious storm, Wes is laughing.

8

Somebody Rescue Me

IN 1990, WOODY JASPER WENT to a picnic for his employer, Continental Water Company, at a county park called Otter Springs near the Suwannee River. He was enjoying himself when, all of a sudden, one of his coworkers came running up in a panic. Four novice scuba divers, all in their early twenties and not trained or equipped for cave diving, had ventured back into a cave, and three had not come back up.

The men had just been certified for open-water diving the day before, and they were on their "graduation dive" with their female instructor. She was familiar with the area, and later explained to rescuers that she had told the men to stay in the spring's cavern—where they could still see sunlight—and not go inside the caves. All five went down and were swimming around, peering into the cave. She says she gave them the "thumbs up" sign, to indicate it was time to go back to the surface. She swam upward, and when she came to the water's surface, she realized the four were not behind her. Several minutes later, one of the four popped up, gravely concerned about the others' survival.

Someone on his way to the company picnic saw the distressed woman standing in her wetsuit by the spring and stopped. Hearing her story and fearing the worst, he ran to get Jasper. Jasper always traveled with his cave diving gear in his truck, and he quickly suited up and dove into Otter Spring—a spring he had explored and knew well—to search for the missing men. Inside the cave, he followed the left tunnel, and he could see stirred-up silt that the lost divers had left in their wake.

When he saw a mask and snorkel lying on the cave floor, he knew things weren't good. Panicked divers running out of air sometimes desperately throw off their equipment. As he looked up, Jasper's light flashed on four fins hanging down above his head. Two men were floating ten feet above, with their heads in an air pocket created by the last of the air from their scuba tanks. Jasper couldn't fit beside them, but he tried to signal to them by blasting air from his spare regulator. After he got no response, he reached up and pulled the first man down. He was unconscious, and Jasper quickly swam him out of the cave toward help.

At the rocky edge of the spring, a group stood ready to tend to the man. Jasper's wife, Kathy, and another man performed CPR. Amazingly, the man started breathing. Ambulances were on the way.

After handing the first man off, Jasper dove straight back into the spring to help the second man. It turned out that something remarkable had happened: Jasper's scuba air bubbles, along with the exhalations he made when he was rescuing the first diver, had sent more bubbles to fill the ceiling air pocket—enough to revive the man. When Jasper reached him, the diver was breathing. Jasper swam him out, handed him off to the team onshore, and dove back into the spring again.

The third man was further into the cave. He was lifeless. Jasper took hold of the diver's body and swam back up to the surface. Ambulances rushed the three men to Shands Hospital in Gainesville. Two survived.

Jasper's dramatic rural rescue made the news wire. That's when television producers telephoned Jasper. They were calling from a show hosted by the actor William Shatner (Captain Kirk from *Star Trek*) called *Rescue 911*. It featured reenactments of dramatic rescues, just like the one at Otter Spring.

They wanted to reenact the Otter Spring rescue for *Rescue 911*. Jasper said yes, and not only could they reenact it, they could do it right where it happened. Jasper could play himself, and—by the way—his dive buddy was Wes Skiles, a world-renowned cave diver and underwater cameraman who had worked for *National Geographic*. Jasper told the producers that he'd do the show on one condition: they had to hire Wes to film it. The *Rescue 911* producers tentatively agreed.

It was just a reenactment for a cheesy TV show, but when you see the episodes today (a double segment that's available on YouTube), Wes's camera work is top-notch for the technology of that era. His experience shows in the way he lights the stunning underwater landscapes, creating spooky shadows during the rescue parts. Tom Morris worked as a diving stunt double, and Jasper recreated the rescues he did that scary day at Otter Spring, this time for the cameras.

Just like that, Wes became the go-to guy for underwater scenes for *Rescue 911*, a mainstay for the network prime-time TV show lineup.

"Wes kept telling the *Rescue 911* people, 'Look, we can shoot above water too,'" says Wes's filming partner, Jeffrey Haupt. Wes got hired to do camera work for several shoots across the country. "When the next call came from *Rescue 911*, asking for more underwater film work, Wes says, 'We can shoot the whole episode.' So then he and I became the above-water and the underwater cameras, and we brought our team, and it became our show then. Once they see you can do the thing, then they keep piling it on."

Wes and his crew out of High Springs were soon getting steady work filming *Rescue 911* episodes. They scouted locations, did the camera work, and provided the stunt divers (sometimes using Wes's wife, Terri, and Haupt's wife, Ruby) to reenact the rescues.

One of the best aspects of working on *Rescue 911* was the connections it brought in the TV film business. Through people they met on *Rescue 911*, Wes and Haupt learned about an adventure documentary series called *The New Explorers*, which would be produced by Bill Kurtis, a nationally known television announcer and host. Wes and Haupt soon were pitching Kurtis on the idea of hiring them to do an episode about cave diving.

Before that came together, Wes got another assignment, and this one was at his home base in springs country. His Australian friends Liz and Andrew Wight—the same cave-diving filmmakers who hired Wes to shoot the documentary at Nullarbor Plain, when they were buried alive and rescued—came to produce an adventure film about cave diving in Florida for Australian television. They hired Wes as cinematographer.

This was Wes's creative dream: someone agreeing to finance a film showcasing the springs and caves he spent his life exploring. This 1991 documentary, called *Florida: Window to a Hidden World*, would not become a big success, but it was an early template for Wes's later groundbreaking film series, *Water's Journey*.

"Wes wanted to tell *Water's Journey* from the moment I met him," says Jasper. "It took him fifteen years maybe to sell it and get it made."

The Florida documentary he did with Liz and Andrew Wight described, head on, the threats that Florida's permissive land-use policies were posing to one of the most abundant freshwater aquifers on the planet. Telling this story clearly set Wes apart from the other cave divers.

He was speaking out. He was evolving from Cave Explorer to Cave Protector.

It's hard to say which environment would prove more hostile—dark, subterranean stone caverns or dark, subterranean Florida politics.

Wes at sixteen with his homemade skateboard in Jacksonville. Courtesy of Terri Skiles.

Wes, approximately seventeen, walking toward Devil's Eye in Gilchrist County, Florida, for a dive. Courtesy of Terri Skiles.

Wes at Merritt's Mill Pond in Jackson County, Florida. Photo by Terri Skiles.

Wes and Jeffrey Haupt filming at Devil's Eye. Courtesy of Terri Skiles.

Wes and Jim Skiles on a surf trip in Puerto Rico. Courtesy of Terri Skiles.

Mole Tribe members diving the Suwannee River: Wes and Woody Jasper, photographed by Mark Long. Courtesy of Terri Skiles.

Mole Tribe members discussing a dive plan at another Suwannee River site: Wes, Ron Simmons, Woody Jasper, Tom Morris, and Bucky McMahon, with Nathan Skiles, photographed by Mark Long. Courtesy of Terri Skiles.

Wes and Bob Wray putting dye in a well for a dye trace, Ginnie Springs, Gilchrist County. Courtesy of Terri Skiles.

Wes on the deck at Devil's Eye with his gear. Photo by Terri Skiles.

Wes and Jeffrey Haupt in Queen Charlotte Strait, British Columbia, during a shoot for the series *The New Explorers*. Courtesy of Terri Skiles.

Wes, Joel Tower, and Georgia Shemitz navigating with the *Log Hopper* johnboat during a *National Geographic* shoot. (This is how Wes's trusty *Log Hopper* earned her name—and yes, a boat can jump!) Courtesy of Terri Skiles.

Tripod platform that Wes and his buddies created for bird's-eye-view images for *National Geographic*. Wes directing Woody, Mark, and Joel. Courtesy of Terri Skiles.

Karst Productions gear room, early on before it grew. Courtesy of Terri Skiles.

Wes during the second Wakulla expedition, undertaken with Bill Stone in 1998. Courtesy of Terri Skiles.

9

Lions and Rhinos

EVEN THOUGH WES FOUND HIMSELF called to expose the cavalier disregard that Florida was showing to one of the world's greatest storehouses of fresh water, he was still being pulled all over the globe, putting himself in dangerous circumstances and delivering killer footage. He was doing his dream, but the truth was that the role of cameraman was beginning to chafe. No matter how many adventures he was having, Wes was always chasing the thrills he had as a cave diver, the kind that few explorers get in life, namely, being the first person ever in a wild place. Coming up as a young cave diver when technology was allowing explorers to go deeper into virgin landscapes, he'd experienced that rush over and over again. He was used to being on top of the adrenaline cliff. Working as a freelance cameraman on wildlife movies didn't have that autonomy or that edge. Despite the work's glamorous image, it took an enormous amount of waiting around and logistics. These were expensive, unpredictable projects. During one frustrating day searching for crocodiles and sharks on a documentary called *Predators of the North* with Liz and Andrew Wight in Australia, Wes started venting in his journal:

> *We couldn't get out of our Zodiac boats and sneak up on the crocs from land. Every time we tried, we just sunk in mud and became sitting ducks for big crocs. We couldn't film on the shore, in most places you couldn't even*

go ashore—to do so it was necessary to build a ladder or raft to stay afloat in a sea of mud. The mud began to prey on our attitudes. Nothing could be done without confronting mud. Mud would always end up on everything; cameras, clothes, furniture . . . the only thing mud didn't seem to stick to was crocodiles, and we couldn't get near any of those.

On the same trip, he wrote:

Out of frustration at the apparent lack of sharks, I schemed up a short horror feature, aptly named "Attack of the Killer Sea Cucumber"—The story of one lone diver and how he meets his ultimate demise, facing what certainly must be the most disgusting creature in the sea.

At home, Wes had supreme confidence in both his abilities and his environment. Overseas, the pressure from the money people was always present. And even though Wes was the shooter, he was not always the one calling the shots. During another frustrating day on the *Predators of the North* documentary, Wes griped:

Going crazy on the boat! I've considered giving up what I presently do. The problem is that I can't quite seem to get a grasp on what it is that I do for a living. Maybe I should start over. That would be easier than giving up, especially since I don't know what it is I do. Whatever it is I do, I sure seem to stay busy at it, but it doesn't pay very well. I find myself constantly saying the next job will be my big break, everything will be great then. Unfortunately, every new job brings some new version of the same old thing. The job doesn't pan out, they don't pay what they promised, the rules change at the last minute, etc. I just seem to continue on, paying my dues, knowing one day, just maybe I'll get the break I know I deserve.

With the freelance gigs and the checks dangling in front of him, Wes kept pressing on. At the beginning of 1992, he took some R&R to go on a dive trip to the Abaco Islands in the Bahamas with friends and family, and his journal entry at the time shows how much he was feeling the pressure of being self-employed and keeping his businesses afloat.

If you could only bottle the synergism and focus of a trip like this, the possibilities would be boggling. The nightmare of returning home is setting in only hours after our departure. I feel the stress and anxiety building in me this very second . . . I feel the edge of my attitude as if it were a razor.

Every time Wes went back home, he was faced with having to gin up new work for the two businesses, Karst Environmental and Karst Productions.

"He used to say to me, 'You get to do all the fun stuff. You don't have to spend endless hours on the phone to get people to back these projects,'" says Tom Morris.

Like most creative people, Wes hated office work. Plus, even the creative work he did in the office could be a chore. Going places and shooting photographs and movies was the fun part. The long hours he had to spend later, sorting and editing, could be a letdown. Wes was constantly second-guessing the choices he made in the field, always thinking he could have taken a better picture if only he'd pointed the lights a different way, or gotten closer, or choreographed it better beforehand.

Once at home in his office, he was pulled in too many directions. While deep into the process of editing photos from one adventure, he would suddenly have to pivot to deal with last-minute changes on a film that was about to air—one he might have shot during an expedition months earlier. Underwater cameramen are used to multitasking, but even for someone as skilled and energetic as Wes, these were a lot of balls to keep in the air.

Wes was thirty-four, and he was now responsible for several employees, as well as supporting his family. His son Nathan was a rambunctious five-year-old, a Florida water rat just like his dad had been at that age. Wes did his best to stay connected with his family, but he was always loading and unloading mounds of gear and getting on and off airplanes.

In the fall of 1992, Wes decided to take a freelance filming job in Africa, a place all wildlife photographers hope to go. As a hired cameraman for a show called *Worldwide Travel Quest*, he would be shooting local people, wild animals, and landscapes—the whole experience of a safari trip. Once again, someone was willing to pay him to trek across the globe, and once again, he headed to the airport with towering luggage carts.

Reading his journal, it seems Wes turned philosophical as soon as he got to Africa, calling it

a spiritual place . . . not entirely ruled by man. . . . You just feel so naked here, so powerless . . . you feel the intelligence, the design of the creatures around you. They are aware, alert, and in control of the place.

As part of the project, Wes and crew got to meet Richard Leakey, the world-famous explorer and paleoanthropologist who was serving as director of the Kenya Wildlife Service. Leakey was involved in a battle against poachers who were killing elephants and rhinoceros to sell tusks to the ivory trade.

> *During his presentation, he brought to light that the African people were gaining in their cause to save threatened and endangered wildlife. I felt a little better hearing this, but know the battle is far from over. I now know, more so than ever, to anticipate my first visual encounters of these beasts in the wild.*

For days, Wes and the other members of the crew filmed cheetahs, lions, rhinoceros, giraffes, elephants, hippos, leopards, crocodiles, hyenas, and swift herds of buffalo, wildebeest, waterbuck, antelope, impala, and oryx. Here were a million great shots for TV, every day. But it was frustrating to try to work creatively while having to follow an agenda set by others. The African guides wanted Wes to stay in, or near, the Jeep, and not go wandering out among predators.

> *We finished the day seeing my first leopards in the wild. They were hanging out at the edge of a small node-like hill. . . . On the way back to the Park Hotel, we spotted a hyena on the move, and filmed a beautiful herd of buffalo backlit by a magenta sky. Again, Sammy let me work outside of the Land Rover to get the shot. More so than ever, I could sense the power and the presence of the place, standing alone filming what many termed a foul-tempered and dangerous beast. The herd, about 30 yards away, stood facing me, no doubt waiting to see what my next move would be. Quietly, I climbed back inside the vehicle, now starting to feel I was experiencing the Africa that I wanted to see, an Africa where I could always assume the risk of my actions and gain the rewards of taking those risks. As we drove back to the lodge, I smiled quietly to myself, feeling that inner-satisfaction of having been THERE.*

Wes was getting the hang of filming African wildlife, but his attempts to get natural scenes of the region's people were less successful and, in one case, deeply embarrassing.

> *We took time to stop and film sights that would establish the sense of journey along the route. It seemed that every time we would stop, Maasai or*

other tribes would show up out of nowhere expecting to have their picture taken, and subsequently be paid. Typically, one would show up first and then suddenly there would be 5, 10, 15 people all wanting, and expecting, money. It was a sad reminder of the kind of impact Western civilization has had on these people.

Not all tribes had become like this, but the fact is that where we do go, the change is obvious. It seemed that any tribe near the road has been impacted by people just like us. Once again, I was reminded that while we were trying to do something unique, we were just the most recent in a long line of travelers that have permanently upset a natural system.

Their African guide warned Wes that if the documentary crew wanted to film tribe members, they would have to pay for the privilege or face trouble.

So sad that human relationships get reduced to simple red-light district economics. What's fascinating to see and photograph is the transitional evolution these people make in the process. The more they interface with Western culture, the more they evolve to be like us, and the less interested we are in them. It's the fact that people are different that attracts us, and, in being attracted to them, we accidentally make them like us. This morning we met with the Maasai people on their turf, which, in this case, I was surprised to find out was mostly cow manure.

The plan that day was to go into a typical village and record daily life there.

Unfortunately, it's quite impossible to invisibly show up and film. Just the act of Westerners entering a village such as this changes the whole mood of the place, not to mention introducing the concept of retakes for the camera. These people, especially the women and children, had hardly ever been exposed to contact with the Western world. Their response to us at first was tentative and shy, and basically remained so throughout the day—although it did get progressively easier to film them as they adjusted to the cameras. One of the ways we knew we were on virgin turf, photographically speaking, was the response we were receiving here as opposed to other areas we had photographed the Maasai. Here on the edge of the crater, far off the beaten track of tourists, we were on a sacred ground of a sort; one that had not been ruined by the "ugly tourist" syndrome. Here, shooting photos of the people elicited nothing more than mild curiosity over the technology we seemed to possess. My fear, as I rolled tape and snapped photos, was that I was the one that was inflicting the first western germs of influence, and that my presence here would forever change these kind people's attitudes toward people like myself.

Throughout the day we attempted to maintain a respectful profile with the Maasai, but never were really sure of where we stood. At the end of our day, I accidentally crossed the line and was made aware of that by the mood of the tribe. The women had been singing various beautiful Maasai songs for us out in the field. When they were through, I thought I would share some harmonica music with them. After a short blow, I heard a warrior yell something at the women. Their mood changed immediately from smiling and happy to nervous. I knew then that my serenade was considered flirtatious and in bad taste, and quite by accident I had made myself an unwelcome guest. It was the last thing I would have ever wanted to do and I learned an important lesson I should have already known. A moment like this really underlines how awkward it can be to be off your turf, yet want to be liked and accepted. In my own attempt to break the ice with these people, I only managed to greatly embarrass myself. The whole way back to the lodge I felt like a large, loud, white, obnoxious kook.

10

And Sharks, Oh My!

IT'S NOT EASY TO PARENT by yourself, but by this point in her life, Terri was used to it. It wasn't typical family life, but Terri knew this drill; she grew up with a military father who was out of town a lot. She had friends and neighbors in High Springs, and grandparents not too far away. When he wasn't on assignment, Wes was a dedicated father, and he tried to spend as much time as possible with Nathan. Wes and Terri had long ago accepted the fact that Nathan would be an only child, because, doctors said, Terri had a medical condition that would prevent her from having another pregnancy. Then—bam, while Wes was off in Africa, she started feeling ill and went to the doctor, who delivered a surprise: at thirty-seven years of age, Terri was three months pregnant.

She immediately contacted Wes in Africa via satellite phone. He had finished the safari portion of his trip and was about to shoot one of his most dangerous and high-profile assignments ever: he planned to go underwater in a shark cage and film great white sharks for Discovery Channel's annual Shark Week—a coveted notch in any wildlife photographer's belt. The way Terri recalls it, when she told Wes she was pregnant, "he panicked!" If Terri was flipped out to learn that the father of her children was about to jump into some of the most shark-infested waters on Earth, she didn't show it. That was the rule.

Wes actually liked sharks, even though he'd been bitten once in Florida. He was dangling his feet off a surfboard when the shark bit him on his foot, then circled back for a second bite. Just like he did when an alligator charged him deep inside a spring, he punched the creature in the nose to make it go away. Wes paddled back to shore with his bloody foot and then refused to go to the hospital, because he knew that shark bites always generate publicity, and he didn't want to add to the species's already bad reputation. Instead he got a nurse friend to tend his wound, put on a dive bootie, and then headed back out surfing with his bandaged leg. He seemed unconcerned about the fact that sharks are notoriously good at detecting tiny amounts of blood in the water. The only reason he quit surfing that day was because the salt water irritated his puncture wound when he rode waves.

The great white sharks that Wes came to film off the African coast are the dead-eyed creatures of horror films, growing 11 to 20 feet long and weighing as much as 5,000 pounds—heavier than a car. Great whites are among the oldest marine species, with fossil specimens found that predate dinosaurs. To capture close-ups of the great whites that he hoped would impress the editors at Discovery Channel, Wes came up with a special camera rig he called the bite-cam. Basically, it was a contraption tied to a line from the boat that had bloody bait wrapped around extra-sturdy underwater camera housing. Was it sturdy enough to survive the force of three hundred shark teeth clamping down? He hoped so.

If things go as planned, this unique camera will give the world its first glimpses of what it would be like to be eaten by a great white, Wes wrote in his journal from South Africa's Dyer Island. The shoreline there is crowded with seals and penguins, and the waters are filled with predatory dolphins, whales, and sharks. About a two-hour drive south from Cape Town, the area is world famous as the best place to see great white sharks. Wes and several colleagues hired a boat and headed to an offshore area that's long been nicknamed Shark Alley.

Well, the day has come, he wrote. *My first real encounter under water with a great white. What am I to experience? Will I be scared? Awed?* As he psyched himself up for the first day of diving in the shark cage, he turned inward. *Everyone is always saying to me, "Are you alright?" "Is there something wrong?" "You're not yourself." "What's up?" It's pretty annoying at times, but makes me realize that on the surface, my ways and moods are quite clear.*

Standing on the deck of the rocking boat putting on his dive gear, Wes spotted a baby seal swimming toward the boat. Then, in an instant, a great white came out of the water and swallowed the seal whole. If watching the shark snap that seal up made Wes think twice about his plan, he didn't show it. He climbed into the shark cage, the crew lowered him into the ocean, and the sharks started coming in after the bait.

I experienced a twang of being scared when a big white really charged into my cage—really hard. At one point, a larger one drove his powerful body up to my cage, ignoring the meat hanging nearby entirely. This beast clearly showed his interest in inspecting me inside the cage. For the first time, I felt both intimidation and fear. There was no doubt in my mind that I was connecting with this shark, and as well, it was very aware of me. I could sense its intelligence and could clearly tell it was not in the least intimidated by me.

The shark cage held, and when the crew raised Wes out of the water, they all felt the surge of success. That first day, they tinkered with the system, replaced a bad regulator, and figured out how much weight to use to control buoyancy. The next day, they again threw bait in the water and deployed Wes and the bite-cam in front of a pack of sharks.

It was absolutely thrilling to see a great white actually coming at the camera, Wes wrote. *Out of the haze came the beast himself, a strong and powerful great white, around four meters. It had already made several passes, and this time it was lined up, ready to consume its prey.*

On the final pass, the shark came straight at the camera with gaping jaws and clamped down, as hoped, on the wad of bait. After capturing the initial chomp, the camera was sideways in the shark's jaws, tossing about wildly. Up on the boat, the recording unit's screen went black.

I yelled, "Get it up! Get it up!" but much to my horror, the worst case scenario had happened on the first round—the shark ate the camera, bit through the rope, and was gone, never to be seen again. I had put considerable energy into this concept, only to have it disappear in one single chomp. What was worse was that I didn't lose the camera because it was destroyed, but instead, simply because the original lure I had tied it to had been re-tied differently when we switched the camera around in its housing. As for the concept, it was a true success. To see a great white coming at you straight on, bearing down at you without veering, then actually eating you is, without a doubt, a horrifying and awesome visual experience.

After the dive, Wes was tired and pissed off. He wanted to be alone but he was trapped on a boat full of similarly disappointed crew members.

The entire crew was sympathetic at a time when I would have rather not heard sympathy. Shortly after the sympathy came the inevitable—a "you should have" series of worthless and irritating suggestions. It occurred to me, as everyone put in their overwhelmingly intelligent two-cents worth, that it would have been nice if some of these folks would have been involved in the process before I lost my invention. I felt like screaming, "Leave me alone!" In their own way, everyone was trying to be kind, but in my mood it was like a maniacal nightmare—all these faces shoving their way into my vision in rapid fire, saying, "Sorry Wes, you should have . . ." "Why didn't you?" "That's too bad Wes, did you have insurance?" "I'll tell you what I would have done," "Oh, certainly you have insurance." GO AWAY. I should have had a bloody bazooka.

Everyone still had frayed nerves the day after the shark swallowed the camera. On top of that, it was too choppy to film underwater. Having decided to go ashore to a nearby island, the filmmakers loaded up into a small inflatable boat, and as they ventured offshore, a monster wave appeared, standing the boat on its edge, everybody hanging on with white knuckles.

My years of surfing and canoeing took over. I instinctively made a mad dive across the boat, throwing my weight to the other side, just as the boat started to go over. It was just enough to bring us back down. We took on a lot of water and much of our gear got wet, but we survived.

As the shark-hunting expedition's days ground on, the sharks continued to prove difficult to find, even in Shark Alley. Day after day, they threw bloody bait overboard, hoping to attract great whites. Wes was planning to do something brave, or foolhardy, depending on your perspective.

Two great whites showed up to play. I knew the minute they arrived that this was the day I would attempt to dive outside of the cage. The surge was quite strong, which made it a bit difficult to stay in one place. . . . It was in one of these surging drifts that I had my first encounter with my friend, the apex predator. I was looking up towards the baits when I saw her familiar shape drive in on one of the baits. She disappeared before I could get my camera into position. Not to worry, it was only seconds before the strong, powerful beast was back again, tearing away at the baits at will. Just then, as if it was a gift from heaven, the sun came piercing through the gray sky, creating a magnificent burst of sunrays backlighting the shark as it swam directly over my head.

Wes swam off to alert two fellow divers, and then he started filming them, hoping to get valuable footage of both the great white and divers outside the protective cage in the same frame. As he filmed, Wes felt the overwhelming urge to spin around.

> *Then, out of the gloom she came. This time her interest was not the cage but us instead. She was on a dead-flat plane headed straight for me—her body large and round and strong. For a moment, I flashed back to the image that the bite-cam had recorded before its death. It was the exact same view; pectorals down, mouth slightly agape. She drove forward toward me, making no indication that she was planning to veer. For the first time I felt the cold chill. . . . As she bore down on me, I began to think that she might attack. My first thought was: "Oh no! I'm going to lose another camera," then worse; "Is she going to get me?" When she was only two feet from the front of my lens, I instinctively lunged forward at her to let her know I was not to be her prey. Her reaction was both fast and formidable. She turned effortlessly and scanned into high gear and disappeared into the gloom. Over the next few minutes, she made a few shy passes alongside of us, but none like the first.*
>
> *Not wanting to stretch our luck, we decided to ascend, knowing the crew would be both anxious for us to surface safely and to share with them our encounter. On the bow, Mike and I discussed our experience together and explored our own reactions to the great white. Both of us felt a similar emotion, that we were not scared or intimidated by her and wondered if that was a healthy attitude to have. After giving it some thought, we both agreed that your focus must be placed on control of your emotions while diving under these circumstances instead of placing energy into fear—to do so is to invite the worst possible beast within us to rise and take control: Panic. In reality, all of the pursuits I've enjoyed most of my life require constant attention to this point. The discipline developed from years of life-and-death encounters within the depths of caves have prepared me well for such scenarios. When you can keep control of your fears, you can survive what others would call their worst nightmare.*

Wes finally had the footage he needed for Discovery Channel. With film of the safari locations and the great whites in hand, Wes left Africa, anxious to travel the seven thousand miles home, where Terri, Nathan, and his soon-to-be second child were waiting.

Wes made the transition from life-and-death wilderness encounters to the more pedestrian demands of home and office, and learned that Karst Productions had scored another business coup: they were hired to do a cave-diving documentary, this one featuring a scientist named Jill Yager, who was studying strange and very rare aquatic cave creatures in the Bahamas. They hoped this job was their "in" to Bill Kurtis's prime-time television documentary series, *The New Explorers*. But it turned out that Wes wouldn't make it to the Bahamas after all. When he went to review his film of the shark encounters, professional disaster struck. In his journal he wrote:

> *I've made what has to be the single largest mistake of my filmmaking career. This is not an easy subject for me, in that it exposes me in a light that I would rather not be seen in. But the truth is that it did happen. I loaded the film backwards in the camera. No way! How could you do that? Easy. I did.*
>
> *I've explored all the reasons it happened a thousand times, spent several sleepless nights replaying the horror of my error. I have never felt so low in my life. Not only was I extremely hurt that I made such a barney, I also felt I let down an awful lot of people. The embarrassment and pain of such a bungling will stay with me throughout life. At this point, I'm not so sure how it happened is worth talking about. It's only important to know that I did it and it's my fault.*
>
> *It was my paid responsibility to come film sharks for The Discovery Channel. I had the perfect chance, great action, everything just right . . . and I captured zipola. Nothing.*

When he discovered his screw-up, Wes realized he was going to have to make things right. He had a busy schedule of new assignments, but he ended up borrowing money to go back to South Africa, once again find great white sharks, and film them—successfully this time.

Not until I've captured five, even ten times, the footage I originally shot will I feel the relief that I so desperately seek, he wrote in his journal during that second trip aboard the *Gay Jane*, cruising through shark country.

> *Several things occur simultaneously when you make a bad mistake or judgment in your life. The first, and foremost, is that your friends, family, and loved ones will rally to your aid, and your detractors quickly go into action*

swinging a broad sword. Even if the mistake is one you can recover from, it will take some form of toll. It is my belief that if you take the positive road and accept the love and support of those behind you, you will come out of such ordeals stronger, wiser, and more careful. Don't get me wrong, the pain will stay as a reminder. Your detractors will never let you, or others, forget. But the strength to be gained from such experiences can help you rise above and beyond the negative effect. In my case, even though I've been set back both mentally and financially, I am quite glad for the second opportunity to return. I expect several extremely valuable things will come from it. It's strange how defenseless you become around your teammates when you are the one that has dropped the ball. You actually feel like you are standing there naked for all to gaze at with no ability to cover yourself up. This emotion makes it difficult, at best, to stand behind your ego or pride. It's an interesting test, although I'm not the person to judge how I'm doing. I do know something more now about human character in the face of adversity. Only when I have returned home and seen the results of developed film will I exhale this painful breath.

Again he was spending long hours on the boat deck tossing bait overboard with the film crew, hoping to spot great whites. It was monotonous and humiliating. On one night, though, it turned magical. He witnessed a sight that (almost) made the return South Africa trip worthwhile.

The sea around the boat began to glow with an intensity only equaled by the stars themselves; an eerie, green glow with a supernatural quality about it. At first, I was not at all sure whether it was real or my imagination. As I exclaimed, "Look at that!" Bill, the first mate, immediately said, "Oh, dat is just phosphorescence." Certainly I had seen this phenomena before, but never on the scale or intensity I was seeing before me now. What was the source of such a massive phantom glow? My initial thought was immediately echoed by the captain, "It must be a flippin' whale." Once again, our soft-spoken, nonchalant first mate said, "Ah no, it is just a school of sardines or anchovies." He went on to explain to me how they had used the magical glow for years to identify schools of fish at night. He quickly schooled me on all the various techniques for identifying the type of fish by reading various and distinct glow-patterns. Here I am standing on the warm, wooden deck of a fishing trawler, miles off the coast of South Africa, over 6,800 miles from my home, in what certainly is one of the most wild, sea-wise, dangerous places on earth, learning to read fish-patterns from the phosphorescence qualities of the glowing sea on a moonless night.

    Within seconds, our entire vessel was engulfed in a sea of luminescence. The radiating light began to break into groups and patterns too numerous to follow from beyond. I began to see the reason. This was more than the flight of the mystic anchovies—this was fight or flight of the mystic anchovies. The dance of thousands of fish on the run from the predator became a show that I am at a loss to describe. It was as if Neptune was throwing balls of liquid electricity at an invisible challenger. The predators that revealed themselves over the night were often as impressive, if not more impressive, than the prey. Each time their synchronized attacks caused the green balls of trailing anchovies to fire off in different directions. For a while, a large cape fur seal dove into the school. We knew it was a seal, both from its regular surfacing puffs for new air and its graceful arcing loops under water. Later, four bronze whales moved in, dispersing the anchovies in a wide arc.

The mackerels, Wes wrote, *came in for the kill in a pattern quite like one would expect from 100 pissed-off Tinker Bells.*

    Over the years, Wes would enjoy recounting his remarkable night. He didn't get to see a spectacle like that during the rest of the trip, but he did have another memorable encounter with the great whites—one so harrowing that it would be mentioned in the story that ran in the *Washington Post* after his death. Reading his journal entry from that time feels like he was putting down a draft of a story he'd later refine and try to sell to an adventure magazine:

Dive gear check, cameras loaded, you enter the cage for the first time. Safely in the cage, you wait for that first true encounter. Nothing can prepare you for this. What will it be like to face such a powerful, dangerous fish on its terms? Out of the gloom, your question is about to be answered. Passing the baits, cautiously at first, a beautiful, 17-foot female swims slowly by with a cold, dark stare from a large, black eye . . . You've dove with other sharks, but never have you felt the presence that you feel from this great white. It seems to say to you, "I know who I am, and I know what you are. I'm just checking you out now, but should I choose, you could be mine." . . . Even with its torpedo-shaped body built for speed and maneuverability, the great white swings about you and the bait in a nonchalant manner. Only when the other great whites move in on the bait do you see the awesome speed-potential of the creature.

You see in front of you a smaller 12-foot great white move in towards the bait. Suddenly, the largest shark's space is invaded and a swift and powerful response is issued. The head swings with lightning speed as the tailfin whips the attacking beast in a great arc. The smallest great white, even though he is one of the largest sharks you have ever seen, responding to the threat, busts off into the haze. Seconds later it is back now . . . more wary of the pecking order.

As you sit there in wonder of the whole scenario, something new happens, something unexpected. The sharks disappear. Now, the underwater waiting game has begun. For the first time you notice the chill in the water. You sit there, protected by bars of steel, pondering what you have just witnessed.

Just as you start to daydream, you feel the cage suddenly snap forward. You throw your hands back to brace yourself from an invisible force. As you reach for the bars, your hand rubs something foreign. Not steel. Something organic. You whip around as fast as you can—jerking your limbs wildly back as your frantic eyes meet the cold, calm eyes of your quest. Her nose is almost a foot into your cage, her open mouth is biting gently on the bars— testing the wrapper which contains the tender morsel inside. Her eyes convey a simple message, one you will never forget: Tag, you're it. . . . From deep beneath the cage you capture a glance of the vertical white patch as it looms upward out of the green gloom. You see it taking shape; pectorals thrusted out and ridged, mouth slightly agape, complete with menacing snarl. Nothing seems to be powering this vertical torpedo, yet, with deceptive speed, the shark closes her eyes, throws open her mouth, and takes the bait, float, and line in one gulp.

At the last moments, you see one of the most amazing sights one can ever witness. Just before slamming its mouth shut, you see the entire jaw, complete with rows of eating utensils, snap forward—apparently detached from the shark itself—as the rest of the mouth that follows the terrifying energy of the great white is revealed. You laugh, say "Whoa!" and shiver in fear, and smile, glad in knowing it is acceptable for a diver to pee in their suits! There's now a new level of intensity vibrating in the water. The smaller 10- to 12-foot sharks begin to be anxious for their round at you or the baits. Again, your cage is slammed and your heart jumps in your mouth.

This time, your worst fear is realized. She's in the cage with you.

How had a great white gotten inside Wes's supposedly sharkproof cage? It was pretty much his own fault. With help, Wes had modified the cage so he could film out of it better. By tinkering with it for the sake of the film, he'd sacrificed his safety.

The great white's head "hit the cage, really hard, and got stuck," as Wes later described it in an interview. "He went into a frenzy, somehow pried the cage open, and came in. I was yelling out loud, 'This is it!' I knew this had no resolvable scenario—that all the worst imaginable things could happen. The shark was reflexively biting. He was as scared as I was and he was thrashing in the cage, biting things, and things were being ripped off me. I used my camera as a battering ram and managed to whip the shark around, and he left the cage. The camera got banged up, but nothing happened to me."

When Wes bobbed to the frothy surface, one of the crew members was on the deck, vomiting. The man was horrified that Wes, the affable American adventure cameraman who kept everyone on the boat laughing, had certainly been eaten alive by a great white.

11

Swimming with Rays

WES'S FRIENDS AND FAMILY HAD A NAME for the fact that Wes consistently turned disasters into triumphs: "Skiles luck."

Thanks to Skiles luck, the great white shark footage Wes shot on his second trip to South Africa was terrifyingly close up and proved worthy of a coveted spot on Discovery Channel's Shark Week. It was a massive screw-up and a considerable financial setback, but in the end he delivered what he was hired to deliver. That meant he would stay on the roster of go-to adventure cameramen. What a massive relief it was after all the nail-biting and self-flagellation.

Four months after Wes survived the great white ramming into his underwater shark cage, he and Terri celebrated the birth of their baby girl, Tessa. Seven-year-old Nathan, who spent his time after school roaming the Skileses' rural home place and swimming in the springs and rivers, was thrilled to get a baby sister.

Wes had to leave that tender new-baby time faster than he would have liked. Tessa was just four months old when he headed out again for a very unusual assignment, probably one of the most unusual—and, as it turned out, tragic—in his adventure career. It involved the legendary American jam band the Grateful Dead.

Several members of the Dead were heavily into scuba diving, and none more so than Dead drummer Bill Kreutzmann. Kreutzmann had long wanted to film marine animals and make a cinematically beautiful movie with a percussion-heavy musical score.

Kreutzmann says he's always had "really good magic with animals." He wanted to move up from being an amateur photographer and filmmaker to being a professional one. He learned about Wes and Jeffrey Haupt's work through a mutual diving friend and sought them out.

A lifelong music fan, Wes was intrigued and agreed to be a film and photography instructor for the legendary rock 'n' roller. During a break in the Grateful Dead's near-constant touring, which saw them play gigs worldwide from the Egyptian pyramids to psychedelic all-nighters in San Francisco's Haight-Ashbury, Kreutzmann packed up his camera gear and came down to Wes's home in High Springs. The two men went to Ginnie Springs so Kreutzmann—known as BK to his friends—could practice filming underwater.

"After a couple days playing around," Wes later recounted, "Kreutzmann said, 'I'm not really getting this, am I?' I said, 'Hey, you don't just grab this stuff and start using it. It's taken me eighteen years to get halfway competent, and you don't just learn it in two or three days.'"

That's when Kreutzmann invited Wes on a very wild ride.

"He goes, 'Well, why don't you come with me on this expedition,'" Wes recalled. "'I'm going to take a sailboat eighteen hundred miles from San Francisco down to these islands, the Revillagigedos.' So we jumped in this sailboat in San Francisco on what would become an epic journey."

The Revillagigedo Islands are just the kind of rare wilderness Wes craved. And luckily, someone was willing to pay him to go there. A cluster of striking volcanic formations jutting out of the Pacific Ocean, the islands sit about three hundred miles south of Mexico's Cabo San Lucas.

Kreutzmann says the team was "committed to the concept of nonintrusive interaction" with marine life. "We were seeking a way to go beyond our own boundaries as human beings," he said, "to meet with the creatures of the sea on *their* terms. And I hoped somehow to combine film and music to capture that moment of contact."

In San Francisco Kreutzmann chartered a 101-foot sailing yacht called the *Argosy*, the same ship that would be used later to scatter the ashes of Grateful Dead guitarist Jerry Garcia into the sea. They planned to sail for six weeks south along the coast to the main island of the Revillagigedos, a protected wilderness called Isla Socorro.

"I knew that some dive boats went there," Kreutzmann says, "but I was getting very tired of going on a dive boat with people I didn't know. I had a lot of fun doing that early in my dive career, but then I said, 'Heck with that, I can rent a boat and I can put together a crew, a real team,' and so I did."

There were nine on the boat: Kreutzmann, four filmmakers, and four crew. Wes was in the role he liked best—director.

"Wes is the one who taught me how to use a camera and taught me about scenes and how you let an animal swim through the scene. You don't chase it around and film its tail," Kreutzmann says. "He was the best I've ever seen at underwater stuff."

Kreutzmann brought a collection of percussion instruments and sat on the *Argosy*'s bow "calling" marine creatures.

"I just played as hard as I could and you could see them come right in," he said. "You can imagine all they hear out there are boat props and stuff, so to hear something like that probably piques their interest."

For this film, they wanted to make the encounters between people and marine creatures seem fluid and natural. Everyone agreed that doing free diving with a mask, snorkel, and fins, and staying down and holding their breath, would work better than wearing scuba tanks.

Wes told Kreutzmann: "For filming's sake, it's better if you don't have this big bubble mass on your back. You're free."

For Kreutzmann, the Mexico diving trip was a rare break from the Grateful Dead's touring schedule. "It was a dream come true for me to be on the water that much time and not have to play gigs, you know, really do my hobby besides music, my other passion," Kreutzmann says.

"Wes was a big influence for me. I loved the guy a lot. He was like a life coach. He'd say: 'Come on, you can do this, man, come on, you can do this.' Anything that I felt was over my head, I always had a sense of good confidence when he was in the water with us. I was near his side when we were diving, because I knew he would know what to do in a second if something went down. I learned a long time ago, when I first started diving back in '87, that you always dive with people who are better than you for a while. I was a student, and it was fascinating. He'd have us come back from dives when we got some good film and we'd be all excited as hell and he'd say: 'Don't talk. Don't tell the story until you tell it to the camera.' And it was right on, because you're tapping the top of that emotion when you've just come from the event."

Sailing over the clear Pacific, they searched for the dark silhouettes of wide, flat manta rays and dove overboard when they spotted them. They swam close to the massive creatures, carried along by slipstream.

"I could feel their heartbeat through my wetsuit when I laid my chest on their backs," Kreutzmann said.

Slowed down and attuned to the sun, wind, and waves, Kreutzmann says that through the ocean he could physically sense the approach of other big marine creatures: whales.

"You could feel them, the clicking in your chest, before you could see them," he says. "You knew you were on track to get film way before you could see the animal. You would turn your camera on way early, because the clicking was so loud in your chest. And then they would come, just materializing out of the mist."

Even though they were doing free diving, not scuba, *Rodale's SCUBA Diving* magazine bought a freelance article Wes wrote about the experience, in which he noted that some readers "might think it redundant to say that a member of the Grateful Dead took a trip and had a vision."

. . . As a cave diver, I thought that I had died and gone to heaven. Every half mile or so there was a giant sea cave—some 80 feet from floor to ceiling—teeming with life. . . . Above water, high tide spilled water into the "Aquariums," captive pools in the rocks high above the water line.

Getting into the pools meant timing a swell and hoping it lifted us high enough to clear the rocks at the lip. Getting out was trickier; BK took a hideous wipeout trying to swim out against a swell.

On the windward side of Isla San Benedicto, the sea was so rough that at times I thought we should turn back, but BK powered on. The water carried the dark-blue signature of extreme deep water. Passing caves, spiky points, and islets, we arrived at a point where we could clearly see a current line.

Only seconds later we discovered one of the most unique phenomena I've ever seen: within the current line we could see mantas, not a pair, not a handful. A whole herd—14 to 16 huge animals, the smallest one 16 feet across, flying in formation along a line of flotsam at the edge of the current. Slipping quietly into the water with masks and snorkels only, we joined the show in progress. The mantas gather here to feed on microorganisms, which got their revenge by stinging us.

As we filmed for over an hour, the mantas would periodically split off from the group to follow us.

Alongside another sea cave, Wes writes,

> we discovered stacks of pelagics: layer upon layer of jacks, yellowfin, blackfin, and wahoo, all hanging out in the current. At 80 feet, we hit dark green, cold water. Angling down, shapes in the hazy distance caught my eye: the familiar pattern of a large school of hammerheads. Seconds later, a cloud of some 50 scalloped hammerheads enveloped us at 130 feet.

The Grateful Dead drummer and his crew got the marine magic they were looking for.

After twenty-one days at sea, the *Argosy* pulled into the resort town of Cabo San Lucas. They found out that Grateful Dead guitarist Bob Weir was there, playing a benefit concert. The divers all hopped off the boat onto land. In an impromptu scene that would have made Deadheads the world over jealous, Wes watched Kreutzmann join Weir for a jam session in the tropical bar.

> BK's long, strange trip had taken us to a little-known backwater, and in the end, we wound up where we started. BK jamming with Weir, and us photographers hoping the images in our cameras would come close to showing the rest of the world what we experienced.

What Wes never mentions in his scuba magazine article is that the trip to the Revillagigedos was darkened by tragedy. Kreutzmann's friend Tabb Vadon drowned while free diving within a week of their setting sail out of San Francisco.

"He was free diving by himself, which is something you should never do," Kreutzmann says. "What happens when people are really healthy is that they overpush their bounds if they're into diving. A person like myself, I know when I'm running low on oxygen, and I'm really willing to get back to the surface and take a big gulp of air. People who free dive a lot, your body gives you a warning—it's painful and you feel out of breath. You can overpower that reflex in your body and stay too long and, unfortunately, pass out. When you're in the water and you pass out, your reaction is to breathe. It's a mammalian reflex. And salt water in the lungs is a really hard thing.

"His family, his people, God bless them, flew down to San Diego. We had not decided what to do yet, and thanks to the time spent with them, they encouraged me to keep going with the trip. We didn't know how they were going to feel about that. That was the hardest thing that's ever happened to me, I'll tell you. I never want it to happen again."

In his journal, Wes wrote that he privately worried that Vadon seemed morose, distracted, and was constantly drifting out of sight of the boat. After Vadon drowned, Wes noted: *For me, it was the 31st body recovery I had performed in my relatively short 35 years.*

Vadon was the first victim Wes had ever recovered outside of a cave. And of all the people whose bodies he'd brought out over the years, Vadon was the only victim he'd known personally.

12

Swimming with Whales

CHANCES ARE YOU'VE HEARD Bill Kurtis's voice. It's got the timbre of the quintessential old-time anchorman, and he's provided the vocals for hundreds of American television programs over decades. Kurtis has been a reporter, anchorman, and announcer on the *CBS Morning News*, A&E Network's *Cold Case Files*, *Investigative Reports*, *American Greed*, and *American Justice*. You may have also heard him do comedy performances that spoof his announcer persona—including National Public Radio's goofy quiz show *Wait Wait . . . Don't Tell Me* and the movies *Anchorman* and *Anchorman 2*, starring Will Ferrell.

Kurtis's roots run deep in serious journalism. He covered the Charles Manson murders, the unveiling of the Pentagon Papers, the travesty of Agent Orange herbicide spraying in Vietnam, and the nuclear disaster at the Chernobyl atomic power plant in the Soviet Union, just to name a few.

In the 1990s, Kurtis moved into the business side of media and started his own production company. When Wes was trying to break into network television, Kurtis opened the biggest doors. Kurtis's adventure documentary series *The New Explorers* was the perfect vehicle for the sort of films Wes wanted to create, film, and direct. It was also a good match personally, because Kurtis and Wes were kindred spirits; both were down-to-earth storytellers who loved wild places. When I asked Kurtis about Wes, the superlatives started flowing in those famous melodious tones. He sounded like he was narrating a documentary.

"Wes was an explorer of the highest caliber, harkening back to the earliest days when people crossed the ocean without knowing what was on the other side, when they went into space not knowing what was out there, or tried to break the sound barrier, not knowing if they would explode," he said. "Wes would light up as he was saying: 'Can you imagine discovering this pile of Mayan skulls in an underwater cave that no one has seen before?' You would see the fire in his eyes and the smile that would come over his face. It was just like discovering gold would be to other people, only more so, because this was true exploration."

At Wes's urging, Kurtis agreed to produce a *New Explorers* segment about scientists who study sperm whales in the Galápagos Islands off Ecuador. The Galápagos are on all nature lovers' bucket lists. It's the place where Charles Darwin honed his theory of natural selection as he surveyed the wide assemblage of quirky endemic species found nowhere else on the planet. Wes knew that mounting an expedition to this remote area off the coast of South America was bound to be expensive. Fortunately, Kurtis was up for it, and the planning began.

To film the whale encounters, Wes turned to people that he knew had the courage, aquatic skills, and steady hands needed to get the job done, namely Grateful Dead drummer Bill Kreutzmann and Jeffrey Haupt. As they had in Mexico's Revillagigedo Islands, they opted to wear only masks and snorkels when they filmed the whales.

Once again, Wes and his friends headed across the globe, laden with mountains of film and expedition gear. Flying into the Galápagos, he was surprised when he looked below and saw a perfect surfing beach, something he hadn't ever considered in the context of these islands (you don't really ever hear anybody say: "Surf Galápagos!"). His journal reads:

> From 10,000 feet, I could see long, perfect barreling—which certainly must have been six to eight feet and empty. Any place on the earth with good surf instantly qualifies in my book as a good place to be. . . . I giggled as our truck ran down the landing strip as casually as if it were the main highway. Before we had made it to the end, a large bus passed us. I laughed at the comical thought of a 737 jet dodging buses and trucks just to land on the island.

His mind flashed back to another landing he'd experienced in a remote part of Africa, when the plane chased a group of startled zebras off a Serengeti runway. Once they touched land on the Galápagos, Wes and crew unloaded the massive piles of gear onto a bus, then traveled through what Wes called *a bizarre land of volcanic craters, prehistoric creatures, and incredible vegetation,* finally arriving at a beautiful harbor that was home to the Charles Darwin Research Station.

They would be filming a whale tracking project by marine mammal expert Dr. Bruce Mate of the Whale Conservation Institute. Mate's crew planned to place tags linked to space satellites on individual sperm whales. The scientists would attach the tags to darts and shoot the darts at the whales as they passed by in the water—an exceedingly tricky task, even considering that the targets are among the biggest creatures on Earth. The tags would allow scientists to study the whales' feeding habits and to document, for the first time, the location, depth, and duration of a whale's dive. Scientists believed that sperm whales dove more than two miles deep in search of their favored prey, giant squid. The researchers were about to do what the voraciously curious Darwin could only imagine: follow the journey that a gargantuan whale takes when it plunges out of sight.

Once the scientists had their tags in place, Wes, Haupt, and Kreutzmann planned to jump in to film and free-dive with the wild marine creatures. The three knew that they would be absolutely dwarfed by the whales, which can grow longer than a Greyhound bus and weigh more than an 18-wheeler. Their plan was to wait on the surface, treading water. When the crew on the research boat located the whales, the three cameramen would each position themselves in front of the oncoming pod, take a deep breath, submerge, and hope that a) they got usable footage in the ocean's gloom; and b) they did not get eaten. Whales do not typically predate on humans, but still—they do eat giant squid, sea turtles, and seals. Mistakes were possible.

In the harbor near Darwin Research Station, the crew boarded the *Odyssey*, a 94-foot research vessel equipped with a sensitive listening array that could detect the distinctive clicks of sperm whales a full forty miles away. The *Odyssey* would be home for the next twenty days, cruising the very waters Darwin explored from the deck of the *Beagle* in the 1800s. Wes wrote in his journal:

I was instantly sure it was going to be a wonderful learning and growing time in my life. On the way out, we passed a three-and-a-half-foot-long iguana casually swimming across the harbor. For some unknown reason I tried to act casual about the encounter, but inside I was already full of wonder and amazement at this remarkable place.

First they headed out on a mini-trip in a small boat to film dolphins.

We raced at full speed. We were treated to a splendid performance of jumping, spinning, and flipping. . . . At times, groups of 15 to 20 dolphins would hurl themselves into the sky in a choreographed performance. . . . I attempted to shoot video but it was simply a waste. Here we are amidst hundreds of the fastest, most intelligent and beautiful marine animals on the planet, in a rubber boat with gasoline burning, box full of gear, pistons, wires, and a prop bouncing off the tops of the waves, trying our best to hold onto anything—including each other—as our teeth rattle and our eyeballs vibrate . . . all in hopes of experiencing a meaningful interaction. What a joke we are at times.

Back on the *Odyssey*, Wes and his colleagues were energized by the wildlife bonanza around them. But they were about to face the difficult and boring lesson that adventure filmmaking is not always an adventure. It was all about waiting around, scanning the horizon and fiddling with equipment. And so it went for fifteen days cruising the Pacific Ocean off South America, with Galápagos whales nowhere in sight.

On Day 16 they finally found a group of whales—just not the kind they were looking for. These were pilot whales, swift members of the dolphin family nicknamed the "cheetahs of the deep sea" because they plunge fast like wildcats, as deep as 3,000 feet, to take down their prey. While sperm whales have the familiar block-shaped head and the ubiquitous "whale shape" so often stamped onto clothing and knickknacks, pilot whales have dorsal fins and look more like smiling dolphins—except they can grow to a length of twenty feet and tip the scales at three tons. Wes and the *Odyssey* crew were now miles from civilization, about to dive without the security of scuba gear into a pod of enormous, unpredictable creatures. They were ecstatic.

From out of the gloom came a great group of over 20 whales. The water was layered with a thick, low vis[ibility] pea green soup, the top 10 feet with reasonably blue water beneath. With several whales only 20 feet from me on the surface, I dove down, hoping to film them in the clearer water.

Descending, I felt the thrill of a first encounter surging through my system.
With a sudden purpose, I felt my first sonic acoustic hammering from a
whale. They were examining me with their unbelievable acoustic capabili-
ties. It almost hurt it was so intense.

Seeing the pilot whales was apparently the expedition magic they needed,
because they soon encountered their chosen cinematic quarry: deep-diving
sperm whales.

"We had found, not four to five, not 10 to 20 whales, but perhaps over a
hundred sperm whales!" Wes recounted in an article for *Rodale's SCUBA
Diving* magazine.

> I remember the first time two whales came at us . . . Suddenly, two
> gigantic heads charged at us from the gloom. No time to react, I froze,
> waiting for the inevitable collision. Then, to my amazement, the lead
> whale stopped dead and swung his head slowly sideways, taking a
> moment to look me over head to toe. The second whale arched up
> and over the first, then both disappeared into the gloom. . . . The set-
> ting could not have been more spectacular. Juxtaposed between two
> massive islands, a golden sun, distant storms and a vivid rainbow, our
> patience was rewarded with one of the most unbelievable displays of
> nature I have ever witnessed.

The whales' behavior began to look strange, with smaller pods coalescing
into larger groups of densely packed whales.

> I had no doubt they were following some calm and predetermined
> plan. This could be our chance. When we found ourselves a half a mile
> in front of about 40 whales, we scrambled frantically for our camera
> and gear like The Three Stooges. Once in the water, I tried to calm
> down and collect myself as I prepared for the encounter, but a mixture
> of adrenaline, curiosity, and fear still pumped through me. No good
> for my breath-holding ability. My lungs felt tight and tiny. I closed my
> eyes and breathed deeply, trying to push from my mind the fact that
> I was floating on top of 26,000 feet of water about to face 40 of the
> largest carnivores on the planet. . . . I took a big breath and dove down
> to 40 feet and hung there, hoping to film at a dramatic up-angle as the
> whales passed over me. After what seemed a silent, lung-bursting eter-
> nity, the whales were suddenly there. The first line of them had clev-

erly dived beneath us, but the second group was still on the surface, lighted by the sun, swimming directly over us in a magnificent display of power and grace. Within seconds it was over. We surfaced sucking for air and screaming at one another like excited kids. We didn't have long to celebrate. Another pod was coming right at us.

As they bobbed on the surface, Wes and crew noticed a commotion in the distance.

At first we thought it was dolphins, but as this new group moved up toward us, we could sense that it was not a happy-go-lucky pod of dolphins. These animals sliced through the water with a razor-edged intensity unlike anything I have ever seen or felt. Too many and moving too fast to be sharks. Killer whales? I wondered.

The marine biologist, Dr. Mate, was pointing toward the sperm whales. About forty of them were now forming a curious-looking formation, gathering their heads together, with their bodies and tails sticking out like the petals of a daisy. The pod of fast-moving creatures neared the "whale flower," and Dr. Mate identified the aggressors as pseudorcas, also known as false killer whales. The false killer whales are actually in the dolphin, not whale, family, and they join together in packs to kill and eat sperm whales.

As the grisly encounter played out, Wes watched the whale pod become obscured by an ominous reddish brown cloud. When blood is in the water, most people get out. Wes swam straight into the cloud.

As I moved deeper into it, I began to see large chunks of whale skins spiraling downward. A feeling of horror struck me as I watched the feasting, but I didn't have long to stare: I was thrashed by the powerful stroke of a fluke that sent me spinning. Surfacing, gasping for breath, I could see more than 20 sperm whale flukes pointing to the sky. Then, simultaneously, they all disappeared into the safety of the depths where no other mammal could go. It was the last we'd see of the sperm whales on our expedition.

The pseudorcas, however, were still all around, available for filming. Fearlessly, Wes, Haupt, and Kreutzmann grabbed lungfuls of air and went back down with their cameras. A dominant male pseudorca about twenty-two feet long started interacting purposefully with the three photographers.

He spoke continuously, letting out streams of vocalizations mixed with bubbles that sounded so much like human speech that it sent shivers through me. At times, it was as if he were asking us questions, and he toyed with each one of us, as if testing us. If so, we all failed miserably, capable only of staring impotently as he flew around us, having his way.

Haupt was filming intently and didn't see when the big pseudorca rolled upside down and swam beneath him.

As the whale came closer and closer to Jeffrey, I screamed through my snorkel. To no avail, the big male moved closer, his head within a yard of Jeffrey's head, his mouth slightly open and flashing rows of sharp teeth.

At the last moment Kreutzmann was able to get Haupt's attention, and he pointed frantically at the whale.

Jeffrey nearly jumped out of his wetsuit when he looked beneath him. The pseudorca simply burst out in front of Jeffrey and resumed his vocalizations, except this time there was no mistaking the mocking laugh.

Then it was my turn. The big male swooped in front of me. As I had learned the hard way with great white sharks, it's important to show no fear, so I did my best I'm-not-scared-let's-just-play routine. He seemed to buy it, swinging around and offering me his fluke. As I reached out to touch him, he began to tremor in excitement. Bad idea, bad idea, I thought. Just as I retracted my hand, the male whipped around, opened his mouth wide, and let out a series of ear-splitting whines. I immediately balled up and hoped he'd forgive me for being so bold.

Snapping a few last pictures, we surfaced to celebrate one of the most phenomenal encounters of our lives.

13

The Hated Cave

WES FINALLY LANDED HIS second assignment for *National Geographic* magazine, an expedition that would turn out to be grueling, shocking, and dangerous. A team of elite explorers would survey a remote Mexican cave system called Huautla (pronounced WOW-tla), considered the deepest ever explored on the planet. The expedition leader was legendary explorer Bill Stone, who had run the 1987 mission into Florida's Wakulla Springs. Huautla was the site of eighteen previous expeditions since the 1960s. Explorers who traveled deep inside the cave system always had to stop when they reached an underwater tunnel: to go any further, they'd need to cave dive. That's where Wes and his highly experienced colleagues came in.

To even reach the water where they would start swimming into the cave system, the team had to travel miles through the jungle, rig an elaborate system of ropes and climbing equipment, rappel down into a steep-sided dry limestone hole, then pick their way past raging underground waterfalls and through tricky, slick rock passageways with names like Slip 'n' Slide Drop, Cracked Slab, and Dust Devil. Their dive destination was a water-filled chamber called the San Agustín Sump, nearly three-quarters of a mile deep inside the Earth and about two miles from the hole they entered at the surface. It is a treacherous place, filled with roaring waterfalls (ear-splitting in the enclosed space) and swift underground rivers that can rise frighteningly fast when it rains on the surface.

Like a lunar mission, it took a prodigious amount of planning and painstaking execution. The expedition team took three weeks to lower almost a ton of dive equipment and supplies into the cave system. The equipment included Stone's latest MK4 rebreathers, the fourth-generation successors to the self-contained life support systems that he had designed and tested at Wakulla. At Wakulla, Stone's rebreather prototype weighed about 200 pounds. By this time he had trimmed the rebreather weight down to 97 pounds. To transport the rebreathers into the cave system, the team dismantled the components and carried them separately. Broken down like that, the remaining main part of the rebreather was still 43 pounds, not an easy load to carry on rappelling ropes through steep passages.

The way up and down included a passage called the Stairway to Hell because they had to rig climbing ropes to ninety-two vertical drops, using nearly two miles of nylon line total.

The team would live in damp, dark camps, sometimes sleeping in hammocks and on a type of scaffolding platform that Stone designed—a 4-by-12-foot nylon deck made of hollow aluminum tubing that they bolted into the cave's limestone walls. They ate freeze-dried camp food, pulverized and stuffed into plastic bottles; adding water made it into an unappetizing protein mush. They drank cave water treated with iodine. Their "bathroom" was a plastic bottle for urine and one-gallon Ziploc bags for the solid stuff. The pack-it-in-pack-it-out environmental ethos that authorities required from explorers meant they had to seal the Ziplocs, stow them in a vinyl duffel, and haul them out of the cave.

Wes's old friend, Florida cave diving legend Sheck Exley, had previously been invited to join Stone in exploring Huautla, but he said no.

"I don't much like vertical caving," Exley told a reporter for *Outside* magazine. "All that climbing, sleeping for weeks in the cave, eating food I'd just as soon not eat. It's what they have to go through before they even get to the water that intimidates me. It's like trying to dive on Mars—if Mars had water."

Once assembled for the diving part of the adventure, Stone's exploration party was so deep inside the Earth that you could have fit the entire Chicago Sears Tower between them and the surface.

Huautla is revered as a sacred site by the resident Mazatec Indians, and some bad feelings remained from the 1960s, when psychedelic seekers invaded the region to collect its famous psilocybin mushrooms. In previous expeditions into the cave system, the Mazatecs cut a rope on one caver, who luckily fell to a ledge and was unharmed. In 1970, villagers rolled boulders down on top of a cave opening, temporarily trapping an exploration party. During Stone's expedition, a six-mile stretch of fiber optic cable that they spent a week stringing across farm fields and into the cave to transmit video was cut twice before the explorers finally gave up trying.

Wes joined the expedition partway through, showing up with his dive buddy Tom Morris. This time, Wes was the *National Geographic* still photographer assigned to document the team's work. He arrived to a devastating scene.

Cloaked in clouds and mist, very ominous arrival, Wes wrote in his journal. Ian Rolland, a twenty-nine-year-old Scottish caver and father of three, had died while diving in the cave. It took expedition members six days to bring Rolland's body out, and Wes would be the one who photographed the grim-faced villagers carrying the stretcher with his Scottish friend's shrouded body the last quarter-mile to the nearby village.

The rumor was that Stone's rebreather had killed Rolland, but that was false. A diabetic, Rolland had died from insulin shock. The team members didn't know that at the time, and some were wary and furious. Five packed up and left the mission.

Photographed Ian's removal from cave and transit to church, Wes wrote in his journal on April 1, 1994. *Incredibly moving ceremony held by local Mazatecs. Felt full impact of our loss after the service. Took first trip into cave. Entrance defies description, from large to small, all picturesque. This project will most definitely change my life in many ways.*

With palpable grief, the remaining team members settled into a daily rhythm, shuttling in and out of the cave system, in and out of dive gear, and making measurements to document their discoveries. After Rolland's death, everyone involved was in flux, uncertain whether to continue Stone's highwire Huautla quest.

Wes argued that Rolland would have wanted them to continue. In fact, in an interview that Wes filmed before the expedition, Rolland had said: "Everybody, I think, has contemplated the possibility of death, for either themselves or somebody else. It's a subject Bill and I discussed at length . . . we both felt that if something happened to . . . to one of us, the expedition should continue, because it's something we all believe in."

Wes argued that it made little sense for them to come all this way and do all this grueling expedition work without having any pictures to document their mission and nothing to show the sponsors that bankrolled it. Stay here just long enough, Wes pleaded, for us to get *National Geographic* pictures.

Stone and his cave-diving girlfriend, Barbara em Ende, wanted to continue attempting to explore the new stretch of cave that Rolland was exploring when he died—the water-filled San Agustín Sump. The feat required diving on rebreathers, and not everyone on the expedition was willing. Of the nine divers trained on the rebreathers, five had already left and two refused to go beyond the water-filled sump.

Because people didn't have cell phones in those days, reaching the outside world meant finding a land line, and periodically team members would travel to a nearby village to call home. On April 7, Wes and his longtime friend Kenny Broad left the dispirited cave diving expedition and went to the village to make phone calls. Broad had been a good buddy of Rolland's, and Wes took some time to talk things through with his friend as they traveled through the remote Mexican countryside.

At the village, when Wes called to check in with Terri, she gave him a piece of news that took his legs out from under him. Wes's mentor Sheck Exley, the bulletproof macho man who wrote *Basic Cave Diving: A Blueprint for Survival*, was dead. He was forty-five years old.

Someone had called the Skiles house in High Springs, Terri explained, asking if Wes was available to go to help recover Exley's body. As it turned out, Exley was also in Mexico, at a deep sinkhole called Zacatón. He was there trying to break the world record for deepest dive. His equipment showed he was about 905 feet deep when he drowned. His body surfaced three days later as recovery divers were preparing to go down into the sinkhole. It was hard to believe that Wes and Exley, two top North Florida cave divers, were coincidentally both deep inside the deepest holes in the Mexican jungle, and that one of them didn't come out alive.

Low point of all recent memory, Wes wrote in his journal. *After a bad night, I began a bad day, ending with a decision to quit project and go home. Pain over deaths of Ian and Sheck mixed with the dark atmosphere of my living environment took its absolute toll. I shot the cave a bird, glad I would never have to see it again. Took two hours to exit, slept along the way. Packed in the morning, anxious to leave by midday.*

"Not only did I feel like I had been playing dodgeball with the Grim Reaper, but now all my friends were getting taken out," Wes later told *Technical Diving* magazine.

"I've been on some really screwed-up expeditions in my life, but none have been as bad as this," Kenny Broad said, ticking off what he saw as the main problems—Rolland's death, unproven technology, not enough man-power, bad morale, and the rainy season closing in.

"I hate quitters," he said. "I don't want to be a quitter."

Wes was just about gone when Stone was able to sit him down at base camp and talk him out of leaving. Reluctantly, Wes agreed to stay another week to carry out his assignment for *National Geographic*. In his journal entry for April 15 he recorded the depth at 630 meters, or 2,066 feet, and wrote:

> *I'm deeper in the earth than I've ever been. The circumstances are unfavor-able, in that the team I'm here to photograph is in such peril of breaking apart. Nonetheless, the journey down to this point is another world. I'm lying on my Therma-rest in the "environment" that I have created around me. It's quite fantastic. I have everything I need, almost. I have a place to sit and dress, a table for my things, a nice level bed place which I dug with a small shovel, and even a marker-stone at the foot of my bed.*
>
> *It would be great to say that I'm totally comfortable in this place, but I have felt the icy fingers of panic touch my heart in the sudden realization of how deep underground I am. The comfort of my friends and the knowledge of myself keeps me from seeking escape. I'm happy to be here when I don't think about it. I miss my family, and will remember to thank God when I see them again.*

April 16:

> *This place is spooky at times; rocks falling in the distance, rooms so big you lose yourself in them. Without a doubt these will be the most highly earned photographs of my career. Deep inside the earth with thousands of feet of rock atop you, it can be difficult to think freely and artistically. Hope tomorrow will bring a better performance.*

April 17:

> *We're trapped underground for what might be a long stay. Awoke to a heightened sound of water flowing through the gorge. Kenny and I first acknowledged it together, Noel said there was no change. When we arrived at the water, flood, foam, and low visibility water was powering through*

what was all dry passage the night before. The rocks Kenny and I heard the night before were perhaps the first warning signs.

Not again. Not buried alive in a cave like they were in Australia's Pannikin Plain six years earlier.

The realization that I have become trapped inside the earth once again is quite powerful. Fortunately, the panic that one might easily experience in this type of situation is not here to haunt me today—might as well simply enjoy the awesome display of Mother Nature.

We shot five rolls of film today—far better than the day before. I mostly focused on increased water flow through the cave. We discovered that trying to head out was a futile and dangerous endeavor. We have gone onto [food] rations tonight until we know what's happening with our plight.

Hoping to find a route out, one of the team members went to scout an exit route, but he was turned back by violent waters.

April 19:

Day three. Isolated from the surface by cave water force plowing through the upper gorge. This is the second time we've been forced to turn around and return to camp. Today we had a very close call when Steve lost his footing and got swept under a waterfall while on rope. We heard his screams for help, along with Tom's. Noel managed to get to Steve first and was able to help pull him to the side, out of the water's greatest force. Ironically, we were just talking about turning around because it was getting too hairy.

After retreating, we went into the lower gorge, only to be turned around there too. The lower gorge is one of the most beautiful passages I've ever seen. I'm very disappointed I will not get to see more.

Tonight we made the difficult and scary decision to exit the cave, for better or worse, tomorrow. We're running low on food, and the fear factor of our situation is rising. The water has not declined in two days and we fear we have entered a fairly rainy season. . . . My next entry, I hope, will be tomorrow.

April 21:

The morning of the 20th, a mixture of confidence that we would get out, and mixed with deep, emotional feelings of the unknowns we were to face. My agreement with the team to exit was that we would try to get out of

the cave and to take photos. Regardless, we left camp with absolute final-
ity; we were going to exit regardless of the consequences. Steve, who nearly
drowned the day before, acknowledged his anxiety. Tom said it felt like we
were about to go into battle. Tears welled up in my eyes when I admitted to
Kenny I just wanted to get out of this godforsaken place.

Upon our arrival at the gorge, we discovered the water had dropped
another six inches, which was a great relief to all of us. We managed to take
a few pictures. . . . The water had dropped enough to allow us to exit, barely,
and we were all thankful for the good timing.

I actually led the exit, not by design, but by chance and desire to look
for possible shots. The climb out of the pit was relentless but enjoyable, in
an odd, painful sort of way. . . . I faced each climb, 24 total, one at a time.
Some nearly got the best of me. At this point I could have left my pack, but
pride and the fact that I never wanted to go back in the cave got me through
the worst times.

When they finally reached the cave entrance, exhausted, they were dis-
mayed to find that the line they had used to descend had vanished.

We were wet, tired, and trapped once again. It was almost too much to be-
lieve. In the distance a light was on, and aiming into the cave. We took this
as a sign that someone would be back with a rope. We discovered we were
wrong, but it was too late to care for me. Since I had carried my camp gear,
I decided simply to camp in the entrance and deal with the situation in the
morning. . . . It was a miserable night, in that I wasn't out. I was hungry
and dehydrated, but I managed, knowing that the exit would be sweet in
the morning. The climb out was exhausting, even after the rest. . . . Took
pictures of the entrance. Some good shots I hope.

Wes's photography from the ill-fated Huautla expedition ran with a sixteen-
page *National Geographic* article that Stone wrote. A shot Wes took outside
the cave looks like an aerial photograph, showing an explorer hanging, ant-
like, from the rope that dangles into the black hole in the jungle floor leading into the cave system. Another two-page image shows three stern-faced
expedition members trying to keep their balance in raging water inside a
spooky cave passage. It's hard to remember that Wes is sandwiched in there
with them, trying to stay steady in the current to get the shot.

One of the most impressive images Wes made during the exhausting expedition ran in a fold-out three-page section. It was a huge pitch-black dry cave, a cavernous ballroom with soaring ceilings. To show the scale of the lightless place, Wes positioned individual cavers in stages, some in the foreground, some in the middle, and some in the background. The cavers have their backs to the camera, and they each hold lights that pool in front of them, outlining their bodies like shadow figures. Through all that adversity, Wes managed to produce an arresting, unusual image that impressed the editors.

In the end, after eighteen days underground, the team's survey pushed Huautla's rank from the world's twelfth-deepest explored cave to the fifth-deepest. Wes later called the expedition his most difficult to date. Someone died in that cave, the grieving crew had to endure disgusting and harrowing conditions, and he'd lost half the film he shot, between those conditions and equipment failure.

"I was faced with going down into this dark, foreboding, high-stress environment and working creatively on photographic images," he said. "We descended thousands of feet on ropes with the terrific noise of waterfalls crashing all around us through high-current passageways and over large boulder piles with unbelievable quantities of equipment. It was cold, wet, and perpetually dark. When I came out of the earth, I looked back at that sucker and I never wanted to see it again. Now, I want to go back, of course. The caver's curse, you know? You hate it while you're there, then you miss it when you come out.'"

14

High Anxiety

WES BARELY HAD TIME to catch his breath from the traumatic Huautla expedition before he was on the road again. Although few knew it, work stress was making him both sick and anxious. He had chronic digestive problems (later diagnosed, Terri says, as gluten intolerance from celiac disease) and pain in his camera-carrying shoulder from damage caused years earlier by the bends when he didn't get timely treatment to free the gas bubbles trapped in his tissues.

When *Outside* magazine called Wes "one of those rare, fortunate souls who's managed to carve out a living doing precisely what he loves most, deftly blurring the distinction between office and playground," it was both true and not true.

Shooting footage of wildlife and natural phenomenon is always an unpredictable business. In the old days, when Wes filmed and photographed in springs country, he had fun, and capturing something wonderful was a hoped-for gift but never a requirement. On these expensive, high-stakes documentary shoots, the pressure was constant and creativity had to happen on demand. Developments in both dive equipment and photography equipment were moving fast, so keeping up with the latest technology meant he had to constantly make substantial investments with uncertain returns. In his journal he wrote:

> *How wondrous the life I get to lead. Why do I feel so often that I'm throwing it away? It's not that I don't appreciate the experiences I have, I do. It*

just seems sometimes that once I'm having them, I don't get to take full advantage of the situations. I know the experience that I want, I'm in the location, yet for some reason or another, I fail to make it all happen. Some days there's simply not enough hours in the day. Other days I let opportunity knocking stay outside. . . . The big question I must soon address is cliché, but nonetheless exists: What am I here for? and What is it I'm going to do about it? . . . In most cases, I would rather surf or dive my way through life. . . . I want to make films, tell stories, take pictures, and share them in a way that it makes a difference, some way, in people's lives. The how-to-make-that-happen is what continues to loop me around in this full circle of chaos and confusion.

Years later, when an interviewer asked Wes for his thoughts on being a *National Geographic* filmmaker and photographer, his mind went first to the pressure:

When the magazine calls and says, "Hey, we want you to go do this," the worrying starts that moment. It's such a high standard to live up to. There is only one *National Geographic* on Earth, and to be a photographer for them is the ultimate achievement. You put this pressure on yourself. I can't sleep. I dream the photographs. I'm tired and angry and irritable when I wake up, and no one understands what's going on with me. Everybody else is just like "Hey, we're having a great time and Wes is going to get the photograph." They don't know how worried I am about getting the photograph. And I don't usually really worry about a lot of things—but I do about taking pictures for the greatest magazine on Earth.

On the outside, Wes was the gregarious swashbuckler everyone wanted to be around.

"Wes would command everyone's attention at dinner with a client or whoever, and he had his top-ten list of stories. He cranked up, and it was just story after story after story. He got people laughing and crying," Jeffrey Haupt says. "There were years when we spent every waking hour scheming up adventures to go on. And I'll be darned if we didn't figure out a way to do it. I mean, every place we wanted to go, we figured out a way to go there. If we wanted to go to Tahiti, damn we were in Tahiti. If we wanted to go to the Bahamas or Mexico or you know, Africa, we were there."

As much as he complained privately, he didn't want to be doing anything else. He'd done the sort of daredevil feats he always dreamed about when he was a kid watching *The Undersea World of Jacques Cousteau.* He beat off a great white shark by using his camera as a battering ram. A baby cape fur seal bit him in the face in Africa when he picked it up, and then a large adult seal savagely attacked him in the shoulder, slamming into him and biting him as he crept through the waves, filming. He worked hard and delivered the images.

In 1994 Wes got a television network prime-time assignment that he thought would finally give him the chance to bring his lifelong message to the nation's living rooms: Cave diving wasn't just some kooky, reckless sport—it was critical scientific exploration, as valid as missions into space.

It was an episode for *The New Explorers* called "The Most Dangerous Science," and they would film it in Mexico's Nohoch Na Chich cave system, which lies beneath the Yucatán Peninsula on the coast near Cancún and Cozumel. Nohoch Na Chich means "giant birdhouse" in Mayan, named for the thousands of needle-like stalagmites and stalactites on the floor and ceiling, which bring to mind a large wicker birdcage. Wes knew that the spectacular formations inside this cave system would bump up the "wow" factor of his first-ever major cave diving film for network television.

Through singular focus over eight years, a cave diver named Mike Madden got Nohoch Na Chich into the *Guinness Book of World Records* as the world's longest explored underwater cave system—twenty-six miles. Now he wanted to push farther. Madden believed that the system connected all the way to the coast, two miles beyond where he'd explored so far. *The New Explorers* episode would document Madden's push, and give viewers a primer on both cave diving and the latest discoveries in cave science.

Wes was able to bring Terri along on this trip to help with the film while their young children stayed in Florida with friends and relatives. Also along for the expedition were Wes's diving partner Tom Morris, his film partner Jeffrey Haupt, and Jeff's wife, Ruby, who all helped with lighting, sound, and logistics.

To get to the Nohoch Na Chich cave system's entrance, the crew had to bring all their gear for caving, diving, camping, and filmmaking to a remote village. With the help of hired locals, they strapped gear onto horses and picked their way along two miles of slippery limestone trail—a two-thousand-year-old Mayan road—through the Yucatán jungle. The entrance to the remarkable cave system looks unremarkable: a low hole over water in the shape of an eyebrow. It isn't until you get inside that you see the underwater Carlsbad Caverns–like wonderland.

During the shoot, dives spanned as long as seven hours as Wes and crew worked to illuminate the killer scenery. Part of the cave system has air pockets near the ceiling, where all you need to see the cave formations is a mask and snorkel. *The New Explorers* host Bill Kurtis geared up and delivered his opening narration with Madden from inside the cave. At times their heads nearly brushed the pointy stalactites as they moved through tight passages, Wes ahead of them, filming.

"There aren't many places left where true exploration is possible, to shine a light where no one has ever been," Kurtis narrates. "This is such a place. It is exploration's new frontier. These explorers, who came for the adventure, have opened up a new environment for scientists. It's an underground river that offers new sources of fresh water to a thirsty world—and something else. They've discovered organisms here that exist as they might have lived at the beginning of life on Earth. Join us for a dangerous journey deep within a subterranean world where secrets wait—for new explorers."

That's pretty much the message Wes had been trying to convey for the past two decades when he and his friends were slipping in and out of dark holes all over Florida, hearing people call them crazy or, worse, stupid. Now here was Kurtis, a respected television personality, delivering Wes's message for him.

When they suit up in full cave diving gear to explore the underwater part of the cave, Kurtis and Madden wear full-face masks with microphones so the audience can hear what they are saying during the scenic dive. Kurtis, predictably blown away by the haunting underwater landscape, turns to Madden and says: "Now I see why you do this!"

Wes knew that Nohoch Na Chich also had a killer visual: a halocline. Haloclines happen when a layer of salt water rests below the fresh water. Because they have different densities, the layers stratify, like oil and vinegar. The effect is a clear liquid shimmering that Wes was able to capture on film, his camera on one side and a shimmering diver on the other.

Besides focusing on Madden, the film profiles Dr. Tom Iliffe, a Texas

A&M University professor who studies, among other things, the specialized environment of haloclines and underwater caves. "We've discovered two new orders, four new families, three new genera, and nearly a hundred new species of organisms living in these cave systems," Iliffe says in the film. "These animals are not just new species, they're new higher groups of animals—types that had been previously unknown anywhere else on Earth."

Then Iliffe floats a bombshell theory:

> Perhaps caves are found at deeper depths, on the sides of islands, on the sides of continental slopes, going down, perhaps even into the deep sea. In the deep ocean, along mid-Atlantic ridges, are systems of cracks, fissures, and crevices that may offer a habitat similar to the cave habitat we're observing now. If this is true, life may be distributing itself around the world through these systems of micro-caves that are essentially a global network.

A global highway within the crust of the Earth, Kurtis describes it. Other scientists are discovering that tube worms growing around underwater vents in the Pacific are the same as tube worms growing by vents in the Atlantic, suggesting common origins.

When Wes and Morris suit up to help Madden's team make the final push to connect Nohoch Na Chich to the sea, they start at the upstream end of the cave system, dropping into an entrance that sits at the farthest end of Madden's exploration so far. Their plan is to travel swiftly downstream on scooters toward the sea. It's a gnarly section, more like one the Moles might explore in Florida.

"Unfortunately, they'll see more silt than cathedrals on this trip," Kurtis intones in the film.

What they do see are skeletons of an ancient sea-dwelling manatee and a sea turtle, making them even more certain that the cave system will connect to the Caribbean. At one point they leave the scooters behind to fit through the tight passages, then have to turn back when rocks start falling on them. It's undoubtedly good television.

In another cave-diving push ten weeks later, the team would finally make the connection to the Caribbean, a feat that provided the episode's satisfying wrap-up.

"After 'The Most Dangerous Science,' everybody wanted us to make a film down in Mexico," Haupt says. "I can't tell you how many shows we shot down there. We shot for the CBS *The Searchers*, we shot for all kinds of Discovery Channel shows, just one after another after another. We would write and shoot and help with the edits on the whole thing. The whole process of shooting for television got easier and easier for us because we understood what it took to finish a show. And so, you know, it was pretty bankable that, if you hired us, we could come back with a complete episode."

15

Extreme Atomic Diving

IN THE SPRING OF 1996, Wes got to do one of his wackiest assignments yet, filming an episode of *The New Explorers* called "Walking Among the Sharks." *Walking*, not swimming.

Their film quarry was a species called the sixgill shark, a relic from the time before dinosaurs. The giant deep-sea creatures can grow sixteen feet long and weigh as much as a full-grown dairy cow. Most sharks have five gills, so in 1996 the sixgill presented a scientific curiosity worth exploring to a marine researcher named Gregory Stone. The sixgills are known to lurk as deep as a mile below the water's surface, which made studying them quite difficult. Even with special gas mixtures, scuba gear at the time was safe only down to around 1,000 feet.

"We found this spot off of Vancouver where these deep-sea sharks came in to relatively shallow water—relatively being between six and seven hundred feet," Stone says.

The idea was for Wes to film the sharks while he walked on the ocean bottom, 700 feet down, wearing a contraption called a Newtsuit. Nicknamed for its inventor, Phil Nuytten, it was a special atmospheric diving suit, so Wes was basically wearing a submarine on his back. At the time he climbed into the contraption, there were fewer Newtsuit pilots in the world than there were astronauts.

The Newtsuit had articulated arms and legs, which Wes was able to move from inside by maneuvering levers. It had a glass-fronted bubble "head" that looked like the helmets on old-time diving suits, through which Wes could peer to see where he was going. For the film, Stone traveled in a two-man submarine to the sea bottom where Wes was. The two-man sub actually had three people crammed inside—Stone, Bill Kurtis, and Wes's *National Geographic* photographer buddy Emory Kristof, who came to test a new deep-sea digital camera. (The camera flooded on the first try, because one tiny screw wasn't tight enough to withstand the tremendous deep-sea pressure.)

The Newtsuit had two great advantages over diving: it didn't require hours of decompression time, and Wes could stay inside it for forty-five hours at a stretch. A lifelong tinkerer and gadget nerd, Wes imagined a beautiful future with that Newtsuit. He mused in his journal about someday wearing one to explore the deepest underwater reaches of the world. In the *New Explorers* episode, Kurtis says they imagine people wearing these suits and walking across the ocean floor from North America to Hawaii.

This will be a chance for me to achieve a dream and participate in first-order exploration of the bizarre and beautiful part of the planet, Wes wrote in his journal before the mission.

In the film, he climbs into the quirky suit and the crew lowers him into the frigid sea. "I'm feeling the weightlessness of just drifting down slowly," he says.

On the seafloor, he uses one of the "arms" to empty a plastic bag filled with fish parts, chumming the area to attract sixgills. Immediately the current carries the bloody cloud right back toward him, and it drifts into his face bubble and over his head.

"The first thing I'm going to see is the whole jaws coming in on top of my head," he cracks.

Then he waits. And waits. And waits. No sharks. After a frustrating five hours, someone suggests that the lights they are using to see through the gloom might be scaring sharks away. He cuts off the lights and waits on the sea bottom in darkness for two long hours. His eyes adjusted to the darkness now, he spots a shark and yelps.

"Oh. My. God! GIANT sixgill shark! We have a GIANT sixgill shark underneath me! He's circling my body now. He's a big shark! Unbelievable. He's a BIG shark!"

Then he starts laughing.

Later he would write in his journal that the Newtsuit is the powerful undersea tool he's been waiting for: *Goal for ten years: My desire is to use an exploration tool to lead the way in discovering just what is down there, a perfect extension of what I have found most rewarding in my career . . . to make observations and document phenomenon no one knows about or understands.*

He told a reporter: "We know virtually nothing about life at the bottom of the sea. . . . If I can stand down there at the bottom of the ocean and share with people things they've never seen, never imagined existed, they'll care more."

Another *New Explorers* episode was now wrapped, and Wes's career was getting significant attention. He had his photographs of the Mexican Huautla expedition in *National Geographic*. He and the Mole Tribe were the subject of a coveted spot in *Outside* magazine, which was the place to read about up-and-coming adrenaline junkies around the globe. Wes's striking photos accompanied the story, which described the Mole Tribe's outrageous feats in the wild underwater caves of North Florida. *SCUBA* magazine also did a profile of Wes and used one of his spectacular Florida springs shots on the cover. His hometown paper, the *Gainesville Sun*, did a feature story about his growing national profile as a big-time, globe-trotting cameraman. The paper ran a photo of Wes standing face-to-face with a black rhino in Kenya, with a quote from Wes underneath: "The guide said if you don't stand up and run you'll be OK."

"What I do is very hard work," he told the Gainesville reporter. "A lot of people perceive it as glamorous and exciting, and it is all of those things, but it involves long, long, hard days of work."

Wes told the reporter about days that started at four a.m. to catch the dawn light, then underwater diving and photography starting at eight and lasting through midafternoon. After a break for lunch, preparation for the evening shoot began, then they'd shoot above-ground footage through the late afternoon and evening light. When that wrapped up, they spent hours cataloging what they'd got and getting ready for the next day's shoot: charging gear, cleaning equipment, filling tanks. This routine lasted day after day until a project was finished.

"Wes and I were at our peak," Jeffrey Haupt says. "We had won the International Cinematography award, the Golden Eagle Cine Award, and the Bronze Chris Award for 'The Most Dangerous Science,' the only time in Kurtis Productions history that a film won all three awards. We beat *NOVA*, *Nature*, *National Geographic*, all of the big boys. It was a very big deal."

Now Wes and Haupt were about to enter the *National Geographic* fold again to film a new television documentary. This one would force Wes to answer the question "If you got a chance to dive reefs where no human has been for decades BUT it's radioactive—would you?" The documentary was called *Return to Paradise*, and it was an expedition to one of the most radioactive places on Earth.

They were the first film crew given access to the contaminated area, located in the South Pacific's Marshall Islands and closed to visitors ever since U.S. nuclear bomb tests in the 1950s. Also on board were *National Geographic* photographers Emory Kristof and Bill Curtsinger—who planned to test another cutting-edge, remotely operated deep-water camera—and world-renowned marine explorer Teddy Tucker. They traveled into the marine wilderness to probe the environment near one of the world's largest coral reefs, called Rongelap Atoll.

During the expedition Wes wrote a series of vivid journal entries:

Three dives. We dove on a beautiful bombie with great large red snapper resembling caberras. They were so uninhibited by our presence that one of them actually bit Bill to see what he tasted like. They had obviously never seen humans before.

A large resident nurse shark showed up right in front of my lens unannounced. Jeffrey free dove down several times and we built a nice sequence of the encounter. After the dive we headed into the Tufa Lagoon—this was without a doubt the most beautiful uninhabited lagoon I have ever seen. No one, no thing, no power, no lights, no structures. . . . The irony is that it's man's destructive nature which has created one of the last bastions of Utopia. This is the "Blue Lagoon." Inside the lagoon were incredible corals and fish of every description, white sand beaches, and coconut palms. It's shaped like a fat C and made for a great protective harbor for our boat, the Mystique.

Towards the end of my dive, I got my first taste of the aggressive behavior of the grey reef sharks—a small, sleek, and very fast shark. No one was around when this grey suit showed up. As I would normally do, I showed the shark I was not scared of it by moving towards it with my camera. Never before had I seen such a reaction from a shark. Almost instantly it went into a frenzied, arched-back, pecs-down position, and darted around me like a misdirected lightning bolt. I was really taken aback by such a dramatic response. I knew right then that I was in an ocean environment that I knew very little about. This one shark had gotten my attention—fast. It was a good warning for me to watch my back. I kept my eye on the little bugger and slowly returned back to the boat.

When I surfaced, the guys were ready to go. Climbing in the boat, I noticed great congregation of terns and boobies hitting the surface of the water about a quarter mile away. With a mixture of fear and electrifying excitement, we decided to go check it out. We knew that beneath the birds would be some kind of feeding. Exactly what, we did not yet know.

Entering this water with mask and fins, we were immediately surrounded by rainbow runners in great quantities. Seconds later, the wall of fish cleared to reveal too many sharks to count. They bulleted by us with great energy . . . maybe great energy isn't the right term—call it nervous excitement. The sharks circled Jeffrey and I, coming from all directions and getting much too close to keep track of. Within what seemed like seconds, the boat was a hundred yards away and I was all alone. Swimming with purpose towards the boat made the sharks more excited, so I decided to take my chances drifting away from the boat with a great circling mass of grey reefs.

The *Mystique* puttered over to rescue Wes, and right after he climbed aboard, a giant gray shape circled the boat: a silver-tipped shark, notoriously aggressive. *Just think,* he wrote. *Minutes before, I was all alone surrounded by sharks.*

While the documentary crew had been diving, the boat's owner, Nigel, went ashore to one of the idyllic beaches and set up a special picnic. *A row of chairs were carefully placed on the edge of the water, each with their own foot mats and palm umbrellas. A cooler full of Victoria Bitter, a grand beer from Australia, was served with sunset.* Everybody partied on the isolated island, eating barbecued chicken and telling stories around a campfire fueled by coconut husks.

Oftentimes in life, I've found myself telling stories of my adventures around the world, Wes wrote once they were back on the boat. *With this crew, I feel I have no stories to tell. The things they have seen and done are so fantastic it's hard to believe.*

One of their colleagues walked away from the firelight and came back holding up what Wes called a "hideous but beautiful" coconut crab.

It looked like a cross between a crayfish, lobster, and stone crab. It was blue in color and absolutely terrifying in its strength. They actually climb coconut trees and cut down the coconuts, then back on the ground they are capable of de-husking the coconuts with their claws and consuming the coconut! The evening finished with Nigel teaching the die-hards a New Zealand game called paklunk—too much fun to be legal.

The morning after the big beach party, it was time to load the deep-water camera with bait to attract marine life and test it out. Tucker and Kristof lowered it off the boat to 3,000 feet—almost three-quarters of a mile deep. The digital camera would stay in the "on" position and record whatever swam by. Because the rig wasn't equipped with a remote screen, they had to wait for hours until they retrieved it to see what images they had captured. Six hours later, they pulled the camera up.

Much to everyone's excitement, the camera captured first-ever images of a Sixgill shark on the bottom at 2,000 feet. The first dive of the deep underwater camera was a huge success, revealing much about an ocean bottom that has never before been seen. I couldn't help but feel the same kind of giddy excitement I feel when I'm exploring virgin underwater caves. By successfully utilizing technology, we were able to go to an absolutely fantastic and bizarre world where giant creatures roam in perpetual darkness. It was a real treat to see so much of Emory's, Mike's, and Teddy's hard work and expertise pay off. It was also quite a milestone in that Emory proved, for the first time, that exploration and documentation of the world's deepest ocean bottoms could be achieved without submarines or remote operating vehicles. The big issue here is economics. Armed with this technology, small remote units can now visit, explore, photograph and study regions that have never been available. . . . We celebrated that night with a huge Japanese sushi dinner that was out of this world. The main course was fresh tuna that we had caught earlier that day.

Wes was amazed how easy it was to catch fish in the remote region: *You know you're in an area that is seldom, if ever, visited when you only have to fish for seconds before your first strike.*

The day after their sushi feast, the team lowered a shark cage down to film at a depth of 20 feet. Two expedition members stayed inside the cage, but Wes opted to hang unprotected in the water and film outside the cage. (Cue *Jaws* music.)

> *At one point, the sharks went into a classic frenzy. They were completely out of control, darting about with great unpredictability. Eric and Bill were physically pushing the sharks out of the cage with camera and hands. I couldn't help but think back to the encounters that I had had with great whites in South Africa. After great whites, all other sharks strike you as impotent no matter how dangerous they really may be, the grey reef shark being a good example. Small, sleek, and very fast, the grey reef strikes you as a predator, but not threatening to humans.*
>
> *Growing only up to six feet, they seem more like toy sharks than real ones. Such is not the case in reality. The grey reef may be one of the most dangerous, in that they are easily excited, territorial, and tend to hang out in packs. When one goes into an aggressive mode, all of them do.*

During one day's experiment with Kristof's camera, the team lowered it even deeper than before, this time more than a mile. They pulled it up and took a look.

> *The bottom at 6,000 feet-plus was very different than the 2,500 feet range. Gone was the rough, rocky shelf contours, instead we were viewing a beautifully landscaped sand bottom with an occasional boulder. The rippling in the sand was expressive of the deep, yet also dynamic, like waves had pushed and shoved the sand into an endless array of patterns. I knew I should be filming, but I wanted to finish dinner while watching the tape with everyone else. Just as I was finishing Teddy's fish stew, an odd creature entered the frame. Teddy felt it was some form of shark, while I was sure it was some form of fish—all of us were sure that none of us had ever seen it before, and we were all suddenly very excited. Jeffrey and I grabbed the digital camera and began filming everyone's reactions. . . . Next was a real treat, a beautiful thing thought to be a chimera: part shark, part ray, with giant iridescent green eyes. It hypnotized us with its graceful arching motions and use of its pectoral fins, which looked more like wings than fins. Its color was brown, and appeared to be four to five feet in length. It, and other unidentified creatures, continued to float in and out of our view as the tape rolled on towards its end.*

Just as we were preparing for the end of the tape, the main event showed up. An enormous shape loomed just out of the frame, completely blocking out the left-hand light. Emory screamed for joy, positive it was a Pacific sleeper, though all we saw was its shadow.

The Pacific sleeper is a rare bottom-dwelling snout-nosed shark that can grow as long as twenty-three feet. With that sighting, all aboard knew that they needed to try one more time with the camera, to see if they could catch definitive footage of the mysterious creature.

The next morning during the last test of the deep water rig, the crew caught a forty-three-pound barracuda, sawed it into chunks, and attached it to the camera. They waited for hours before raising the camera to review what it had recorded.

About 20 minutes into the program, we were once again visited by the chimera—this time they were larger, six to seven feet, and seemed to hang in pairs. The team hooted and hollered as the chimera choreographed the most amazing dance for us, right in front of the camera. . . . Three quarters of the way in, we were all frozen by an image of great magnitude and importance in size. The main event was here, and it was now time to determine just what type of shark that it might be. Soon the shark rolled, and twisted and turned through the frame, giving us our first good look at this massive leviathan of the deep. The room erupted as the frames revealed the true size and girth of the monster. As the final third of the shark swished through the frame, Emory got exactly what he wanted— a confirmation that it was indeed a Pacific sleeper shark. Emory was ecstatic. His vision had become reality and his hypothesis confirmed— two truly great moments in the life of one of the world's greatest—but least-recognized—explorers passed as he watched his work roll by on the screen.

Persistence had paid off and they got the kind of rare video they hoped to find in the South Pacific. They had a good, unique documentary in the works, and they all knew it.

Bobbing in the Pacific during the expedition's down time, Wes again fretted privately in his journal about wanting to do more than just work as a cameraman.

Here today and now, I'm making someone else's movie, and it simply does not hold this passion for me that I feel it should and I wish to be completely in control of my ideas and work as an artist. The goal must be to achieve a product of ownership, something that I can call my own and pass on to Nathan and Tessa. Ideally, it will be a great library of stories and images that will forever mark this time on our planet.

When Wes made the long journey back to Florida, he was determined to put the musings he'd written on the boat into action. He wanted to make a movie—his own movie—that would inspire people to protect Florida's springs. In the South Pacific, he'd been surrounded by pure wilderness, the kind he almost took for granted back when he spent hours exploring Florida's untouched freshwater caves. Given the worrisome pollution that he and his cave diver friends were seeing in the state's underground drinking-water conduits, Wes felt he had little time to waste.

16

Crusader

IT'S A TWO-HOUR DRIVE from Florida's capitol building in Tallahassee to High Springs, the epicenter of springs country.

Leaving the leafy city, you plunge right into backwoods Florida—timber farms, country churches, and deep swamps. Wild rivers wind their way through Florida's deep bend to the Gulf of Mexico. The coast is shallow and buggy here, which is why developers have mostly stayed away. An hour outside Tallahassee, you hit the town of Perry, heralded by the stink from the giant paper pulp mill and the staggeringly polluted Fenholloway River. The stench makes drivers roll up their windows and shut their air vents. Most people have no idea that tourists once traveled for days to get to this place to take the healing waters.

In 1912 the Hampton Springs Resort rose like an exotic castle beside a bubbling mineral spring that flowed into the Fenholloway. The chief draw was the spring water, a treasured health elixir. Guests soaked in the spring pools and bought samples to take back home from the nearby bottling plant. The 108-room resort showcasing the remote Fenholloway lured wealthy northern travelers south for a spa vacation. They came by train, getting off at an exclusive resort station, which also served as a band shell. Elaborate walkways led to gardens, fountains, and pools filled with tropical fish.

"A stay of two or three weeks at Hampton Spring will afford a new glory to health," the resort's printed advertisement promised. "A different phase of life—a real delight in the knowledge that you still live in a world of such wonderful beauty—and inspiring, amazing miracles."

After the Great Depression hit, the resort struggled; it housed military men during World War II, became a rooming house, grew decrepit, and eventually burned down.

Worst was what happened to the healing springs along the Fenholloway—the kind that Wes and his buddies would have surely explored. They virtually vanished. Their death warrant was signed in 1947 when local civic leaders went to Tallahassee to persuade the Florida Legislature to pass a law that seems astonishing today. Industry in Taylor County, the legislation said bluntly, may "deposit sewage, industrial and chemical wastes and effluents, or any of them, into the waters of the Fenholloway River and the waters of the Gulf of Mexico." With those words, the only throwaway Florida spring-fed river, the only one classified as "industrial," was born.

For Wes and his dive buddies, the Fenholloway's story lingered like its foul smell. The underground limestone around the river was full of holes and caves, just like the ones the Mole Tribe were exploring an hour's drive north or south. During droughts, the chemical-filled Fenholloway disappeared into that limestone maze and the local health department got complaints from people reporting smelly water from their wells. No one wanted to drink it, and no one wanted to dive around there.

In the 1950s, armed with its go-ahead-and-pollute law, the rural county had snared one of America's most coveted industrial prizes: consumer products powerhouse Procter & Gamble. The P&G mill opened for its first shift in 1954, producing high-grade wood cellulose that's used in everything from disposable diapers to explosives and sausage casings. It takes a lot of harsh chemicals to break down trees that way. At the shoreline where the Fenholloway meets the Gulf, the very spot that the river's life-giving estuary should be, there's a dead zone spanning several square miles. Every creature and plant that wanders near or through it is affected.

Today, some local leaders in Perry will tell you that the loss of their river and springs is worth the money P&G brought the town. But all these decades later, the area is run down, the average income is very low, and it is irrevocably, dangerously polluted. One local mother, Gwen Faulkner, kept drawing nasty water from her taps and had the county health department test her private well.

"There were chemicals in there that they could not analyze, but they told me it was okay to drink," she told me. "That doesn't make sense."

Like most polluting Florida industries, the mill did its own water monitoring and reported the results to the state. With no real pollution requirements in place in Taylor County, P&G was hardly ever found to be in violation, even though the mill's discharge was potent enough to snuff out just about all the aquatic life in its path. Some fish and insects that frequented the river were changing sex, drawing curious scientists to study the phenomenon. Although federal and state environmental regulations grew stricter over the years, the Fenholloway's special "industrial" label sealed its fate as the state's most polluted. P&G eventually sold the mill and moved elsewhere.

Here is how much of a lost cause this river and springs became: In the late 1980s the federal Environmental Protection Agency began taking a hard look around America at pollution from pulp and paper mills, and EPA scientists came to test fish from the Fenholloway. The fish were contaminated by the potent poison dioxin. The EPA sent a letter to Florida officials, telling the state it needed to warn people not to eat the fish. Amazingly, state officials didn't issue the health warning. The EPA office in Atlanta made more phone calls and sent another letter. Finally, a full year and a half after the EPA found toxic fish and told Florida to warn people, the state issued an official advisory. "We have information that suggests there may be a health risk" from consuming the fish, it said. "This health advisory is being issued as a precautionary measure while additional information is being obtained." The state didn't even post warning signs along the river. Florida officials claimed, straight-faced, that they didn't have the money for the signs. Hearing that ridiculous pronouncement, a local woman named Joy Towles Ezell printed warning fliers with a skull and crossbones on her home computer, wrapped them in protective plastic, tromped through the overgrown swamps and nailed the fliers to the trees on the river banks.

In a way, this is what Wes would end up doing with *Water's Journey*. He saw that leaders weren't sounding the alarm about the pollution entering Florida's springs, and he took it upon himself to tell people. Instead of posting fliers, he made films.

People don't talk about the way the Fenholloway's spring water was once treasured and sold for health. I had to poke around the old stone foundations left at the Hampton Springs Resort site to find evidence down in the weeds: a lone rusty bottle cap marked with the logo of the Fenholloway spring water bottling company.

Eighty-five years after tourism boosters built that resort to take advantage of Fenholloway springs, the largest private water bottling company in America at the time came to High Springs and broke ground for a plant near Wes and Terri's house. It was 1997, and Aquapenn Spring Water planned to pump water from Ginnie Spring and sell it across the country.

Aquapenn got a permit to pump 300,000 gallons a day out of the spring, which was a fraction of the 262 million gallons Ginnie discharged every day. While Florida was taking its springs for granted, the world's water bottling companies were not. They saw a cheap and available resource, and they started moving in to profit off it.

Aquapenn investigated different springs in the area when scouting for a bottling plant site, and rejected one along the Suwannee River because tests showed high levels of nitrates, a sure sign that the water is polluted by sewage, fertilizer, and manure.

"We have prided ourselves in going the extra length to find the cleanest water sources in the country," Aquapenn's president said at the time. "The Ginnie Springs area is extremely unique."

He was about to find out how badly Florida treated its springs. As soon as the company started building at Ginnie, Aquapenn found itself facing an enormous water pollution threat. Local politicians approved a 1,000-acre industrial dairy cow operation just a mile from the Santa Fe River. Wes knew from swimming in the aquifer that the groundwater under the dairy site flowed right toward Ginnie and the other eighteen springs along that stretch of the Santa Fe, the very spring water that Aquapenn planned to bottle.

He also knew that the new dairy cattle operation would produce massive amounts of manure, and nitrates could make their way into the porous karst landscape and pollute the rivers and springs. Already, manure from dairies in the area had fouled some private wells, and the landowners now had polluted water coming from their taps. It was crazy, but these homeowners living in the heart of springs country now had to buy bottled water.

Wes knew what had happened to the Fenholloway. He knew that big industry could have its way with politicians. And he knew that the vast network of spring water he dove in around the Suwannee, Santa Fe, and Ichetucknee Rivers was irreplaceable, probably the most important and neglected natural resource in a state that worshipped its crowded shorelines.

"When he started to find funny long white streams of 'yuck' oozing through the walls of underwater caves, he was so upset, it propelled him on a mission with a passion," says Terri Skiles.

By 1998, news of nitrate pollution in the springs was just emerging as a statewide environmental issue. But compared to well-known crises like Big Agriculture's decimation of the Everglades, development wiping out natural ecosystems, and massive erosion on coastal beaches, the trouble boiling up from the state's springs was not well known. Who better than Wes to get the word out?

A story in the state's largest newspaper, the *St. Petersburg Times*, read:

Wes Skiles has been diving into Florida's cobalt-blue heart for two decades. Down into the ground water he goes, flippers propelling him into the dark rivers that flow under houses, parking lots, roads and forests. He swims past a pipe that is someone's well. He surprises strange albino crayfish. Sometimes, in the bottom of an underwater cave, he sees things that were swallowed up by sinkholes—a plastic baby doll, a van.

"Basically, I'm swimming in your drinking water," said Skiles, a Gainesville man who has done films for *National Geographic* and television networks. Back on land, Skiles delivers a message that scientists around the state are echoing: Florida's spring water is becoming polluted. Water that was icy blue is getting a green or tan tint. Algae is appearing where it never has before.

"There's no place in the world with a greater natural discharge of pure, potable freshwater than Florida," Skiles said. "Having the advantage of exploring wild Florida inside out, I see the changes occurring to these places. I'm deeply concerned."

Since the proposed dairy near Wes's house threatened the water supply, the locals decided to fight back. The Alachua County Commission in nearby Gainesville voted to join the owners of two High Springs recreation businesses, Ginnie Springs and Blue Springs, in a lawsuit to block the huge dairy operation.

"We have been blessed with an abundance of almost pristine quality of water. It's chilling to understand that with the blink of an eye, it could be lost forever," Alachua County Commissioner Penny Wheat said.

The fight was on, and Wes and Ginnie Springs owner Bobbie Wray were at the forefront. Wray dug through public records and reported that the state agriculture department had recorded an estimated 13,500 cows in the county—more cows, in fact, than people. Each lactating dairy cow, she discovered from the state records, was estimated to produce more than 47,000 pounds of manure and urine a year. The new dairy planned to have 850 cows. To the commissioners, Wray wrote: "Do we really need another 40,353,750 pounds of raw manure that a new dairy consisting of 850 cows would add to the amount of animal waste that we already have?"

Wes and the other dairy opponents soon learned a frustrating reality: the government had few rules to stop agricultural pollution. Lobbyists for the powerful industry—at the time it was the state's second biggest, right after tourism—diligently kept regulations at bay, year after year, at the state legislature in Tallahassee. Big Agriculture is one of the largest political contributors in the state, to Republicans and Democrats alike. The industry's campaign dollars consistently earn agri-industry political favors in Congress and in state legislatures all over America.

Getting nowhere with state regulators, Wes and Wray and the other dairy opponents took their case to the public, calling reporters and writing letters to the editor, like this one from Wes to the *Gainesville Sun*:

March 6th, 1998

To The Editor:

Based on present trends and projected growth of the livestock industries, it is evident that we are headed for the contamination and ultimate destruction of one of the largest and most valuable aquifers in the world.

Presently, the Florida Department of Environmental Protection has no rules to protect groundwater from the direct discharge of pollution into the Floridan Aquifer. Despite the repeated warning of degrading water quality in North Florida springs and rivers, the FDEP has permitted 15 dairies out of the last 15 requests for dairy-related industrial waste discharge permits.

Despite overwhelming statistics and documented violations of safe drinking water standards directly beneath already permitted dairies, the FDEP has given its approval for the permitting of yet another dairy, this one up-gradient of several critical springs along the Santa Fe River. Citizens have come forward to oppose the siting of these dairies in order to protect springs and rivers and to prevent the threat of pollution of their own nearby household wells. Public resources and private property values are at risk because of this threat.

However, when these citizens turn out to the Florida DEP, they find out there is no protection. If the right boxes are checked on the permit applications, the applicant is all too easily off the hook concerning groundwater, and the DEP is powerless to do anything more about it because of current statutes.

In order to fully protect the aquifer and springs, and correct the current deficiencies, rule changes must be initiated by the FDEP that properly protect groundwater from the discharge of contaminants to the aquifer. Until FDEP is willing to regulate discharge of contaminants to the aquifer, the people of the state of Florida are powerless to protect their quality of life.

Sincerely,

Wes Skiles

Wes had been attending a state-sponsored committee called the Ichetucknee Springs Working Group. The Ichetucknee River was designated as a state park for most of its length, revered for its otherworldly air-clear water, bone-white bottom, and tropical fairyland forest along its banks. Thousands of people descended on the park every summer to float in inner tubes, and a little trolley picked them up and took them back to the spot where their cars were parked.

In the 1990s, gross-looking brown algae were beginning to coat the bright green native grass at one of its feeder springs, a sure sign of nitrogen pollution. Water testing confirmed elevated nitrates, and state and regional water officials started focusing on the problem.

Jim Stevenson, an ecosystem manager with many years' experience tackling Florida's environmental problems at the Florida Department of Environmental Protection, formed a working group to investigate where the Ichetucknee was picking up its excess nutrients and try to prevent it.

Skiles was a faithful attendee at the meetings whenever he was in town and not off filming some adventure. He and Stevenson became close. They had a lot in common—Stevenson and his wife were cave divers, they lived close to Wakulla Springs, and Stevenson's wife was one of the elite divers on the 1987 Wakulla Springs expedition with Bill Stone that Wes had filmed for *National Geographic*. Stevenson could see that Wes had a way about him, a certain confidence mixed with relatability, that would help move pollution prevention ideas forward.

"People were drawn to Wes's energy because he was a self-made man," says Florida nature photographer John Moran, who made a career capturing the beauty of springs country. "His level of expertise was boots on the ground. He put that to good use and he had a remarkable ability to meet people where they were. He was comfortable speaking to schoolchildren and governors and everybody in between."

Wes and Stevenson developed a behind-the-scenes partnership to try to move the bureaucracy in the right direction. We're talking bureaucracy with a capital *B*. At the time, Florida had a patchwork of environmental agencies. The Department of Environmental Protection dealt with permitting, pollution, land preservation, and cleanups, among other things; the Florida Game and Fresh Water Fish Commission dealt mainly with land management, outdoor sports, and wildlife; and the Marine Fisheries Commission managed species in the sea. Plus there was another critical layer: the state's water policy and permitting were, and are, handled by five water management districts in different parts of the state, with power to tax people in their areas. Each water management district has a board whose members are appointed by the sitting governor. Frequently these appointments are payback for political contributions. More often than not, the boards are packed with people from the agricultural, development, and utility industries, with the odd environmental or scientific person scattered among one or two of the district boards around the state. The water management district boards have enormous power to shape the state, but very few citizens pay any attention to what they do.

As a state worker who dealt with politicians and the industries affected by regulations, Stevenson had to be careful about what he said in public.

"Being in an agency, I was always walking on eggshells," he says. "I'd call Wes and say, 'Here's the strategy.' I'd tell Wes what he needed to do, and he'd do it. He'd come on strong and rattle the cages. He understood that he didn't know anything about bureaucracies and I did, so we made a good team."

In 1998, as the fight over the dairy went on in High Springs, the state elected as its new governor a forty-five-year-old Miami real estate developer and son of a U.S. president: Jeb Bush. Republicans also gained majorities in the Florida House and Senate in that election, making Florida the first southern state since Reconstruction to elect both a Republican governor and a Republican-controlled legislature. The long reign of the Dixie Democrats' assured majority was over.

Protecting the environment is a bedrock populist issue in Florida. In northern states, Democrats generally "own" the issue, but in Florida it's more complicated. Old-school "yellow dog" conservative Democrats, like Bush's predecessor, Governor Lawton Chiles, generally thought land ought to work for a living, not just sit there looking pretty. They were avid hunters and held business interests in citrus, timber, and cattle operations. Among Republicans in the late 1980s and 1990s, a moderate group became evident, at least as far as the environment was concerned. These Republican politicians and their big political donors lived in pricey waterfront communities, and they liked boating and sport fishing.

Jeb Bush was not one of these. His idea of "environment" was, basically, a golf course. But the polls showed that environmental issues were a big priority among the public. Raised in the most political of households, Bush was obviously politically attuned. The moderates in his party, especially those from Florida's upscale coastal areas, made it clear that it would be good for the governor to burnish his environmental image.

Bush appointed David Struhs from Massachusetts as his secretary of environmental protection. Struhs knew well how to make nice with environmentalists while ensuring that the Republican party's industry friends were not overly burdened by limits on pollution. He learned his trade first as an executive assistant at a federal Environmental Protection Agency regional office, and then later at the White House, as chief of staff for a key advisory group, the President's Council on Environmental Quality.

Along with the dairy fight, another high-profile battle broke out shortly after Bush took office. The controversy was over a proposed cement manufacturing plant not far from Ichetucknee State Park, to be built by the state's largest road builder, Anderson Columbia. After hearing about the cement plant from riled-up environmentalists, Struhs and Bush decided to tackle the issue head on. They came to see the Ichetucknee for themselves in June 1999.

In a canoe flotilla that had reporters, a security detail, state scientists, and some locals trailing along, the new governor and his new environmental chief seemed bowled over by the drop-dead gorgeousness surrounding them. Halfway through the trip, Bush stopped and made a speech, praising the Ichetucknee's postcard beauty and mentioning that other paddlers he passed on the river urged him to stop Anderson Columbia from building the cement plant. One chief concern was mercury coming out of the plant's smokestacks and falling into the springs and rivers. Another was Anderson Columbia's history of state environmental violations.

On that trip, Struhs directed Stevenson to form a statewide Springs Task Force to delve into the springs' problems and recommend solutions. Within five months Stevenson did so, and Wes was one of the first people appointed to serve on it. The way Stevenson saw it, Wes was a perfect person to appoint to the Florida Springs Task Force. With more firsthand knowledge than probably anyone in the state, Wes had another critical credential for the time and place: he was a registered Republican.

"When Wes began attending the working group meetings," Stevenson says, "he had found a home with like-minded people where he could express his frustrations and take meaningful action."

"Everybody on the task force had the attitude of 'Our springs are in trouble. Let's really dig in, let's really look at this,'" says Pam McVety, a top Florida DEP official at the time. "This was before there was awareness, and a consensus, that our springs were all turning green. I grew up in Florida. I had enough of a memory to know they didn't look the way they looked now."

Wes was "the very kind of person a government employee wants on a committee," McVety says. "He understood the seriousness of the issue, and he was gung-ho. He was like an enzyme in a chemical reaction. He's making things happen."

Russ Frydenborg, a DEP scientist and administrator who served on the Springs Task Force, says the state was trying to grasp the problem of springs pollution.

"We went out and did some testing, and we were surprised to see that the highest nitrate levels were near the spring vents," he says, referring to the places where the spring water boiled out of the aquifer. "We were surprised that it wasn't near parking lots and other sources. That was kind of an eye opener—that maybe these contaminants are *in* the aquifer."

Wes was still traveling around the world on assignments, but when he was home, he focused on film and photography projects to publicize the problems that he and his friends were seeing in the springs. He had the outlook that if people knew better, they would do better.

He again went to Bill Kurtis, this time with an idea for a *New Explorers* episode, focused on the Ichetucknee, that would be called "Polluting the Fountain of Youth." He had made a sort of prototype film a few years earlier with his Australian friends Liz and Andrew Wight. That 1991 film, *Florida: Window to a Hidden World*, opens with touristy shots of beachy Florida, then shows divers moving through the limestone aquifer, cuts to an aerial view of the dark Santa Fe River, then focuses down to a single canoe. Then the camera is underwater, looking up from inside a spring at the canoe above, and then the camera is topside again, with the canoe approaching with Liz and Andrew Wight paddling toward Wes on a dock at Ginnie Springs. He's wearing a backwards baseball cap and wailing on a harmonica, looking like the backwoods river rat he is. He splashes Liz when the canoe comes close.

"It's the world's fah-nest water," he says in a redneck drawl that the Aussies always found charming. The Australian narrator says: "Liz and Andrew Wight are two of the most experienced cave divers in the world. They've explored and documented underground water systems across the globe, and the challenge to investigate the Floridan aquifer proved irresistible. The third member of the team is one of America's finest underwater photographers and cave divers, Wes Skiles. He's a native of Florida, and these springs are his backyard."

Wes explains: "This whole region around here is recharged over a great area, and the water that's coming out of the spring here now is water that got into the aquifer before the drought even. That's really interesting."

"Does a spring like Ginnie ever dry up?" Andrew Wight asks.

"I don't think that's a worry," Wes says. "Pollution, the destruction of this water, the contamination of our drinking water for our planet—that's really the issue. Not running out, just destroying the water instead.

"One of my most favorite stories," Wes continues, "is that Jacques Cousteau himself was here in the 1960s, and when he saw this spring for the first time, he proclaimed it to be 'visibility forever.'"

They tramp through the woods toward a nearby spring that's fenced off, protected for the endangered red-eyed crayfish that makes its home in the dark water there. The camera points at household trash scattered on the cave floor.

"It's really sad," Wes says, "because they don't realize that they are actually polluting the water they also want to drink."

The narrator says: "Most forms of agriculture are successful here, but there is a long-term cost."

To make the point plainly, Wes interspersed shots of fertilized farm fields and dairy cows crapping in manure-filled feedlots.

"Several new dairies are proposed for surrounding land which lies on top of the aquifer," the narrator says. "A cow's daily waste output is about equal to twenty people, and at these new dairies, there will be around five thousand cows. That's roughly equivalent to a city of a hundred thousand people, whose sewage would simply be allowed to seep into the ground. The waste from these dairies could contaminate the groundwater, then the springs, and finally the river."

"One of these days," Wes says in the film, "if more people can see this stuff, there will be a different appreciation of how we have to treat water."

Wes was now among a small army of people doing their damnedest to get more people to see the crisis unfolding in Florida's groundwater. Not only was he filming the Ichetucknee nitrate pollution story for the *New Explorers* "Polluting the Fountain of Youth" episode to air nationally on A&E Television, he'd lined up another major international story about Florida's springs, this one for the "yellow border," *National Geographic* magazine.

By all rights, it should have been the uber-connected governor Jeb Bush who got national attention focused on the plight of Florida's springs, but for many reasons, that wasn't going to happen. If anyone was going to do it, it was going to have to be Wes.

Wes reloading the cameras between dives . . . before digital was available. Courtesy of Terri Skiles.

Wes preparing an underwater scooter for a dive at Huautla. Courtesy of Terri Skiles.

Wes entertaining and educating Tessa Skiles's classmates, during an actual underwater shoot at Ginnie Springs Outdoors. Courtesy of Terri Skiles.

Wes gathering his photo gear as he prepares to climb out of the Azure Blue cavern in Branford, Florida. Courtesy of Terri Skiles.

Wes filming topside on the Ichetucknee River, Columbia County. Photo by Georgia Shemitz. Courtesy of Terri Skiles.

Wes with his HD underwater camera. Courtesy of Terri Skiles.

Above: Crew members of the *Braveheart* lowering Wes into the Antarctic during *Ice Island* filming, 2001. Courtesy of Terri Skiles.

Right: Wes filming water flow. Photo by Nathan Skiles. Courtesy of Terri Skiles.

Wes happily at home in Gilchrist County, Florida. Courtesy of Terri Skiles.

17

The Aquifer's Secrets

IN 1999, WES'S PHOTOS went all around the world with the *National Geographic* story "Unlocking the Labyrinth of North Florida's Springs." He was more than photographer in the story; writer Ken Ringle made Wes a central character. "There are very few places nowadays where the average person without a lot of money can still extend human knowledge as an explorer," Wes says in the article. "But deep in the cave systems of the Florida springs, that's what you are."

He took one of the arresting photos from high above remote Cypress Spring in the Florida Panhandle. His camera captured two people down below in a red canoe, with the spring water so clear it appears that the canoe is suspended in air. Another dramatic photograph showed a diver underwater at Ginnie Spring, emerging from the river's dark tannic water into the blue spring water. Knowing the light as he did, Wes waited until the sun was in the exact right place to send rays through the tannic water, making it look like a fiery starburst. The photo was so striking that the editors ran it on a page-and-a-half spread.

Georgia Shemitz was Wes's assistant for fifteen years, accompanying him on various photography adventures, including the *National Geographic* springs shoot. (She's married to Wes's longtime business partner, Pete Butt.) She says one of Wes's secret photography weapons was a contraption he designed and built with the help of friends. Called the "ladder pod" (a play on "tripod"), it was made from three extension ladders, welded together with metal sheeting to keep it stable. Climbing atop it, Wes had a vantage point from twenty feet in the air.

"This is a big, huge, cumbersome thing that would take three big guys to set it up," Shemitz says, "but when Wes was up there, he took some really nice pictures with it."

One of the *National Geographic* photos is a long view of the Santa Fe River, shot from the ladder pod at dawn. A canoe heads away from the camera, and Devil's Eye spring is in the foreground, divers heading toward it. To highlight the spring, Wes submerged lights deep inside to make it glow blue in the dark river. It took numerous dives for Wes to get the composition and lighting right for his two-page photo of the cavernous Diepolder Cave, 250 feet beneath a dark water hole near Central Florida's Weeki Wachee Spring. The photo looks like a space mission with four aquanauts (instead of astronauts) suspended in the blue void. With that picture, Wes sparked awe in millions of people who had never seen such a place. And that, of course, was his goal.

In the late 1990s, although most of these springs still looked lovely, the invisible nitrates were beginning to do their destructive work, fueling unwanted algae and noxious plant growth. The pressing task was to find out how to stop it. That meant solving some mysteries: Was pollution (fertilizer, for example) percolating directly down through the ground, or was it washing overland into streams, lakes, sinks, and springs during rains? And when, exactly, had the pollution appearing now made its way into the groundwater?

Scientists found a way to check the age of the water surging out of Florida springs by looking for certain chemical signatures. Tritium isotopes, for example, got into the world's surface waters when they rained down from the atmosphere after nuclear bomb testing in the 1950s and 1960s. Chlorofluorocarbons, which floated into the Earth's atmosphere from refrigerators, air conditioners, aerosols and foam, offered more information. Since scientists had been recording CFC levels in the atmosphere for years, they could compare atmospheric levels against the levels found in the spring water to calculate the water's age.

Through this high-tech testing, they discovered that springs pump out a mixture of both old and new water. The water that floats people in inner tubes on the Ichetucknee River is an average of twenty years old. Some of the water got into the aquifer just days or weeks ago, and some of it is very old. That means pollution from decades ago still moves through the underground system. In some parts of the state, dye tracing tests proved that groundwater moves miles each day, and in other places it moves more slowly. The main idea that Wes and his cave diver friends had been pushing for years—that there are underground rivers with currents and eddies—was finally being accepted by mainstream institutions.

Wes and Pete Butt helped with what was then one of the largest underwater dye traces in history, featured in the "Polluting the Fountain of Youth" episode for *The New Explorers*. Divers wriggled through a limestone hole so small they had to take off their tanks to do it. In the dark cave at a place called Russell's Rub, near Rose Sink outside Lake City, they emptied a five-gallon container of fluorescein dye and swam back to the surface to wait. Rose Sink is six miles away from the Ichetucknee. More than a hundred volunteers waited with sampling equipment for the dye to show up at Ichetucknee. They thought it might pop up the next day. But it didn't, and not the day after, or the day after that. In the end, it took eight days for the water to move through the limestone caves and tunnels. Even with dye tests, seismic equipment, ground-penetrating radar, water flow measurements, and maps, and even after cave divers physically went into tunnels to take a look-see all over karst country, Florida's aquifer was still a mystery.

"We have overtaxed the system with manmade chemicals too small, too stable, to be removed," Bill Kurtis narrates in "Polluting the Fountain of Youth." "It's not easy to impose regulations of land use for a problem that can't be seen."

Or, as Suwannee River Water Management District scientist David Hornsby says in the film: "We know that what we're doing on the land we won't see for ten, twelve, fifteen years, so we need to start planning for tomorrow yesterday."

At the Florida Department of Environmental Protection, Jim Stevenson was, like Wes, continually focused on finding ways to elevate the problem of springs pollution in the public eye.

"How do you get the public excited about groundwater?" he mused in 1998. "It isn't saving the whales. It isn't the Everglades. You can't watch a sunset over it. But when you're looking at springs, you're looking at groundwater."

Wes warned: "Life in the underworld is evolving because of things we barely understand."

Cave divers and hydrogeologists were working to get better maps of the aquifer's caves and tunnels, and a new expedition at Wakulla Springs was about to make a huge leap in that regard.

In the years since the record-breaking 1987 Wakulla expedition by Bill Stone and the U.S. Deep Caving Team, technical divers had been making repeated forays into the cave system, breaking the world record for longest explored cave over and over again.

The 1987 explorers had gone back 4,200 feet into the tunnels—about three-quarters of a mile. By 1998 a group of clannish divers organized under the Woodville Karst Plain Project (WKPP) had pushed the exploration at Wakulla Springs nearly three and a half miles into the Earth.

"The fact that there is so much water moving is bad, in terms of pollution, because things are carried far," the WKPP's leader, cave diver George Irvine, said in 1998. "We're running a race to get as much information on this system as we can, before it is destroyed."

The WKPP and the U.S. Deep Caving Team had a rivalry, and it was especially bitter when Stone returned to Wakulla in the winter of 1998 to lead another *National Geographic* expedition there. Stone's new expedition, Wakulla 2, was a showcase for the latest inventions.

"There was so much going on in terms of technology. It was more like a space mission," Stone says. "It was the kind of thing where we had to have simulations for each of the trips we were going to do in there, because there were so many complicated things that they had to be scripted out and rehearsed."

They had dive scooters with a 12.5-mile range, and the latest twin rebreathers that allowed divers to do eighteen-hour missions without switching out air tanks. By now the rebreathers were lighter and about the size of a hotel mini-fridge. Each diver wore two on his or her back. The prize piece of technology at the center of it all was Stone's latest invention: a Digital Wall Mapper that collected more than ten million points of data to create the first three-dimensional images of Wakulla's cave system. The $750,000 3-D Digital Wall Mapper married technologies used in ballistic missile navigation with magnetic radiolocation. The mapper was a little over a foot in diameter and seven feet long. A diver swam the mapper through the cave system while the device sent signals pinging against the walls. Divers affixed magnetic wire "beacons" at various points as they explored the cave system, and radiolocation expert Brian Pease (who would later track the divers through Sonny's Barbecue restaurant in Wes's film *Water's Journey: The Hidden Rivers of Florida*), traveled overland, putting little flags in the ground that corresponded to the beacons in the cave system below. In this way they were able to make more accurate maps than ever before.

This time, Wes wasn't doing any exploration diving at all. Back in Stone's 1987 expedition, Wes had been on his first assignment for *National Geographic*, worried about making a good impression. In 1998, he swooped in as a savvy heavy-hitter: the director of photography for the *National Geographic* documentary about the project.

"He had his own team, himself and maybe five others, who were his underwater gaffers and everything," Stone said. "He was shooting both video and stills."

Wes's photos from Wakulla 2 would later appear in a *National Geographic* offshoot publication, the now-defunct *National Geographic Adventurer*. His longtime diving buddy Paul Heinerth says Wes was wistful about not being an explorer this time around, and remembers that when he sat around after his dives telling Wes about what they were seeing below, "I could see the twinkle in his eyes, and his desire to be part of the exploration team."

Since Wes was limiting his deep diving because of the damage he'd suffered from the bends, he attached cameras for divers to take along with them on their scooters.

"When it came time to film some of the deep segments, he asked for a volunteer to help him out, because he didn't particularly want to expose himself or his team to the deep-long penetrations . . . so he wanted someone to carry a camera for him and film deep stuff. And I'm like, 'Pick me! Pick me!'" says cave diver Jill Heinerth.

Jill, an ambitious and talented artist and diver from Canada, had married cave diver Paul Heinerth, and Stone picked the accomplished couple to be part of his expedition. During Wakulla 2, Wes asked Jill to come work for him as a producer, and she became a crucial player, as well as dive-actor, in *Water's Journey*.

"The first time that I drove that mapper into the room under the Wakulla lodge and Wes turned on the cinema lights to film me passing through there and I saw the whole place illuminated for the first time, I nearly dropped my rebreather out of my mouth," Jill says. "It was just unbelievable!"

In mid-January, diving conditions took a turn for the worse. Heavy rains turned Wakulla murky, which affected the photographic side of the project. The disappointed divers pressed on with their tasks as best they could. The Digital Wall Mapper, after all, didn't depend on clear visibility.

As the expedition cooked along, tragedy hit. Henry Way Kendall, a seventy-two-year-old Nobel Prize–winning physicist, died in just ten feet of water at Wakulla Spring as he prepared to go into the cave system to take photographs. He was visiting the expedition as a member of the National Geographic Society. Kendall had failed to wait for his dive buddy and didn't use proper procedures on his rebreather.

"According to fellow Wakulla 2 divers, Kendall ignored the pre-dive safety checks of his equipment, paid no attention to audio and visual alarms honking and flashing on his rebreather (which his diving companions pointed out to him) and got into the spring alone," the *Miami Herald* reported. "Divers said Kendall wasn't himself that day; they speculate he may not have been feeling well before he donned his Cis-Lunar MK-5 and got into the water."

Stone was devastated. Kendall, a larger-than-life man who helped discover the subatomic particles called quarks, who cofounded the Union of Concerned Scientists, who sounded the early warnings about the problems of nuclear waste and global warming, was a friend.

As he had after Ian Rolland's death during the Huautla expedition in Mexico four years earlier, Wes tried to buck Stone up.

"The night after that happened," Stone says, "it was Wes, around that campfire, who basically gave everybody a stern lecture about life, you know? He talked about the fact that Henry pretty much cut his own route, as he had through his entire life, and he bypassed a lot of safety procedures to end up with what happened. You could argue many different ways and say, 'Well, weren't you watching him?' Well, the plan was laid out, he had his diving buddy, he had a diving safety officer he was supposed to report to, you know, all of these things, and he never did any of those. And as a result, he made a mistake. He didn't turn his oxygen on. Wes, basically, in that good southern drawl of his, for lack of a better term, gave everybody a pep talk. He said, look, life and death come together, and sooner or later everybody's going to die. Henry had a pretty amazing life—a pretty staggeringly amazing life if you look into what he had done. And, okay, it wasn't a great thing that he died, but the fact is that everybody is still here.

We're all damn-well alive, and we should do something good with what we've got. So, that was kind of the turning point. For the next three and a half or four weeks, or whatever it was that we had left, we did the best we could—collect the data, get the film done, and do the things that we set out to do. I largely credit Wes with keeping that project together after Henry died.

"I think that was a characteristic of Wes, having that big picture. Wes lived expedition, he breathed expedition. That's what made us brothers, was the fact that Wes was a true *expeditionario*, and I say that with all respect and love for someone who lived in that same genre. Wes was the quintessential team player, and I've seen him equally well assume the leadership role without being overbearing, obnoxious, or disenfranchising . . . he fit right in and worked in a collaborative, collegial sense. So it was 'Hey we're here! Now let's a) have fun, and b) get the job done and come back with some data.' Wes was all about bringing back the data. In his case it was film, in my case it was digital records and survey data and things like that, but we all worked together and we all knew what the game was."

After the expedition, Stone calculated that the Digital Wall Mapper collected ten million data points inside the Wakulla cave system, and he pointed out that it would have taken individual divers their entire lives to record that much data using the conventional methods at the time.

"There was a lot of new technology for cave and technical diving that came out of that project," says Brian Kakuk, a diver who participated. "High Intensity Discharge Lighting—that became commonplace in cave diving, we used the first ones on that project."

The groundbreaking magnetic underground-to-surface location system used on the Wakulla 2 project would later be used in Antarctica to track submerged unmanned vehicles under ice, and may one day be used to explore beneath the ice of Jupiter's moon Europa. Wes had been pestering Brian Pease, their techie inventor, to make it possible for divers submerged in the caves to actually talk (through three hundred feet of earth) to people on the surface through microphones in their masks. It had never been done before, but Pease figured it out.

"I modified some gear that Wes had that's normally diver-to-diver acoustic communication, like an underground walkie-talkie using high-frequency sound waves," Pease says.

"The first time we tried it was at Wakulla Springs," Jill Heinerth says, "and I remember we had a whole bunch of schoolkids topside, and [Florida DEP secretary] David Struhs was there. We were doing a little educational day. And we were talking to the kids. It was the day of the Gator-Seminole football game. And we [divers underground] were like, 'Hey, are the Gators winning?' We were talking back and forth with the kids."

You would think that an invention like this, one that enabled people on the surface to talk to cave divers two or three hundred feet below for the first time ever, would be a major, sought-after technology. Not so.

"I'm not aware of anybody who's done it other than me," Pease says nonchalantly.

It turns out most cave divers don't like wearing the full-face masks that the technology requires. And even more than that, they aren't especially interested in talking to people above ground when they are down inside the aquifer, a place that's about as far away from civilization as you can get while still remaining on planet Earth.

"This is like a distraction for the divers," Pease explains. "They are busy. They are doing things down there, things like mapping the caves."

With the remarkable Wakulla 2 expedition behind him, Wes found himself pushing through more than just tight cave tunnels—he was now pushing through politics, and it wasn't a pretty landscape. Two years after the Wakulla 2 expedition, the world's eyes were on Florida for thirty-six days as scrambling officials tried to sort out a balloting fiasco that would determine whether George W. Bush or Al Gore won the incredibly close U.S. presidential election.

It couldn't have been a worse time for the Florida Springs Task Force to unveil its final report, the fruit of a year's worth of meetings and study. But that's when the report arrived in the office of the soon-to-be U.S. president's brother, Florida governor Jeb Bush.

The thick report detailed the disturbing changes showing up in the state's springs from overpumping and from sewage, manure, and fertilizer pollution that was getting inside Florida's aquifer. The Springs Task Force recommended that the state start developing regulations right away to protect the vast water source before it was too late. Politically, it was a tough sell. Both the Bush in the White House and the Bush in the Florida governor's mansion were constantly preaching about how government regulations hindered businesses. (They were fine with handing out fat government subsidies to politically powerful agricultural polluters, however.) The truth was that neither Bush was especially moved by environmental issues.

Wes was in his forties, and in addition to his political and expedition work, he and the Mole Tribe were still actively out there in wild Florida, as he liked to say, "leaving nothing unexplored for the next generation." His physical damage from the bends meant he had to avoid extremely deep dives, but exploration in the North Florida caves around his home base seemed to pose few problems for him.

His repeated forays into the meeting rooms at local and state government offices were a different story. He'd started out as a concerned citizen observer, and when he witnessed firsthand the pollution invading the fresh water supply, he went to alert his local politicians. After they brushed him off, he turned to the regional water management district, certain that they would want to see his cave maps and hear about what he had seen. They, too, brushed him off. When he went higher in the bureaucracy, to the Florida Department of Environmental Protection, he learned the reality behind the snarky nickname that some people gave the politicized DEP—Don't Expect Protection.

Politicians and officials were friendly, they liked to talk about protecting springs, and they especially liked to stand before a pretty backdrop and make speeches about the "precious resources" we all share. The reality was that the bureaucracy in Florida was loath to do anything meaningful about the pollution. It was scientifically complicated, with many unknowns, and that was a nightmare for any state regulator, who was sure to face lawsuits from giant corporations questioning every picky aspect of a proposed state rule. Solving the issue required tough decisions and enforcement, resources in short supply on both the federal and state levels.

Whenever anyone brought up the tie between water pollution and fertilizer, it drew attention from Big Sugar, one of the largest campaign contributors in the nation. The fertilizer that sugar corporations use on their Everglades operations is a source of consternation and constant legal battling. Big Cattle and the national and state Farm Bureau chapters were also well-heeled and active opponents. Legions of agricultural lobbyists in the halls of Congress and the Florida statehouse perk their ears for even the slightest whisper that government leaders might utter about controlling fertilizer and manure pollution, and they are ever-ready to fight.

In Wes's home turf of High Springs, the local battle to protect the springs from pollution took a turn for the worse. Despite the lawsuits and the predicted pollution to one of the planet's best caches of fresh water, the dairy near Ginnie Springs got its state permit. The modest pollution-control measures the state required were voluntary—the same as for all Florida agricultural operations. Incredibly, the state and federal governments rely largely on the honor system to protect the public's water supplies from agricultural pollution. As one Florida environmental lawyer put it, all a corporation has to do is *say* it is implementing a plan to control pollution, and it is exempt from monitoring. It's as if a big trucking company were allowed to blow through speed traps as long as it submitted a "speed-limit compliance plan" to the Highway Patrol.

Wes also saw, over and over, that people were still ignorant about the resource under their feet. In rural counties rich with some of the best water on Earth, people were still pulling up pickup trucks and dumping garbage into the spring bowls. Wes and a friend once found an entire professional-sized pesticide sprayer dumped inside an underwater cave, still filled with pesticide. Wes also caught a county government crew dumping 55-gallon drums of something into a spring not far from the public water plant. He told them he wouldn't report them if they'd pull the drums out and never try something like that again.

"People were in total denial that there were even such things as conduits, caves, and passageways—that water can move this way," says Mark Wray, one of Ginnie Springs' owners.

The state's leaders were no better. Despite Governor Jeb Bush's populist talk on his Ichetucknee River canoe trip about stopping the cement plant near the river, Bush permitted the plant after all, blowing off protests from top state park officials in his own administration. There was clearly a disconnect between what politicians were saying in public and what was actually happening in Florida's behind-the-scenes power plays.

Instead of doing what most people do—become cynical or give up—Wes elected to do the same thing he did when he faced an obstacle inside a cave. He decided to try another approach.

If scientific testing showed that the water flowing out of the springs was, on average, twenty years old, Wes knew that there was no time to wait to take meaningful action. Since the adults were continuing business as usual in the face of growing environmental harm to the water supply, Wes decided that the best thing to do now was to reach out to the next generation.

He began to conceive his *Water's Journey* film as an educational endeavor, geared to middle school students. He turned to his teacher sister Shirley to help develop a classroom curriculum to go with the film. During the next two years, he worked to raise money for *Water's Journey* in between paying gigs that still had him traveling all over the world.

18

Ice Island

FOR SOME WHO ARRIVED to join the *National Geographic* expedition that Wes had organized to Antarctica, the first shock was seeing the boat. At 118 feet, the *Braveheart* looked, well, *small*.

It looked too small for what they knew could lie ahead: hurricane-force winds, waves as high as ten-story buildings, and killer ice. Everyone who prepared to board the *Braveheart* in New Zealand that day knew that ice had doomed many previous explorers, their boats trapped and squeezed to splinters.

The expedition's aim was to dive beneath icebergs, do scientific exploration, and produce a documentary film in high definition (new technology at the time), a glossy color book, and a *National Geographic* magazine story.

Like other Antarctic expeditions, this one planned to take advantage of the brief two-month window in January and February when the ice cover on the Southern Ocean thaws a little. The crossing between New Zealand and Antarctica is one of the most treacherous in the world. At that latitude the wind blows from east to west, and it's the only place on the globe where there are no land masses to slow waves as they careen around the planet.

"It'll be like traveling from Florida to California at ten miles per hour while being whipped by mountainous seas and gale force winds," producer and host Bill Kurtis narrates in the film that documents the trip, *Ice Island*.

"Every day the ocean got rougher, the air colder, and the hours of daylight longer," Wes's co–expedition leader, marine biologist Gregory S. Stone, writes in his book about the expedition.

Stone was forty-four and had been to Antarctica twice before, specializing in Antarctica's ecology for his graduate degree. This expedition with Wes was Stone's first-ever time writing a story for *National Geographic,* and it was a plum opportunity for him. Usually scientists don't write the articles, writers do. Stone jokes that the reason he got the gig was that they couldn't find a writer who wanted to go on such a perilous journey. But it's more likely that the editors had found something special: a scientist who could write in a way that engaged regular people. For the Antarctica trip, Wes was *National Geographic* magazine's photographer and the principal documentary filmmaker.

Wes and Stone had met several years earlier, when they were working on the "Walking Among the Sharks" episode for *The New Explorers.*

"We really hit it off, the two of us," Stone says, "because we were like two sides of the coin. I always called him my favorite redneck friend. He was from Florida and kind of the good ol' boy, and I was this guy from Boston— you know, this scientist guy with a PhD. But we both shared a passion and an interest in ocean exploration. I was able to bring the scientific context to the situation and he was able to push the exploration edge with his vision and his diving ability."

You may be wondering, as I was: why choose a 118-foot boat for a two-thousand-mile journey through the planet's roughest seas? The simple answer is cost. The expedition didn't have the budget for an icebreaker, the large boats that most sea captains use in the Arctic.

"I think the biggest waves I have ever seen were on that trip," Stone says. "And if you have a smallish boat like that, it's actually good, because you would go up and down the waves, and the boat doesn't get caught between two waves. If you get [a boat] up in the two- to three-hundred-foot range, you can get caught between two crests and really slammed around. So if you have a small boat, it sort of becomes insignificant from the wave's point of view."

Jill Heinerth remembers that the tough-talking Kiwi boat captain, Nigel Jolly, had a laconic way to describe the physical reality of boats in those seas: "The big ones break," he told her. "The little ones bob."

The boat may have been smaller than expected, but the expedition was full of the latest high-tech equipment and hand-picked and ultra-qualified personnel.

On January 17, 2001, summertime in New Zealand, the scientists, divers, and crew of the *Braveheart* sailed out of Lyttelton Harbour. It didn't stay summery for long.

"About an hour into the trip, the captain says, 'It looks like the satellite phone's not going to work,'" Jill Heinerth recalls. "We had about twenty minutes of connectivity before it went out. So everybody on the boat sent a quick message: 'Sorry, no phone as promised, talk to you in sixty days.'"

Their destination was a mammoth iceberg with the utilitarian name of B-15, which corresponded to specific categories of icebergs and Antarctic quadrant designations.

Wes had wanted to go to Antarctica for a very long time. He thought he'd cooked up an expedition that would appeal to *National Geographic*. The idea: to retrace the route of Sir Ernest Shackleton's 1914 Antarctic voyage and report back for the rest of us.

Shackleton hadn't had good luck, but his expedition is legendary. Nearing Antarctica, his ship, *Endurance*, became hopelessly trapped in sea ice. It was frozen fast for ten months, and then was crushed and destroyed by ice pressure. The crew abandoned ship and struggled to survive in the frozen wilderness. After camping on the ice for five long months, Shackleton made two open-boat journeys, one of which—a treacherous eight-hundred-mile ocean crossing to the remote and mountainous South Georgia Island—is considered one of the greatest boat journeys in history. Trekking overland across frozen mountains, Shackleton reached the island's lonely whaling station, organized a rescue team, went back, and brought out all of the men left at the ice camp.

Wes hatched his idea for a modern Shackleton expedition when he ran into his *National Geographic* photographer friend Emory Kristof at a diving equipment expo. Wes confided to Kristof that he was looking for a good project to use the newly introduced high-definition filming equipment. It turned out that Kristof knew someone who might be up for such an adventure: Nigel Jolly, a rough-and-tumble New Zealand sea captain who owned a former Japanese research vessel called the *Braveheart*. Kristof warned Wes that while the Shackleton idea had some appeal, it might not have enough pizzazz for the notoriously fickle editors. But he encouraged Wes to make a pitch anyway, especially knowing that Wes had bona fide world explorer chops and that beguiling southern charm.

Wes set up a meeting with the bigwigs at *National Geographic* headquarters in Washington, D.C. Then something unexpected happened. The night before his meeting, Wes was in his hotel searching the Internet for fresh new Antarctica facts to punch up his presentation. And there on the screen it was: an exquisite gift from the journalism gods.

It was a news story about a giant iceberg that cleaved off Antarctica on March 17, 2000, astonishing scientists and raising new questions about the effects of global warming. The B-15 iceberg was a half-mile thick and as big as Connecticut. Scientists calculated that it had a thousand cubic miles of ice—enough fresh water to supply the needs of the entire United States for five years.

At the time, it was "the largest moving object on earth, easily seen with the naked eye from space," Stone writes.

The pitch to *National Geographic* would now be an expedition to check out B-15 up close, a chance to send divers down under the ice to take samples and see what lurked there.

"When Wes saw that story about B-15, he just shot from the hip and said: 'This is what I want to go do,'" says Terri Skiles. "He had not done anything towards doing it, he just came up with a bizarre idea. And they loved it. So he had a 'go' from there."

"That's the kind of guy he was," says Stone. "He reads about something in the newspaper and he says: 'I'm going to go!' It was a very audacious trip."

The expedition was able to get sponsorship from Kurtis of *The New Explorers* and three heavy-hitting scientific organizations: the New England Aquarium, the Bermuda Underwater Exploration Institute, and the National Geographic Society.

"I still can't believe we actually did it, looking back on it now," Stone says. "That we did it and we all came back alive."

The more she learned about the harsh conditions, Terri says, the more worried she got. Before he left, Wes gave their daughter Tessa two little yellow chicks to comfort her during her dad's absence. "That was the beginning of the chickens in the yard," Terri says.

"I started to get worried when I realized they'd be on a ship and meet things like rogue waves. And then they were going to go dive underneath icebergs that no one had ever really done. I was like 'Holy crap, Wes!' This was the only one of his trips that everybody knew I was concerned about. We did talk about it, but he just—it didn't really matter to him that I was concerned. He would give me a little bit of 'Well, I'll be okay, don't worry about it. I've got good people.' That was the extent of it."

The amount of specialized equipment and survival gear they needed to haul was daunting. They shipped it across the world and spent several days loading it into the boat. Among other things, they hauled 10,000 liters of diesel fuel, tons of food, scuba gear with dozens of 25-pound air tanks, three large computerized rebreathers, high-definition camera equipment specially adapted to survive the subzero temperatures, lights to make the photos of the all-white ice-scape pop, scientific testing equipment, dart guns to collect samples of whale tissue if they were lucky enough to spot whales (they were), ice survival gear, sea survival gear, skiffs, a helicopter, special dive suits, ice goggles (because the cold would freeze your tears), and defensive equipment in case they needed to ward off aggressive leopard seals.

"We had been warned that leopard seals had knocked over ice floes with scientists on them," Jill says. "We were told that was the most dangerous thing in Antarctica, animal-wise. I remember Wes spent one whole night sitting on this cliff-like iceberg, looking down and filming this leopard seal who was swimming back and forth, back and forth, huffing—which is predation behavior."

The expedition recruited an eighteen-member team of divers, environmental scientists, and crew. Laurie Prouting, a New Zealand sheep farmer, brought a helicopter he used on his ranch, which he would now pilot for the expedition.

The team that would dive inside and beneath icebergs in the 29-degree water included Jill and Paul Heinerth, who were a married couple at the time and both experts at extreme diving and using closed-circuit rebreathers. The recycled air in the rebreathers was much warmer than the air in traditional tanks—a bonus in these conditions.

Everyone knew big waves and high winds were coming when they crossed the Southern Ocean between New Zealand and Antarctica. The latitudes had long been known as the Roaring Forties, the Furious Fifties, and the Screaming Sixties, meaning that the farther you went toward the South Pole, the taller the waves and the fiercer the conditions.

The experience was one of those things you simply can't imagine until you are in the midst of it, Jill Heinerth says. Not long before they set out on their journey, a ship in the Southern Ocean had hit 100-foot waves. The *Braveheart* hit 60-foot seas, the height of a six-story building. As the boat got sucked up, up, up the sides of these enormous waves, then lurched back down the other side like some screwed-up roller coaster, they almost all got seasick and were confined to their berths. It just wasn't safe to move around anymore.

"We were still filming when the waves were at twenty feet, and then we stopped filming. Matt Jolly, the first mate and the son of the captain—he was about twenty years old—he climbed the mast and secured the camera to the mast," says Jill Heinerth, who was thirty-five at the time. "After that, everything was secured for a week. All we were doing was lying in our bunks feeling miserable, hearing things crash and break. I never felt scared, I just felt sick. I just kept thinking: Is it going to be like this for two months? Because we're not going to get much done. Some of the people were just paralyzed with fear. People had different ways of coping, from completely turning inside themselves, to aggression, to bipolar behavior, to heavy drinking. For the captain, fuel was constantly on his mind. Every time we turned on a generator, we used fuel. They kept the temperature on the boat at 55 degrees; it was like a meat locker."

Later, on the way back from the expedition, they sat around and asked one another: "What was your scariest experience—when you were afraid you might die?"

"The captain said he had lost the bailing pumps and he thought we might sink," Jill says. "The engine room was filling with water. I didn't even *know* we were near having to jump in lifeboats. I mean, how's that going to work? Imagine a lifeboat dinghy in sixty-foot seas. All that's going to do is prolong the agony before you die."

Three days into their crossing came a wave that they would remember for the rest of their lives. People were thrown from their bunks, dishes smashed in the galley, and two fuel tanks came loose and careened across the wildly pitching deck.

"There was an inclinometer—a small pendulum that records the degree of swing port or starboard a ship rolls," Stone writes. "The maximum roll an inclinometer can measure is 45 degrees—and that was where ours was stuck, which meant we had actually rolled farther than that. How much farther we will never know. After that, we were more careful about slowing down for big waves."

"I thought we were going to go over," Stone says, "and that would have been the end of us."

"Wes, to his credit," Jill Heinerth says, "got out there on that deck with the first mate, which was unbelievably dangerous, with these huge—I don't know how much those fuel tanks weighed, maybe a ton?—sliding around the deck, out of control, and they managed to secure them in probably thirty- or forty-foot seas that night."

In the *Ice Island* documentary, there's footage shot on the deck of the lurching ship, filled with sea spray and roaring winds. You see a bundled-up man knocked off his feet and skittering across the frozen, pitching deck of the boat. It's Wes, trying to grab the fuel tanks. He's sliding across the deck, prone, and he's laughing.

"An absolutely nice day!" he shouts, cracking up the crew.

Wes and Stone spent time each day discussing how to handle the psychological toll that the conditions were taking on the expedition team. At one point the cook locked herself in her cabin, declaring that she quit. Right there in the middle of the ocean wilderness, with eighteen people to feed, at a time when each person needed several thousand calories a day to handle the freezing temperatures.

"It took me a whole day of talking to her through the door through her tears to get her to even come out and face the day," Jill Heinerth says.

After eleven days on rough seas, they made it across the Southern Ocean, two thousand miles between New Zealand and Antarctica. On January 28, 2001, they entered Antarctica's Ross Sea, a place so cold that the ocean spray froze instantly on the rails and deck. Everyone had to go out on deck periodically with hammers and baseball bats to break ice off so the boat wouldn't get too top-heavy.

Now they were in the area where they planned to dive under the icebergs. Each berg had its own fantastical shape and personality. Some had bright little blue "bays" beside them where the melting fresh ice water met the saline ocean.

Wes enthusiastically started putting his new Sony high-definition camera through its paces. It was somewhat nerve-wracking, because Wes wasn't familiar with the new technology, and neither were the other folks who would help film. They'd assumed they would be able to reach tech support at Sony during the trip, but when the satellite phone quit working an hour into the journey, they knew they had to figure it out on their own.

The only communication the ship had with the outside world was through a New Zealand woman's ham radio station called Bluff Fisherman's

Radio. She faithfully kept contact with some 100 fishing vessels out in the Antarctic, noting their positions and checking on them if they weren't heard from for several days. On the radio over such long distances, voices sounded like they were speaking from the bottom of a well, but having that connection was a great comfort for everyone.

In this wide white world, the precision high-definition camera technology was a godsend for Wes. The equipment was able to provide detail in the glaring whiteness that shone twenty-four hours a day. Wes's footage would turn out to be some of his most stunning creative work. The icebergs look like floating cartoon mountains and mesas, surprising and breathtaking.

When the *Braveheart* made it to the Ross Sea, it was ten months after the B-15 iceberg they came to explore had calved off the Ross Ice Shelf. By this time it had broken into two big chunks and hundreds of smaller pieces.

"Then one morning they wake up to an ominous sign," Kurtis narrates gravely in the documentary. "It's supposed to be icy here in Antarctica . . . but this much is early, and the *Braveheart* is not an icebreaker. If the seas freeze too early, she's in trouble."

The pack ice was indeed closing in, and it looked impossible for the ship to reach B-15.

"I remember I was up on deck with Wes and we were freezing our butts off," Stone says. "I looked out to the ice and I said: 'Wes, that ice could crush the ship! You think that we should start getting all of our stuff out on deck— all of our supplies and food and, you know, gear?' And he said: 'I don't know, maybe we should . . . ' I mean, that was the kind of situation we were in."

They were also running low on fuel. Wes and Prouting, the helicopter pilot, prepared to make a trip above the ship, to take a look at the ice around them and see if there might be a route through. From the air, they could see it was no use. There was no safe route for the *Braveheart* through the ice. They decided the safest thing to do was to find a place to tie up for a while, and the captain maneuvered the boat into a picturesque bright blue curved cove, cradled by an ice "mountain" that provided hours of entertainment for the cooped-up explorers.

"I decided to film a segment of Wes talking about how bad the situation was," Jill says. "You know, *how do you feel at this point?* So I am filming, and just behind Wes, Matt Jolly, the first mate and the captain's son, is running stark naked across the ice back and forth in front of the boat. Wes is talking to the camera and has no idea Matt's doing this behind him!

"Wes was always a pretty good cheerleader. At one point, when the sun came out for a little bit, he said, 'Let's go.' It was right around Super Bowl time. He got everybody off the boat to play football on the ice. It was just something to break the tension. That's really leadership."

Stone, Wes, and other key members of the expedition held a powwow to talk about Wes and Prouting taking the helicopter to the largest chunk of B-15, so Wes could film it and take still photographs for *National Geographic*. They'd been in radio contact with a fishing vessel and determined that the *Braveheart* was about sixty-five miles away from the iceberg.

There were lingering worries about the chopper's safety. When it was secured on deck in New Zealand for the journey, Jill says, its battery was inadvertently left connected to its electrical system, and key components were now corroded by salt water. Wes jumped in to figure out how to get it running again.

"Wes and our audio guy fixed the chopper up," Jill says. "It was literally best-guess mechanics. They were like 'It kind of looks like a trolling motor. It looks like there was a wire here. Well, something's got to give power to that.'"

The helicopter had enough fuel to go on a three-hour trip, so they could go to B-15, stay a minute without turning the engine off, and Wes could jump out and film while pilot Prouting refueled for the trip back to the *Braveheart*. They knew they'd be out of radio contact with the *Braveheart,* and that was another worry.

"There was no chance that, if something went wrong, that we could rescue them," Jill says.

Prouting took the helicopter for a wobbly test flight, where it hovered like a wasp just above the ship's deck, then flew just fine. Prouting landed the helicopter back on deck and loaded Wes, fuel, safety equipment, and the filming gear aboard. When they tried to take off the second time, the helicopter was too heavy. So Wes removed his seat and some gear and sat on the floorboards, where he was able to film gorgeous aerials of the iceberg's imposing white cliffs.

Wes filmed himself that day, with Prouting's help. They documented being the first humans on what was then the world's largest iceberg.

"We're on B-15!" Wes shouts in the film, laughing hard. "It's the ultimate experience in life to make it to such a place and to see such things!"

On the *Braveheart*, everyone was tense, waiting for Wes and Prouting to return. They shot flares off the deck at timed intervals to guide the helicopter and were grateful to welcome the explorers back aboard.

With icebergs all around, the team began taking samples and exploring. Stone took basic measurements to determine the levels of chlorophyll, salinity, and temperature of the water around the icebergs. What he found was that the water got warmer as it got deeper, and there was an increase in phytoplankton along the berg's edges. They had brought along a remote-controlled aquatic robot to film along an iceberg's edges when the water was too deep for the divers.

Seawater in the Antarctic freezes at about 29 degrees Fahrenheit—cold enough to kill most people in a matter of minutes. Sometimes the team was diving in water that was turning to ice as they swam. To dive here, everyone carried along special gear. The Heinerths and Wes planned to use the rebreathers, because their recycled breath would be warmer than gas supplied by tanks, and the lack of bubbles would make better film.

"There's nothing you can do to keep your fingers and toes warm," Jill says. "We had a little heating pad by our kidneys. You're wearing basically a snowmobile suit under your dry [diving] suit. When you're submerged in water, the cold is much worse than being in the cold air."

The first Antarctic dive they took was at the iceberg nicknamed the Ice Palace, where they were docked.

"Wes had electric boots and electric socks. He got an electric undergarment to wear under his dry suit to keep himself warm," Jill says. "He rolled off the boat and reached up for his camera, and he goes: 'I'm leaking.' I advised him to get out right away. He said, 'I just want to get a minute of footage.' He had a brand-new high-definition camera, and he wanted to test it. . . . Even though his suit was leaking, he decided to drop down anyway and shoot a minute of footage. He comes up and he's incapacitated from the cold. He can't get into the Zodiac boat. He's got no muscle control."

The expedition members moved quickly to rush the now-hypothermic Wes back to the *Braveheart*.

"Hauling him into the Zodiac was near impossible now that his suit was filled with many pounds of freezing water weighing him down," Jill says. "It was a really close call for his very first dive."

Wes recovered with a hot shower and getting wrapped in a sleeping bag.

"After that dive, it was kind of sobering for him, and he was saying, 'Maybe this is more than I can handle.' It scared him," Jill says. "He decided to switch from the rebreather to the open circuit. The open circuit is actually much colder, because you are breathing cold air. When we finally arrived at what appeared to be a spacious crevasse reaching inside an iceberg, Wes asked Paul and I to make the first explorations. If it looked promising for footage, he would consider diving again. On one dive, Paul and I had just gotten into the tunnels when a large piece of ice at the opening calved off and closed the entrance that we had come in. To Wes, who was topside, he saw that the opening to our cave was gone and he was feeling that we were dead or trapped. He spent about twenty minutes convinced that Paul and I were not coming back, but we did.

"Then Paul and I did another dive, and the current shifted and we couldn't get out. We were just being sucked into the iceberg. We made a hasty decision. I saw light, an opening which the current was moving toward, so we decided to go toward that.

"We were forty-five minutes overdue. We were down so long that we had to decompress, and we hadn't planned to do that on this dive. It was 130 feet deep. We surfaced from the decompression and I look around, and I'm next to this giant iceberg, and I don't see the boat anywhere, so I know the boat can't see me."

Jill inflated a "safety sausage"—a four-foot-long bright orange balloon— to make them visible. She started orienting herself in her mind, retracing the route they had gone during the dive. They started moving through the icy water in that direction. Then they saw part of the boat peeking around the end of the iceberg. It turned out that the *Braveheart* had come loose from its anchor and drifted. They reached the boat and ended their dive safely.

Jill, Paul, and Wes weren't the only ones who had a harrowing Arctic dive. Greg Stone and the ship's medical officer Porter Turnbull weren't sure they would survive their venture.

"We knew this was the most dangerous diving in the world and we were ready for every scenario except what actually happened," Stone writes. Swimming along an ice wall, they suddenly started getting sucked downward.

We kicked up but could not stop the descent. The wall of ice was now rushing past us, as the sunny day and outline of our boat above got smaller and smaller. I looked over and saw Porter's eyes wide and intense. We were at 80 feet and still sinking. We channeled air into our dry-suits and buoyancy jackets, but nothing slowed us. Finally, at 100 feet, we began to rise and regain control of our dive. We moved away from the berg and realized we had been caught in a density-driven downdraft by the berg's edge. Our first discovery was that large icebergs in the open ocean cool the water around them, creating powerful down-currents at their edges, too strong for divers to fight.

Later they decided to release biodegradable fluorescent dye to measure the downdrafts, and the current clocked in at 1.15 miles per hour.

Wes was still shaken from his experience with hypothermia, Jill says, but when he saw the film that she and Paul shot with a small movie camera under a stationary iceberg, he decided to go diving again.

"We're here at Ice Island cave number 4," Wes says in the film. "By far, this is going to be the most dangerous and risky dive of our trip, but one we're looking forward to making. We're physically going inside the iceberg. It's incredible to describe the feeling of being encompassed in ice, but it's also a feeling that you're out there at the virtual limit of mental, physical, and technological limits."

The film they shot beneath the iceberg turned out to be the visual surprise they needed for the documentary. The iceberg had been stationary for three to five years. Instead of finding the typical blank seafloor left behind where icebergs constantly scour the sea bottom, this "fixed" berg had ice columns and caves connecting it to the seafloor. Venturing into the caves, Wes and the Heinerths filmed a remarkable multicolored undersea garden that looked like it belonged in a Dr. Seuss book. As the iceberg sat in one place, phytoplankton colonized it, providing building blocks to attract marine life.

"I was in wonderment," Paul Heinerth says. "I couldn't believe so much life could exist there."

The seafloor was carpeted with sponges, sea cucumbers, starfish, and other creatures. Jellyfish with rainbow-colored glow-in-the-dark stripes swam through the fantastical landscape.

"I think the biggest discovery was how much life was under some of these icebergs," Stone says. "We were basically the first ones to point to the fact that icebergs increase ocean productivity, that they were a driver of ocean life. Prior to that, no one had ever looked at it."

The dive that Wes and the Heinerths did under the stationary iceberg turned out to be another perilous adventure. The current grew incredibly stiff, and, Jill wrote later, "getting out of the cave became a frightening fight for our lives."

The cave walls were slick ice, and the only things they could grab onto were finger-sized holes made by tiny ice fish. They had been down for an hour, twice as long as most Antarctic ice dives, and the current was so strong that Jill could make no progress swimming. Wes was carrying the bulky high-definition camera, and Paul and Jill knew perfectly well that even though conditions were dire, Wes would not let that expensive equipment get swept away. Paul quickly moved to help Wes painstakingly drag the camera upward. At 90 feet of depth, they were finally able to get around to a part of the iceberg that was shielded from the current and catch their breath. The upside was that their frantic fight to get out made for some nice adventure tension in the documentary, especially with the spooky underwater light inside the ice cave.

"Holy shit!" Jill says in the film as she climbs out of the water. "The cave tried to keep us today!"

Everyone was safe and back on the *Braveheart* that evening, and they planned to do another dive inside the berg the next day. But at one a.m. they heard a loud crashing and ran out on deck. The iceberg they had just been exploring exploded.

"This minefield of ice that you see right out here was the iceberg we were just filming inside of," Wes tells the camera. "Our cave system is absolutely obliterated."

Narrator Kurtis intones: "This too is a major discovery. No one has ever seen, perhaps even predicted, that disintegration could happen so suddenly. The expedition is stunned."

Kurtis summarizes the scientific explanation for viewers. Icebergs melt a little when temperatures warm, and then, at night, those melted fissures refreeze. At a certain point, like an ice cube in a glass of water, their internal structure gives way and they pop apart.

"On this night," Kurtis narrates, "the tired internal lattice of cracks reached its breaking point and shattered from the thermal shock."

Everyone was disappointed that they had not gotten film of the iceberg's explosion. When the berg blew, all the cameras were already stored for the night, their batteries on their chargers. The explosion happened so fast, the only footage they got was the vast field of floating ice shards where the iceberg had been. The shards covered two square miles.

"We had moved our boat only two hours before the berg flipped and exploded," Stone writes. "We had no reason to move the boat other than wanting a change of scenery that night. A lucky decision."

And one more time that Wes narrowly avoided death.

19

Making *Water's Journey*

GOING TO ANTARCTICA WAS A MILESTONE for everyone, and for Wes it was a passage into an even higher professional realm at *National Geographic*. But he still chafed to make his mark with the film project he had been planning for years, *Water's Journey*.

Jill Heinerth was now working for him as a producer. Wes was hustling again for money. Since his concept for *Water's Journey* was to make it educational, Wes came up with the idea of turning to his contacts in state government for funding. Politically, he had some advantages. He was a Republican businessman approaching a Republican administration. He was on first-name terms with the state environmental secretary, David Struhs, and with Jim King, a prominent state senator from Jacksonville who helped shape the state budget each year in Tallahassee. Wes's main goal, the one he'd long pursued, was to give young viewers a lifelong visual connection between the water that flows from their faucets and the water that runs, unseen, beneath their feet. For hours, Wes and Jill brainstormed in Wes's office in High Springs.

"It all started with a roll of about forty feet of brown kraft paper on the floor over at Karst Productions," Jill remembers. "We had colorful markers, and we started drawing the connections. I drew this huge, long, visual storyboard showing: 'Okay, you flush the toilet, and here is where it goes. Well, it goes to a sewage treatment plant in some cases, and so then what happens from there?' So we drew all these connective paths, and then we started thinking about where you could illustrate those connected paths.

Where were cave systems that we knew that went under interesting places like bowling alleys and golf courses and homes and Sonny's Barbecue restaurants and things like that? And so we drew this all out on this giant piece of paper. We didn't know how it was going to all come together, but we knew it was a concept that would make this all *real* for people—fun and less abstract."

Wes took his rolled-up kraft paper outline to Tallahassee for a meeting with DEP secretary Struhs.

"He walked into that office and he said, 'Here's what I want to do,' and, in typical Wes fashion, with all the enthusiasm, he knocked David Struhs's socks off. And David Struhs just looked at him and he said, 'I have never had such an outrageous and bizarre presentation in my life. A guy comes in with a roll of kraft paper and crayons and asks me for two hundred and fifty thousand dollars. I'm blown away, and I am going to give it to you.'"

With the encouragement and help of key state officials, Wes was also able to get some funding from the Florida Departments of Agriculture and Education. In between his other paying film gigs, he started to craft *Water's Journey: Hidden Rivers*, which would eventually air on PBS.

By necessity, all moviemaking contains elements of trickery. While we watch the divers in *Water's Journey: Hidden Rivers* go on an "uncharted expedition" under the Sonny's Barbecue restaurant, the bowling alley, and the golf course community, the truth is that all these routes were well known to Wes and crew. All were dive sites they had long explored and knew would work well on film. As a viewer, you may know this intellectually, but there's a sense of suspending that knowledge as you watch the story unfold. When diver Tom Morris gets "stuck" in a tiny cave passage restriction, for example, you are worried for him even though, if you stop to think, cameraman Wes has obviously already made it through the restriction safely, because he's inside the next cave passage, pointing his camera back at Morris.

During filming, Jill, Wes, and Tom wore identical scuba outfits, so they could serve as interchangeable models when the need arose. Wes also employed a filming trick that he and his team had honed over the years. In the film, it looks as if the handheld lights that divers use are illuminating the whole cave as they swim through. In truth, the hand lights aren't that powerful. So Wes had extra divers hidden off the frame, holding more powerful lights. As the actor divers swam past, the lighting divers would cover and uncover the powerful lights, so it looked as if those little handheld lights were doing all the illuminating. By the time he made *Water's Journey: Hidden Rivers,* Wes was seasoned at this type of creative engineering, and shooting the film was relatively quick and painless. For one thing, it was a local project—a luxury for Wes and crew, who could go home to their families at the end of the day. He was even able to cast his children, Nate and Tessa, in the film.

Wes was finally making *his* movie, not someone else's. He cast himself in the role of friendly guide, instead of hiring outside talent. Jill says they were later criticized for this at some film festivals by people who thought they should have used an outside scientific "expert," which was the standard style for nature documentaries at the time. But really, who was a greater expert on Florida's aquifer cave systems than Wes? By knowing his subject so intimately, he was able to easily showcase the detailed scientific and exploration work he and his friends had been doing, unseen, for years. It manifested in passages like this one, from the film:

> Jill Heinerth (diving inside the cave): Okay, Tom, let me jot down our data here. This is going to be profile sample number four, looking at the general water chemistry and, let's see . . . depth is 82 feet, the right time—okay, I got it, let's go, Tom.
>
> Brian Pease (above ground, tracking the divers): I got them really clearly right here, it looks like they are heading for those houses right over there.
>
> Wes (above ground with Brian, walking across a golf course): Right there, huh? Excuse us, cave survey coming through. I'm going to mark this just because it's right in the middle of the fairway here, and it's kind of an interesting spot to have.
>
> Narrator: Deep below the golf course, the divers continued to transmit the signal to Wes and Brian.
>
> Wes: This just goes to show you there's no facet of life that these underground systems aren't able to travel under. Here we're literally going underneath somebody's patio here and into their sliding glass door and into the Florida room.
>
> Brian: How close should I go to the house?

Tom and Jill swim to the well pipe for someone's house, then the film cuts to Wes and Pease back on the surface.

Wes: They're in the plumbing of the Earth, underneath the water plumbing of the house. . . .

Brian: Yeah, now they're heading out towards the driveway. They're heading this way.

. . .

Narrator: Finally, an encouraging sign, they can feel the current of the water at their back. . . . They finally found their way forward.

Jill: Looks like we found the flow, Tom.

Tom: Wow, this is gorgeous.

Jill: Yeah. . . .

Brian: I'm right over the top of them here.

. . .

Narrator: Finally, after twists and turns, crawling through the cracks, victory is within their grasp.

Wes: All right, well, here they are. They're coming through a sinkhole. Ya know, here we are at the end of the water's journey and most people think of this as the beginning. In reality this water has come all this way through all these features, underneath golf courses, restaurants, highways. Just unbelievable.

As Tom and Jill emerge from the sinkhole, Wes tells them: "You would not believe the places y'all have been underneath!"

It is a quirky approach, and *Water's Journey: Hidden Rivers* makes an immediate impact on anyone who sees it.

"I thought that when I brushed my teeth and let the water run, it went right back into the plumbing and was reused again. I was obviously wrong," reads a note from one student who saw the film at Fort Clarke Middle School in Gainesville.

"I didn't know that sinkholes led to aquifers, so when you dump garbage into a sinkhole, you're really dumping garbage into the aquifer," another student wrote.

"From now on," another student wrote, "when I see someone wasting water or polluting it, I'll think of your movie and tell them to stop!"

20

Hydrillasaurus

STARTING IN THE 1970S, an alien invader began to pillage Florida's clear, white-sand-bottomed rivers, one by one. A bushy aquatic plant called hydrilla, which was likely tossed into a Florida canal when someone cleaned out a fish tank, began to march across the underwater landscape. Like many of the alien creatures that have colonized Florida—including Burmese pythons big enough to swallow alligators, giant African snails that eat stucco houses, and African lizards from the Nile River that can grow seven feet long and eat cats—hydrilla appears here to stay. Many of the lovely river bottoms we've enjoyed in Florida for hundreds, if not thousands, of years, disappeared beneath the deep green underwater hydrilla forest in just two decades, fueled by fertilizer, manure, and sewage runoff.

In 2003, Wes started work on a film called *Monsters Put to the Test* for the Discovery Channel. He was hired by his friend John Tindall, a television producer he'd met while working on *Rescue 911* episodes. The film was a spoof featuring a monster called, appropriately, Hydrillasaurus. The fake story was that Hydrillasaurus came from South America, had no known predators, and lived in the Santa Fe River near Wes's home. In fact, the elaborate costume, which looked a lot like the Creature from the Black Lagoon, was manufactured in Wes's shop at home.

Pulling off a hoax like this in a town as small as High Springs, Florida, especially with a colorful and well-known resident like Wes involved, was no small task. They put together a sham barbecue competition with a $1,000 prize, held along the banks of the Santa Fe River. The contestants thought the competition was real. As they cooked, Tindall interviewed each hopeful barbecue chef, and carefully positioned them facing the Santa Fe River so that, as they looked at the camera and interviewer, they would also see the river in the distance. While the "contestants" talked, a diver partially surfaced in a Hydrillasaurus suit, à la Nessie, the Loch Ness Monster.

"We'd start the interview, and the interview was set up in such a way so that they would look past me and the camera and Wes, and they'd see the river, and this creature would make a bubbling noise," Tindall says. "It was all cued. We had walkie-talkies and people everywhere. During their interview, this creature would go by, just barely breaching the surface, and they, of course, would be slack jawed, going 'Oh, I've never seen anything like that!' And I'm like 'Yeah, yeah, yeah,' asking them: 'Do you use the barbecue juices? Do you use Tennessee wet? Do you use Kansas City?'"

At the end of the hoax, they had two guys in a boat pulling up to shore, yelling, "We've got it! We've got it!" The creature was in the boat, under a cover.

"Then we pull the covers off, and this goofy thing stands up," Tindall says. "And everybody knew it was a joke at that point."

The Hydrillasaurus was just the kind of prank Wes loved. But among those who dove and floated the wild rivers and springs, it was gallows humor. Our waters were changing for the worse before our eyes. It was happening so fast, and no one in power seemed to be taking action to stop it.

There was the perennial problem of the polluters' great political influence in Florida, as well as the fact that the springs were located in sparsely populated areas where fewer people witnessed the devastation. But there was something else critically important that escaped the public's eye.

The very assumptions that state regulators used to determine whether to issue permits to draw water or to put in a dairy operation or build a gas station were wrong. The models that hydrologists learn in school to explain how contamination moves through underground water supplies were developed in the Midwest, where uniform sand and gravel deposits assure that groundwater percolates steadily through the layers. In these models, it is easier to predict, for example, how far and how fast spilled oil will move through the ground. But even though cave divers were discovering that Florida's Swiss-cheese limestone acted like a siphon in some places and like a great underground river in others, state regulators continued to use the model developed for a different kind of aquifer altogether. The public was unaware of this major disconnect in public policy.

"As cave divers, we knew there were these big caves, and water flows really fast through the caves, so contaminants can move really fast. And the computer models that people were using—and still are—to manage the resource, don't consider any of those caves," says Todd Kincaid, a cave-diving hydrogeologist who worked as a consultant with Karst Environmental Services.

"All the models were reaching incorrect conclusions," agrees Rodney De-Han, who worked as a senior research scientist for the Florida Geological Survey. "Wes was the first to convince me of that. Wes was interested in seeing that his explorations generated some real results that eventually translated into real rule-making. He was a quick study for somebody who was not trained in science. He understood these highly complicated concepts."

"Early on," Kincaid says, "the fact that Wes was a cave diver worked against him when he was talking to scientists. Across the spectrum, people regarded cave divers as crazy—as somebody who had a death wish or someone that was an adrenaline junkie. Just all these labels, I think, got in the way of being taken seriously about what you were trying to present. I think towards the end that changed, I think especially after people saw *Water's Journey*, it started to add an air of legitimacy to Wes's opinion. But that didn't happen for a while."

At one point Wes took a series of large topographic maps of the Santa Fe River basin and taped them together. Then, working from what he'd seen and recorded underground, he drew scale maps of all the caves he had explored and put arrows for how the water flowed in the huge karst region.

"I was blown away," says Kincaid. "It was a more comprehensive detailing of groundwater flows than any professional in my field would make."

Wes brought his one-of-a-kind map to officials at the Suwannee River Water Management District.

"They told him they didn't want the map because they didn't think there was anything useful in it, because he's not a hydrogeologist and blah, blah, blah," Kincaid says. "Just the idea that the water management district didn't want to look at that, it just blew my mind, the level of hubris. As hydrogeologists, we strive to make those kinds of maps ourselves, and we make them by measuring water levels, and we contour the water levels, and we get that data from wells, and you can also get that data from sinkholes and springs, and you compile all the stuff together, but what we *don't* have are the flow directions. We have to infer the flow directions from water levels, which are ultimately a very sparse data set. The fact that he could draw arrows on that map and show the direction of water flow, that's his amazing level of knowledge that, to me, any professional hydrogeologist would just love to have that. That's something that we strive to make, and here he has this firsthand observation of it."

One of the other glaring regulatory problems was that the state had different rules governing pollution to surface waters—streams, lakes, and the like—and groundwater, even though in Florida they are pretty much one and the same.

"What we're saying with our laws is that it's not all right to contaminate a surface stream, but it's OK to destroy our drinking water," Wes said. "I'm not against people and their rights, but I don't think that gives someone the right to damage the water of our entire state. The rules need to be changed."

Wes started to feel that the time he spent in government meetings and talking to officials was a waste. More and more he could see that his first instinct, to bring the information straight to the public, was the right one.

"That film, *Water's Journey*, changed so many people's mindsets," Kincaid said. "If somebody sees *Water's Journey*, and they see the cave going underneath the Sonny's Barbecue and then they go to a meeting and they listen to some official trying to tell them that water doesn't flow like that, they have no patience for that."

Years later, Karst Environmental Services was part of a team that poured fluorescein dye into lakes, sinkholes, and wells a few miles from Central Florida's famous Silver Springs to determine how fast groundwater moves through the karst landscape. The state's official scientific model predicted that it would take years, decades, or even centuries for the water to move through the system.

The dye reached Silver Springs in two weeks.

21

Water's Journey Grows

WES WAS ANNOYED WHEN OFFICIALS dismissed his critical message about the government's obviously flawed models for groundwater movement, but the fact remained that his films, his employees, and his family all depended on government contracts.

Water's Journey: Hidden Rivers was funded by the government, and Karst Productions was also doing public service videos and publications for environmental agencies. The water management districts, state environmental agencies, and county governments all hired scientists and divers from Karst Environmental Services to do aquifer investigation work. Among other things, Karst Environmental developed ways to install and monitor equipment to gauge spring levels and flow, did radiolocation for well drilling sites, and conducted thermal imagery, ground truthing, and underground dye tests to find flow direction.

The water bottling operation at Ginnie Springs was a client. Coca-Cola came into High Springs to take over the plant, and right away the company recognized that the state's groundwater modeling would not protect its investment, because it wouldn't accurately predict contamination that could wreck its water source. Coca-Cola hired Karst Environmental, with hydrogeologist Kincaid on the project, to develop a new groundwater flow model that would actually reflect the reality of karst terrain. It took four years, and when it was finished, Wes and Kincaid offered it to the Suwannee River Water Management District. The government declined the offer. They said that a study done by government scientists, rather than by a multinational corporation, would have more validity in the public arena.

But the money for that government study never came, the state kept using its flawed model, and the permits for groundwater withdrawals were handed out pretty much when anyone asked for one. Every year, more people wanted to stick straws into Florida's groundwater.

Wes focused on his role as environmental educator. His creative baby, *Water's Journey*: *Hidden Rivers*, was now being shown in schools, paired with a classroom curriculum for teachers and students. As Wes made the film, daughter Tessa had served the valuable role of "kid consultant" to make sure the message was understandable and interesting to young people.

When Wes was at home in High Springs, "it was one hundred percent 'kid time,'" says Nathan. "He was everything, and more, I could ask from a dad. I could always talk to him about whatever. He was my best friend every minute."

Both Tessa and Nathan were involved in school sports, and Wes was a fixture at their games, often coaching.

"He would always be picking up trash at my baseball games," says Nathan. "I was playing traveling baseball, and we'd go to these random cities, and while I was warming up, I'd see him out there with a bag he'd found, picking up trash. That was classic."

Terri and Wes took their kids to Costa Rica to surf, to Bermuda and the Keys and the Bahamas to dive, and to Mexico to see ruins and swim the springs. At home, they had horses and rode together on their land in High Springs. Most Thanksgivings, they'd hold a campout at Blue Springs, right next to Ginnie and just across the rural highway from their house.

"Dad would give us all dive lights to light up the spring, and we would play music and just jam out," says Tessa. "No matter what, no matter where he was, if I called him, he would pick up the phone. I feel his favorite thing— on top of the filming, the photography, and trying to protect our springs— was that he loved to have fun. He loved to hang out with me and Nate. He would do anything to make us happy. I could go up to my dad and say, 'Hey, Dad, I really want to go to this place,' and he'd be like 'All right, let me get a month to get my stuff together and we'll go.'"

At work, Wes could be a stickler and a perfectionist, but both Tessa and Nathan say their dad never made them feel judged, and that he was a cheerleader for whatever they wanted to do.

"In his mind, there was never a roadblock for anything," Nathan says. "It wasn't like 'Oh, we can't do this because of that.' There's always a way to get things done. He just made a way. He jumped into the unknown—that was his whole life, you know, surfing, diving, whatever—just 'Let's go!'"

When Nathan was graduating from high school and Tessa was middle-school age, Wes and his team got government funding to work on more projects close to home. They would do two more *Water's Journey* films: one to showcase Northeast Florida's three-hundred-mile-long St. Johns River, which runs through Jacksonville, and another focusing on the thorny hydrological puzzle that is the diked-and-drained Florida Everglades. Both watersheds were considered at the time to be among the largest man-made environmental restoration projects in the world.

The new *Water's Journey* films had multimillion-dollar budgets, and the subject material was a complex mix—part recitation of the grave pollution threats facing the waterways, part environmental education about where the water comes from and where it goes, part spotlight on solutions, and part chest-thumping for the state's environmental policies.

Wes was bulking up his staff at Karst Productions as his workload boomed. At a trade show he met Ross Ambrose, who was working for a camera company in Chicago. He persuaded Ambrose to move to High Springs, and Ambrose jumped in as production manager and coordinator for the two new *Water's Journey* films. Wherever they went to arrange places to shoot the documentary series, Ambrose saw Wes work his gregarious magic.

"Whether it was a politician or a farmer or a country boy, they all could relate to Wes," Ambrose says. "That's how Wes was able to build bridges, and that's how he was able to make the *Water's Journey* films."

The St. Johns River film, called *Water's Journey: The River Returns*, is an upbeat travelogue of a three-hundred-mile journey in a flotilla of house-boats and kayaks. The St. Johns is a big river, and its length is filled with intriguing stories. For one thing, the river flows south to north, collecting water from the surrounding springs, tributaries, and wetlands along the way. Its Native American name translates as "river of lakes," because of its slow flow and large, lake-like basins. White settlers arrived at the banks of the St. Johns when Florida was still a Spanish territory.

As a cautionary tale of how waterways can get wrecked by adjacent land uses, the St. Johns is a poster child. It's been polluted by paper mill waste, by Jacksonville's sewage and urban runoff, and by industrial agriculture operations in the rural areas farther south. Its headwaters were ditched and drained by early settlers and its wetland forests clear-cut in the name of progress.

The river is periodically plagued by toxic algae outbreaks locals call the Green Monster, because the waterway turns a scary-looking fluorescent green and thousands of fish go belly up when too much fertilizer, manure, sewage, and industrial waste contaminates it. It's so bad that authorities warn people not to swim, fish, boat, or even touch the water during outbreaks. At the time of the film, taxpayers were on the hook for a massive restoration project designed to filter the polluted water flowing off agricultural operations. Critics pointed out that the agricultural companies should be required to clean up their pollution before it goes into the public's water supplies. But the government wasn't interested in regulations. Instead, the film—funded by the Florida Department of Agriculture and the St. Johns Water Management District—showcased the voluntary "best management practices" that some agricultural operations were using, such as slow-release fertilizers and precise irrigation systems to water roots instead of spraying a whole field. Spotlighting these voluntary forward-thinking practices in the film was important, because it showed people a better way. But the big water cleanup was happening in the multimillion-dollar settling ponds, with taxpayers footing the bill.

While the state paid Wes and crew to do the film describing all the ways everyone could pitch in to clean up the St. Johns River, state officials were also allowing the multinational corporation Georgia Pacific to dump 28 million gallons a day of its polluted waste into Rice Creek, which flows into the St. Johns. As in the Fenholloway River, the paper mill waste contaminates the waterway with toxic chemicals, including cancer-causing dioxin. Given the political realities of a state-funded film project, it's not surprising that nothing about the Georgia Pacific mill's pollution was included. This frustrated Wes, but it was the reality of working on the state's behalf.

Water's Journey: The River Returns gave the Jacksonville boy Wes a chance to work closely with family and friends who lived nearby. And he got to play with a supercool toy: an actual flying boat. In the film, Wes climbs into a two-man inflatable raft that has an ultralight aircraft attached to it. The contraption looks terrifying, with no proper sides to keep you from falling out, and a pilot in front maneuvering with a metal bar in the open air.

Like a duck gaining speed for liftoff, the raft sputters across the river "runway," then zooms into the sky, dramatically soaring over the wide St. Johns and the vast wetlands around it. Wes uses a fish-eye camera to capture the huge scene below, truly an eagle's-eye view. During the trip, no matter where they are on the river, they can just jump in the flying boat and zoom up to see what the ospreys and eagles see.

Jill Heinerth and Tom Morris cave-dive inside the enchanting Silver Glen Springs along the river, with Wes capturing gorgeous underwater footage as the crew expertly lights the scenic cave system. The film has striking scenes where manatees float languorously in Blue Spring State Park. In one memorable passage Jill and Tom, clad in cave exploration gear, follow a tributary up from the river, then work their way, stooping, through a series of dark, dank giant storm-water pipes for hours, and end their journey by peeking out a manhole cover beside a busy street. An elderly lady out walking her dog comes up to ask them politely what the heck they are doing. She is stunned to learn that the manhole cover eventually leads to the St. Johns, and seems shocked that there's no special filtering system that cleans the city's runoff before it reaches the river.

For the next installment of the *Water's Journey* series, Wes and crew had to travel south, working for months in and around the Florida Everglades. Of the three films, *Water's Journey: Everglades* is the most cinematically beautiful, because Wes had the project budget for great equipment. The subject matter was another story. It's not easy for anyone to sort through the complicated maze of actions and reactions over decades of civil engineering projects, some designed to drain the great marsh and some designed to fix it back the way it was before they drained it. In untangling the Everglades' story, Wes would come to learn what many have discovered in trying to parse what happened to the ecosystem and how to fix it—it's a big old mess, tangled up in hubris, greed, idiocy, scientific duels, and billions of our tax dollars. To me, as an environmental journalist, reporting on the Everglades always felt a little like covering the Middle East, with fighting factions resurrecting hurts from battles won and lost, far back in history. Doing the documentary in a way that would please his government sponsors and the PBS was a high-wire act, and Wes certainly felt the strain.

Wes asked his son, Nathan, to go with him to be part of the film crew. At first Nathan was reluctant.

"I was just dying to go to this music festival, Bonnaroo," Nathan remembers. "All my friends were going, and I was working real hard and saved up the money to go. I was kind of pissed that I wasn't going to get to go because I had to go to the Everglades in the middle of nowhere for a month and live in a trailer, you know, walking around the swamp. Well, that turned out to be the best time of my life. I just spent quality time with my dad. After we got done shooting what we needed to shoot, I got on this four-wheeler, I rode and rode and rode and never saw a single person or a house. Instead I saw snakes and gators. I saw a panther and a black bear."

The Everglades film ended up being a two-part documentary. Artistically, it was top-shelf. The final product looked like the best of the nature specials you see on television, with sweeping aerials of the sawgrass marsh and close-ups of alligators, panthers, otters, fish, snakes, corals, and even the rare ghost orchid deep in a remote swamp called the Fakahatchee Strand. The top-notch equipment and ample resources showed. As in the other films, Tom and Jill were the featured explorers, kayaking through deep mangrove forests, slogging on a night hike past alligators, and sleeping in mosquito-netted hammocks suspended in the wild Everglades night.

Like the St. Johns film, the state-funded Everglades episodes ended up being an upbeat recitation of Bush administration accomplishments, which was preferable to the powers that be who paid for it. Big Agriculture was portrayed as a willing partner in Everglades cleanup, busily engaged in voluntary efforts to clean its pollution. In fact, giant agricultural corporations were spending millions in court to get out of cleaning up their mess. The government was actively enabling the Everglades ruin by allowing the corporations to pump their waste into government-run canals leading to public waters.

Around the same time that Wes and crew were making the last two *Water's Journey* films, and some shorter Florida public service videos about springs protection, Hollywood came calling. Wes knew he had to go where the work was, and soon he and his crew were off to a cinematic project that filmed in both Mexico and Romania. Wes was hired to handle underwater operations for a Sony Pictures horror thriller called *The Cave*.

The film meant good money for Karst Productions, and Wes got high marks for his ability to light the underwater caves and deliver high-quality imagery in difficult conditions. For the first time, Wes found himself filming somewhere he never thought he'd be—in a fake underwater cave. The moviemakers built a football-field-sized aquarium set in Romania, with the specially designed fake caves inside. To film an avalanche, they used fiberglass boulders filled with sand, and to create an underwater volcanic eruption, they used natural gas to ignite fire on water. The film's plot had underwater cave explorers getting infected by creepy subterranean life-forms à la *Alien*. When it was released, critics panned it, saying the plot was full of clichés. One movie critic called it "a generic slice of ho-hum horror that begins underground and keeps on heading south."

In private, Wes let friends know that, while he appreciated getting work from Hollywood, he agreed with the critics who panned it.

22

Meltdown

WES WAS ALWAYS CLOSE to his mom, Marjorie. She named him after her father, Wesley R. Cofer. Marjorie was from Newport News, Virginia, and she'd met Wes's dad, who was from Pittsburgh, when both were at an Air Force base in the southeast Florida town of Pompano Beach during World War II. Wes's dad, James Edward Skiles II, was stationed at the air base, and Marjorie worked in administrative support. Throughout Wes's life Marjorie was his touchstone, and he reached out to her when he had a big decision to make. She had always been chief cheerleader for her high-profile, daredevil son. Starting in her seventies, her health began to fail, and she battled cancer for more than ten years. She endured surgeries and treatments, but the cancer was tenacious. When she died at age eighty-two in 2005, Wes lost his way.

He had been hustling television and movie jobs, on top of filming and editing the St. Johns and Everglades *Water's Journey* films. He set aside no real time for grieving. Everybody knows you can't be all things to all people, but sometimes you convince yourself you can. Wes's demeanor took a turn southward, and it affected his relationships, marriage, and work. Things got so bad, they had to shut down the Everglades shoot so that Wes could get himself together. He took a timeout with his old Jacksonville dive buddy and friend Spencer Slate, who now ran a dive operation in the Florida Keys.

Like most meltdowns, this one was a long time in the making. Wes had been playing hurt for a long time. His camera-carrying shoulder, which had suffered permanent tissue damage when he got the bends years before, was a source of constant pain. His doctor prescribed painkillers, and he took them so he could keep up his hectic work pace. Over time his tolerance increased, and so did his intake and his dependence. The grief, exhaustion, and the daily battle with chronic pain piled up. Alarmed, Terri called Wes's brother and sister. Together the family surrounded Wes and convinced him to seek help to get control over the pain medications. It was tricky, because there weren't many options for him to manage his pain. Wes had a powerful swimmer's build, and the damaged tissue was deep beneath his hefty shoulder muscles. He tried massage, but it was tough, Terri says, for even for the strongest practitioners to reach the damaged tissues. Most people outside Wes's family didn't know how he suffered from the shoulder pain, from severe allergies, awful sinus headaches, and a messed-up digestive system from celiac disease and his past bouts with tropical parasites abroad. He was running ragged, had been for many years, and felt it.

Wes went through a medically supervised regimen to reduce his intake of the prescribed painkillers and muscle relaxers he needed, reserving them for the very worst pain episodes. He was never able to abandon the pain meds completely, but he had regular blood screenings to check for painkiller levels in his system for the rest of his life as a safeguard to make sure he didn't drift back into dependence. With a lot of work, Wes finally found the combination of physical therapies, massage, and regimens that offered him relief. He also took a look at his life, and realized he needed a change.

Karst Productions had turned into a many-armed octopus that was smothering him. He'd added a lot of people as subcontractors, but he remained the only one responsible for getting new business and raising money to pay people's wages and buy the expensive equipment.

"He couldn't get away from all of his responsibilities," Terri says. "He had so many people working for him, the stress was ungodly. Money was going out faster than it was coming in. Nobody was bringing money in other than him. He seemed like he wanted the old days back again, you know, being footloose and fancy free."

Wes made the decision to cut loose many of the people who were working with him on projects at Karst Productions. Terri, who had been occupied teaching and tending their children, agreed to go back to work, becoming Wes's bookkeeper. Together, at ages forty-eight and fifty, Wes and Terri started over in their ramshackle office in High Springs, re-creating what they hoped would be a leaner, sweeter Karst Productions.

Wes started approaching his work and his life with vigor again. His jokey personality and creativity emerged. After his reset, Wes got a call from his old friend John Tindall, the producer he had worked with on *Rescue 911*, *Ripley's Believe It or Not*, and the crazy Hydrillasaurus spoof, *Monsters Put to the Test*. Tindall offered Wes a quirky job in Boston with a Discovery Channel TV series called *Time Warp*. It was a science show using ultra-high-speed photography to capture things that happened in a fraction of a second—explosions, roller coasters, water droplets, bullets hitting, mousetraps snapping, and the like. Hosted by Massachusetts Institute of Technology scientist Jeff Lieberman and TV personality Matt Kearney, the *Time Warp* series was a godsend for Wes. For once, he didn't have to work in a physically grueling, hostile environment, and he wasn't responsible for all the personnel issues that come with an expedition into the unknown. On the Boston set, he got to play with cool techno toys, blow stuff up, and hang around other media-savvy science geeks. During 2008 and 2009, he moved north for months at a time to work on the series, putting in twelve-to-fifteen-hour days, six or seven days a week.

High-speed photography is technically challenging, and it can take hours to set up a single shot. To begin with, says one of the segment producers, Andrew Zoz Brooks, "you've got to multiply the light you put on the subject by how fast you're going," which means the photography lights are powerful enough, he says, to spark fires.

"We were very often around explosions, car crashes, and things that we were setting up," says Tindall. "We'd call these times 'balancing a boulder.' It's as though you had a thirty-foot pole with a ten-ton boulder on top, and you're balancing it. And if you screw up, the boulder's going to fall and crush you. You're either comfortable in that place, or you're not. If you're comfortable in that place, you're going to make a level-headed decision and you're going to be fine. Wes and I shared that sensibility, that we're comfortable in that hyper-focused, 'balancing a boulder' state of mind, where anything can happen."

Host Lieberman tells a story about shooting *Time Warp* that shows that Wes was definitely back to his old self. Wes was filming a man who could throw playing cards so fast that the flying card sliced a zucchini in half thirty feet away.

"Of course, Wes wants to get like six inches away from the zucchini to get the perfect shot of the card coming towards the zucchini," Lieberman says. "And the guy misses. He hits Wes right above the eyebrow and slices Wes's forehead open a little bit. It was bleeding, and Wes went to go clean it off. The next minute we see him, he had taped the playing card as if it were lodged in his skull. He wore that around the rest of the day at work."

"I remember Wes saying to me, 'Tindall, you've kept me alive for two years,' like he was saying that by being with me during that time, he was protected somehow," Tindall says.

Everybody knew Wes couldn't stay out of the caves for long. With better health and a renewed outlook, he headed down to the Bahamas to shoot footage of the incredible cathedral-like underwater "blue holes." These stalactite- and stalagmite-filled flooded caves have a thin lens of fresh water lying on top of denser seawater below. It's a one-of-a-kind environment that requires divers to brave toxic hydrogen sulfide gas—a spooky-looking red layer in the water that smells like rotten eggs and can penetrate dive gear and seep into your body. At high levels it can cause delirium or even death. But at low levels it was just likely to produce nausea, dizziness, and headache. Once divers made it through the hydrogen sulfide layer, they found an astonishing landscape, part Carlsbad Caverns and part Grand Canyon, where it seems the Earth's tectonic plates have separated to form bottomless cracks. Some of the glasslike crystal formations have ancient fossils visible inside, like insects caught in amber.

In these magical places, Wes would do some of his best-ever image work. He and a group of divers, including his old friends Tom Morris and Kenny Broad, were part of a BBC documentary called *Oceans*. Cave diver Brian Kakuk, who had been part of the Wakulla 2 expedition and *The Cave*, lived and worked in the area, and had been the first diver to see many of the underwater caverns. Wes also had a new dive buddy, Agnes Milowka, an Australian spitfire in her twenties who was gung-ho on exploring new cave passages. Milowka held a degree in maritime archaeology, and she was ready to go wherever, whenever, just like the Moles. She and another diver had even made a new cave connection in the Suwannee River basin, the heart of Mole Tribe territory.

In December 2008, during one of the Bahamas dive trips, Wes wrote:

Everything is so new and exciting, and full of possibilities. A big part of it stems from fresh blood. Other than Tom, I'm with a new crew. It's hard to describe how invigorating it is to be on new terrain with new people. I guess it felt more like the first time I did something like this, instead of the thousandth time. It reminded me of why I used to love teaching so much—it allows you to vicariously experience the thrills of a new experience through your students.

After diving one of the caves with translucent crystalline calcite deposits that look like drapy curtains in some places and skinny straws in others, Wes gushed: *First cave I've ever filmed that I've ever felt justifies a full-frame book on its own—simply stunning.* And at the turn of the year he mused:

I find myself returning to a more purposeful and fulfilling lifestyle—simpler, more fun, and more productive. This realization is causing me to re-evaluate my life and priorities. Not sure much is likely to change, but as in 2008, things do change by simply doing as opposed to sitting back and waiting. Certainly, having to only worry about self-support over supporting a staff has removed much of the stress and angst of the past. . . .

Karst Productions is now rediscovering the joy and freedom in doing what you do, the best you can, with only the resources of like-minded friends and minimal tools.

Not only was he feeling good for the first time in years, but he was about to venture back into the pages of *National Geographic*, this time with his old friend Kenny Broad. Two decades earlier, Broad had been the eager cave diver, ten years Wes's junior, helping with Karst Productions projects and crashing at the Skiles house in High Springs between forays with the Mole Tribe. Since then, Broad had traveled the world, making his name as an anthropologist. In 2006 the National Geographic Society gave Broad its Emerging Explorer award, and he was now professor and chair of the Department of Marine Ecosystems and Society at the University of Miami's Rosenstiel School of Marine and Atmospheric Science.

Broad asked Wes to be part of a National Geographic Society expedition into the Bahamas blue holes, with both a magazine story and a film to document it. Among other things, they had permission to take samples of a stalagmite out of the cave (which would turn out to hold 36,000 years of history) to look for clues about the Earth's climate change.

"Wes and I teamed up on pitching it to National Geographic and then we worked together, even though technically I was the expedition leader," Broad says.

Wes's son Nathan came along on the shoot, helping haul equipment, holding lights, and working as a diver. Nathan says his friends thought he was so lucky to be in the gorgeous Bahamas, not realizing that the place is a sweltering jungle during the summer and they had to haul tons of equipment over sharp rocks amid poisonwood and swarms of biting insects.

"I'm surprised someone didn't keel over, carrying all that equipment over miles in that heat," Nathan says.

During six weeks, the expedition did more than 150 dives. The aquatic environment below the hydrogen sulfide layer is devoid of oxygen, which means that bones and some tissue are preserved intact, a huge boon to scientists studying the past. Among other things, they discovered a three-thousand-year-old skull of a Cuban crocodile (a species that's no longer found in the Bahamas) and the skull of a Lucayan Indian from a tribe that lived on the islands between the sixth and fifteenth centuries. Like other ancient skulls that archaeologists had found over the years, the Lucayan skull had a flattened forehead. The Lucayans would strap a flat piece of wood to a baby's head to create the shape, but no one knows why.

They also found deposits of red dust, which blew across the globe from the Sahara Desert during prolonged ancient storms. They took samples of the many unique cave creatures that survive without light or oxygen. Wes's friend Kakuk, dive safety officer for the expedition, had discovered more than a dozen creatures new to science during his twenty-one years of exploration in the Bahamas blue holes.

"This was one of my most challenging assignments, in that there was so much going on," Wes later told an interviewer. "We had this multidisciplinary team of scientists working on global climate change, microbiology, paleontology, archaeology, biology. We were also studying water resources and doing conservation work. Then all of that is tied to real exploration. I mean, the stuff that people dream of—going into places, seeing things that no human being has ever seen before. The challenge was to capture that balance and to communicate that this very special team of highly experienced cave divers were the vessels of the scientists. They were the eyes and the ears. They were able to go down in these caves and collect the specimens and make direct observations and bring out fossils that these scientists had never seen before."

Broad and the other scientists were in a hurry to document all they could while the evidence remained in the caves. Sadly, as in Florida, people dump junk and trash into the spectacular blue holes. Even worse, sea level rise threatens to fill the caves with salt water instead of fresh water, altering forever these strange, one-of-a-kind environments. Of more than a thousand blue holes believed to be in the Bahamas, only about 20 percent had been explored then. One of the most intriguing is among the deepest documented caves on Earth, more than 630 feet down, with a bell shape that's as big at the bottom as several football fields.

"This is easily the most important story I've ever photographed or filmed," Wes told an interviewer. "We're revealing a world of majestic beauty and wonder, new things that we've never seen before, but we're also getting answers to questions that are very important to our planet, and to the people of our planet, right here and now. The global climate-change work being done on this expedition is going to be rewriting what we know about the past events of climate change. This notion that climate change occurred over a long period of time, that it took hundreds or thousands of years to occur, is being completely blown out of the water by the results of these studies. We're realizing that catastrophic events were occurring at fairly regular intervals, as far as geologic time, in as little as fifty years. We're in one right now, and it's really exciting and scary at the same time to be part of a team that pulled this information from the depths of a deep and mysterious environment and shared that information with scientists who are able to take it and reveal these remarkable findings."

It was like back in Florida, where Wes and his cave-diving colleagues made new discoveries about how water moved underground, debunking theories that some scientists had stubbornly clung to over decades. The Bahamas expedition photography sessions ended after repeated trips over seven months in 2009. Of course, when he left the Bahamas, Wes had no idea that he was near the end of his life.

He returned to High Springs and started scouting Florida locations for a new project, this one to focus on the battle over the water in Florida, Georgia, and Alabama, and the resources at stake in the middle of the political divide. During the summer of 2010 Wes wrote in his journal:

After a long process of rehabilitation work, massage, adjustments, and working out, I've found new joy and excitement doing dives that used to cause me great pain. With that monkey off my back, last year I did 140-plus dives in Bahamas Blue Holes, relatively free of past symptoms. Stretching is critical. . . . I'm getting back in great shape; thinking clearer and feeling better, more confident about who I am and what I'm doing.

He was back to his favorite pursuit—exploring water-filled Florida caves and, even after all those years, finding some new cave booty.

It was great to be back and visiting one of the best scoops of my life. The new upstream is easily one of the best and most promising caves in Florida. It exhibits a rare and exciting hydrogeology. Bottom line is, the cave continues to get bigger and have higher flow the further you go. This is the polar opposite to most caves, breaking down to smaller with less and less total flow.

He told a reporter at the time:

I was adding it up recently, and I have surpassed 500 miles of virgin exploration in my career. I've been in, and laid line—the first line ever—in 500 miles of virgin cave. That's a *lot* of going places no human being has ever been before. In a world where most everything on the planet has been explored, it's like discovering a state the size of Florida and being the first person on Earth to walk its entire length from the Panhandle to the Florida Keys. I've done this all underground, under water.

23

Making the Cover

THOUGH WES HAD NOW BEEN WORKING off and on as a freelance photographer for *National Geographic* for twenty-five years, he'd never been able to get one of his photographs on the main edition's cover. One of his Mexican cave photos made it onto a limited Latin American edition, but he was always after the Holy Grail—the main cover. In years past, a few of his photos had been slated to run on the cover, but every time, they got knocked off in favor of a special project or a breaking world story.

This time, with the Bahamas Blue Holes Expedition, Wes's dream came true. He snagged not only the cover photo but also a four-panel pull-out poster in the magazine's center, with a perforated edge so people all over the world could tear it out and put it on their walls.

Tragically, by the time the magazine hit the shelves, Wes was dead.

His friends and colleagues were comforted by the fact that Wes had seen the magazine mockup before he died, and he knew he had reached that rare pinnacle among the hopefuls who photographed around the globe for *National Geographic*.

"It gave me some relief to know that he had a chance to see the printed magazine, for him to hold it in his hands and look through it," says Sadie Quarrier, who was the *National Geographic* editor on the Bahamas Blue Holes story.

Wes's son, Nathan, and another diver were on the cover, swimming through the black void and framed between thousands of carefully lit stalactites above and stalagmites below. The cover photo was a sort of teaser for the grand pull-out picture of the whole Cascade Room cave, 80 feet down in a blue hole called Dan's Cave. That photo was chosen as one of *National Geographic*'s top ten photos of the year. It was a "stitcher," meaning it was made up of three images digitally stitched together to form a whole. It's a cross-section of the dramatic cave, with three divers swimming through it. Before his death, Wes did a video interview for a *National Geographic* television program that featured the year's top ten photographs. In it, he gave details on how he made the remarkable image.

"Really," Skiles told the interviewer, "what it's all about is comprehending that we have sometimes hundreds and hundreds of feet of rock above us and hundreds and hundreds of feet of rock below us. We're diving in this very narrow void inside the spaces of the rock. . . . I always loved ant farms when I was a kid, seeing that path the ants went through, and I thought: 'That would be cool, to do an ant-farm-type photograph.' But the big challenge was, how are we going to pull that off? How can a team that can't communicate with each other create a perfect image that tells that story?

"What I came up with was this idea that only the central corridor would be lit, and that above it would be black and below it would be black. That's very much the world we're diving in.

"I was perfectly perpendicular to the team as we worked through the series of shots. The challenge was containing the light, not letting any light come from me or the safety divers or anybody that might have been on the peripheral edge. What that meant is I had to swim through the dark. I worked entirely in the dark. The only light I had was the little LEDs inside my camera to figure out what setting I wanted to be at for that particular photograph. It was an interesting challenge with a grand reward at the end."

Editors were so enamored with Wes's Cascade Room "ant farm" image that they hung a twelve-foot-long print in the photography department at *National Geographic* magazine headquarters in Washington, D.C.

"I think it is one of the best underwater pictures ever made," says *National Geographic* senior photo editor Kurt Mutchler. "The technical challenge is amazing. For a guy wearing all this gear, and to have his vision impaired by wearing that mask, to be able to see that picture and pull it off technically— I am still amazed. There were multiple divers and multiple lights. It's like a symphony down there in total darkness."

In his videotaped interview for the Top 10 Photographs TV show, Wes called the image "a team photograph."

"I get the photo credit—unfairly—because this picture doesn't happen . without this incredible group of divers working with me and contributing their own part," he says. "Ultimately they were positioned like you see them in the photograph. The exception is the big column in the middle, in which I got everybody to cluster behind the column, where I couldn't see them, and they all sprayed their lights in different directions. What we did was, we worked up to it. We did it a number of times and we'd evaluate it. We'd sit there and look at it as a group. We weren't stitching it together at the time. I was just using my 'This is what it will look like' kind of pre-visualization. Tom and Nathan and Kenny and Brian would come to me and say, 'What if I did this?' or 'What if I was here?'

"I laid a line that I could follow, and then I had to be able to level the camera and get the angle correctly. In an underwater cave, there are no straight lines. There is no A to B; you're always blocked by a formation that you have to swim around or something you have to deal with. We managed to overcome those obstacles, and we started getting each segment looking better and better each dive. We practiced it a couple times. We did a trial run with photographs. Then we did another major effort where we went 'Okay, this is going to be the picture!' then 'Not the picture!' which is often the way it goes. Then we did it a final time. So it took five real intensive efforts, major dives. You spend the entire day getting all of the cave diving equipment ready—lights charged and tanks filled and fixing problems from the last dive, and getting all of this stuff together and loaded and driven out into the woods and hauled into the hole and put it all on. Then off we go. It's quite a process. It's not like scuba divers going off the back of the boat and saying, 'I did five dives today.' We do one dive and it's an eighteen-hour day to do one dive."

The Blue Holes article covered nineteen pages of the magazine. Wes got five two-page photo spreads: one showing a diver moving alone through the lit-up, needle-like stalagmite "forest," another showing the red layer of hydrogen sulfide gas in the cave system, another a close-up of Broad swimming out of the cave with the precious stalagmite sample tucked under his arm, another with an archaeologist holding the unearthed Lucayan Indian skull, and another a close-up of Kakuk excavating the three-thousand-year-old Cuban crocodile skull. One of the most arresting images is a close-up of a whirling vortex of water sucking down into a blue hole, which Wes called "your bathtub on steroids." Wes and the others had seen the vortex in action, but it wasn't always there, and it was dangerous to get close to it.

Wes told the *National Geographic* interviewer how he got the image:

"We'd seen it before. We had photographed it before. So, we go back, and we think we know all the rules, and it doesn't happen. We get this little weak vortex. Then I say: 'Okay, maybe it doesn't happen like we thought it happened. Maybe it happens like this . . . ' We went back again, and we got a little bit better result, but we certainly didn't get the photograph. I came home and I started talking to oceanographers. I started talking to geologists and hydrogeologists, and we just really put all of this information together and I made my own prediction about when it was going to be the best. *National Geographic* was done—they were like 'You're done.' My photo editor was fighting for me, saying, 'Give him a chance. He knows exactly when it's happening,' and I'm going 'I'm *guessing* when it exactly is going to happen,' and I knew it could go really badly. We get there to the Bahamas, and there is this horrible storm for four days and we can't even leave the room. Then, on the final day, the last minute, the sky opened up, it got blue. It was the peak day that I had calculated it would happen. We went out there, and it was a raging pillar. It was as strong and big as I had ever seen it, and I was like 'Yes! We got it!'"

In the video recorded for the Top 10 Photographs special, the interviewer asks Wes how he feels about the honor.

"I'm speechless about the photograph being selected as a Top 10," he says, a huge grin on his face. "In my wildest dreams, I couldn't imagine having that happen to me. The cover is also a dream come true. This is my fourth cover that I had; all the other ones got knocked off by major world events. Hurricane Andrew, September eleventh, and other events. I just can't believe I got this incredible honor and the cover. All it makes me want to do is to go out there and get working on the next assignment."

24

Legacy

*For water, springs are a way out. But they
also have a way of drawing people in.*

WES SKILES, APRIL 2008

IN THE MONTHS BEFORE WES DIED, Kenny Broad says, he and his old
friend were planning another large-scale expedition, and they had carte
blanche with the highest levels at *National Geographic* to pursue it.

The idea was a sort of "vertical transect" of water, following it all the way
from space down through the atmosphere, through the ocean, down underground, and showing all the connections that make life on Earth possible.

Instead of pursing that project, Broad was called to Ginnie Springs on
July 28, 2010, to join hundreds of friends and colleagues who had flown in
from around the world to attend a memorial for Wes's life. Tents were set
up around the spring, and chairs sat in rows before a podium. A huge southern potluck supper covered picnic tables lined end to end. A slide projector scrolled photos of a full-of-life Wes having adventures across the world:
standing on icebergs, rock-climbing through cenotes, swimming inside the
planet. It was an impressive visual journey that made his absence all the
more surreal.

Per usual, the North Florida summer afternoon skies grew heavy with dark clouds and threatened to storm. As a speaker memorialized Wes at the podium, thunder rumbled loudly.

"Wes wants it to rain!" one of the mourners shouted. Everyone knew that if it rained, it wouldn't last long, just like that scene in *Water's Journey: Hidden Rivers* where the sun shines when Wes and company go in one door of Sonny's Barbecue and it's pouring rain when they come out.

Before the service, Wes's children Nathan and Tessa and friends dove into Ginnie's cold depths and set up lights inside the spring to make it glow, just like their dad loved to do. The funeral service turned into a party—the kind Wes would have been presiding over—and they floated an eight-foot-long float across the spring's surface and set it ablaze. Then, as people settled on the grass beside the spring, Wes's favorite: fireworks.

Most of Wes's closest friends were used to the ache of loss, but it didn't make it any easier. Wes used to complain about being so involved in a dangerous pursuit where he had to see so many friends die.

"It's my passion," he told a reporter once. "But I guess I could have made a better choice. I picked the deathly hollows of narrow underwater spaces where my friends go to die. I picked the worst thing on the planet to love."

Even at times like these, nobody talked about quitting cave diving. A month before Wes died, his business partner and friend Pete Butt was diving near Central Florida's Silver Springs when a big alligator swam up behind him and attacked. The gator had Butt's head in its mouth, and clamped down hard enough to put serious holes in Butt's throat and head and break his jaw before releasing. When Butt showed up for Wes's memorial, his jaw was still wired together.

The nagging question among everyone at the memorial, of course, was: What the hell happened? Did Wes have a stroke or a heart attack? It wasn't making sense. At the time, an autopsy was pending. For more than three months, Palm Beach County authorities investigated Wes's death. But when the official report finally came on November 1, 2010, it offered no explanation. The Palm Beach County medical examiner's chief investigator, Harold Ruslander, told the *Palm Beach Post* that "there was nothing to indicate natural causes or outside forces. . . . All we're going to be able to say is that it was an accidental drowning."

The investigator's report says that Wes had been diving for about an hour and a half that day, filming scientists studying goliath grouper fish. They said they found him motionless on the bottom after he'd told them he was going to the surface to get more digital tape and a new battery for his camera. His rebreather was flooded, his breathing regulator was out of his mouth, and his camera had drifted about fifty feet away. They gave Wes oxygen, rushed him up to the boat, and tried CPR, to no avail. He was pronounced dead at the hospital. The scientists said that Wes had done all the required pre-checks for his Dive Rite O2ptima FX rebreather, and that he seemed healthy and upbeat before the dive. As those who knew Wes each coped in their own ways with grief, it was frustrating not to know why he died.

After he died, Wes started receiving honors—an avalanche of validation that he would have been thrilled to get while he was alive. On September 22, 2010, the congressman who represented Wes's High Springs electoral district, Cliff Stearns, rose on the floor of the U.S. House of Representatives to read a resolution honoring the "remarkable life of Wes Skiles" who was known as "Florida's Jacques Cousteau."

"Wes died doing what he loved most, exploring the ocean and providing vivid pictures of unusual places," the resolution read in part. "Wes Skiles lived a passionate life full of adventure and excitement. Although he was taken from us too soon, his work will carry on for many years to come."

Two months later, the state of Florida renamed its park at Peacock Springs, the cave system near the Suwannee River that Wes had explored for many years. It was now known forever as Wes Skiles Peacock Springs State Park. Today you can walk a trail in the park that is like a mini *Water's Journey*. As you walk through the sandy-floored forest, interpretive displays give you descriptions and pictures of the underwater cave features that lie beneath you.

"Wes did more to educate Floridians about the plight of Florida's springs than anyone else," Wes's friend, DEP ecosystem manager Jim Stevenson, said at the dedication ceremony.

In 2011 Wes reached what he would have considered an ultimate honor. He and Broad were each named the National Geographic Society's 2010 Explorer of the Year, for the Bahamas Blue Holes Expedition. Terri went to the gala in Washington, D.C., where she sat near famed movie director and ocean explorer James Cameron (*Titanic, Avatar*). Cameron dedicated his 2011 horror movie *Sanctum* to Wes because it was loosely based on Wes's harrowing buried-alive adventure in Australia.

The more Terri looked into the circumstances of her husband's death, the more she believed it had been caused by equipment failure. Two years after

Wes died, Terri filed a wrongful death suit in Palm Beach County, naming Dive Rite, which designed and built the rebreather Wes was using when he died; Juergensen Marine, which manufactured the electronics used in the dive computer; and Analytical Industries, which makes oxygen sensors for rebreathers.

Terri lost her lawsuit, and it was a divisive issue in the cave diving community. They are risk takers, not lawsuit filers. But Terri says she wanted to make sure no one else gets harmed by equipment that she still believes was faulty, and she believed the legal arena was the right place to do that.

It would be a nice wrap-up to say that Wes's warnings about the springs' pollution changed policy. They did, as far as showing people the amazing, unseen resource beneath our feet. But as I write this, Florida's government has eroded many programs to protect springs, and corporate interests continually seek—and get—permits to pump polluted water into our aquifer.

Big Agriculture and lobbyists for developers relentlessly stalk the halls of Congress and the statehouse, beating back cleanup rules that would protect and restore the springs. The City of Jacksonville's utilities department got a permit to pump hundreds of millions of gallons of water out of the Suwannee River, which many people believe will rob local springs of their flow. Housing developments all over Florida are still allowed to use thousands of septic tanks, when we know central sewer systems better protect the aquifer. Huge cattle operations and fertilizer-intensive crops cover the fields over the spring systems where Wes's family still lives outside High Springs.

We see successes when people get organized to protect their local springs. The City of Tallahassee retooled its immense sewer plant, at great expense, after cave divers and scientists proved that the pollution from the city's wastewater sprayfield was soaking through the ground and wrecking Wakulla Springs, twenty miles south. In 2014, citizens held a rally at the Capitol to protest springs pollution and urge state lawmakers to do something about it. There were big demonstrations, too, on both South Florida coasts, where citizens protested the toxic pollution that happens every time the South Florida Water Management District opens floodgates in Lake Okeechobee, dumping agricultural wastewater through canals and rivers out into the Atlantic Ocean and the Gulf of Mexico.

Wes's hunch was right after all: the first order of business is to make people aware.

During 2013 and 2014, reporters and photographers at some of the state's largest newspapers, including the *Orlando Sentinel* and the *Tampa Bay Times*, did major news series about the problems facing Florida's springs. A Florida Geological Survey report came out in 2009 warning that the aquifer is in big trouble. Analyzing data it collected from 1991 to 2003, it showed that the levels of fertilizer, manure, and sewage are rising in the groundwater. State tests also found something else alarming: salinity levels in many springs, including some located far inland from the coasts, have been rising. That raises the specter that by pumping so much, we're depleting the top layer of fresh water in the aquifer and that the ancient, relic sea water located deep below is moving closer to the surface.

An agricultural company bought land near Ginnie Springs and started heavily applying fertilizer. Some of the smaller springs at the Ginnie Springs camping resort (though not Ginnie Spring itself) turned green and algae-filled. Ginnie Springs' owners went to court, spending big bucks in legal fees, trying to protect their springs. But because of the permissive laws around agricultural pollution, they had little luck.

The last time I saw Wes, it was six months before he died. He was at the Capitol in Tallahassee, speaking at a statewide rally for springs protection. He was one of the very few cave divers who showed up. Hundreds of citizens clogged the outdoor courtyard between Florida's Old Capitol and New Capitol buildings while the legislature met inside. They held signs with the names of the local springs they loved.

Wes spoke powerfully about the changes he was seeing, firsthand, inside the springs. He brought along a friend who wore the old creepy Hydrilla-saurus suit; the creature lounged casually against the grand steps of the Old Capitol—a classic dramatic Wes touch.

Cave divers are still launching expeditions into Florida's underground aquifers, and dye tracing tests happen frequently. In 2007, divers mapped an incredible seven miles' worth of underground passages around Wakulla Springs. Some of Wes's buddies still head out on weekends to see what new connections they can find in springs country. Wes's daughter, Tessa, has followed in her father's footsteps, taking gorgeous underwater photos to show the wilderness in the aquifer. In downtown High Springs, there's a new storefront that houses a nonprofit called the Florida Springs Institute. The scientists affiliated with the Institute advocate for protecting the state's springs, they do studies, and, like Wes, they work to get the powers that be to realize that it is insanity to treat this rare resource so carelessly.

Not long ago, I showed *Water's Journey: The Hidden Rivers of Florida* to a friend who teaches science to middle school students in North Florida. The next fall, she called me with a request. Could she get a copy of Wes's *Water's Journey*? (Yes, it's on the Internet.) Isn't there a classroom curriculum that goes with it, also? (Yes, it's on the Internet.)

"Good," she said. "I want my students to see that film. I want them to learn about this."

Wes on a surf trip in Costa Rica. Courtesy of Terri Skiles.

Acknowledgments

FIRST, THANK YOU to those who really *do* go where no one has gone before: especially inner-planetary explorers Woody Jasper, Tom Morris, Pete Butt, and Kenny Broad.

Thanks to Emory Kristof, Kurt Mutchler, and Sadie Quarrier at *National Geographic* magazine, to television personality and producer Bill Kurtis, and to Grateful Dead drummer Bill Kreutzmann; you all made it possible for millions to see what cave diving explorers experience in the depths.

Thank you to Florida writers Carl Hiaasen, Craig Pittman, Diane Roberts, Jeff Klinkenberg, Susan Cerulean, and Cynthia Barnett for your counsel over many years and your work on behalf of our beautiful and heartbreaking state.

It was an honor for me to get to chronicle the amazing life of Wes Skiles. I wrote this book during stolen weekends over several years, sandwiched between my regular jobs working on the issues of wildlife, clean water, citizen justice, and clean air. Thank you to the kick-butt attorneys at Earthjustice for heading polluters off at the pass and for giving me a wonderful job with purpose.

Thanks to intrepid explorers Bill Stone, Jill Heinerth, Paul Heinerth, Jeffrey Haupt, Mark and Annette Long, Brian Kakuk, Greg Stone, and Paul DeLoach, who took the time to describe many expeditions to me. Thanks to Wes's longtime Key West pal Captain Spencer Slate.

Thanks to the scientists who spend their days puzzling out obscure underground mysteries, especially Jim Stevenson, Todd Kincaid, Mike Wisenbaker, Brian Pease, Rodney DeHan, and Harley Means.

The Skiles family generously let me into their world, and I am grateful to Wes's widow Terri Skiles, his brother Jim Skiles, his sister Shirley Spohrer, and his outstanding children, Nathan and Tessa. Thank you to the Wray family of Ginnie Springs, and to Tom at the Rustic Inn in High Springs, where I stayed so comfortably during many reporting and writing trips.

Thank you to Wes's film colleagues who helped describe the cinematic side of things to me, especially Ross Ambrose, Georgia Shemitz, John Tindall, Jeff Lieberman, Howard Hall, and Andrew Zoz Brooks.

Thank you to the late M. C. Davis, a great conservationist gone too soon: he believed in this project and funded a writing fellowship for me to finish this manuscript.

Thank you to John Newton for providing steadfast family and moral support when I was buried in timelines, notes, and transcriptions for days on end.

Thanks to my friends and family who listened all these years and provided input, especially Kathleen Laufenberg, Jan Pudlow, Lucy and Richard Morgan, Steve Willkie, Kelly McGrath, David Rivera, Beth Butler and Randy Van Oss, Linda and Ed Deaton, E'Layne Koenigsberg, Judith Thompson, Brad Bischoff, Jane and Davie Brightbill, Laura and Terry Schneider, Paul and Joanne Chamberlain, Bonnie Gadless and Bob Scanlon, Cliff Thaell and Georjean Machulis, Leslie Jorgensen, Teddy Tollett, the Green Hat Ladies, my daughter Colleen Newton, and my sisters Brook Urban and Jane Rainwater.

Thank you to editor Sian Hunter at University Press of Florida, who conceived this biography in the first place and tapped me to write it.

On her dad's side, my daughter Colleen Newton is part of a family line that first settled near the Florida Panhandle's springs in 1820. As I write this, she is twenty, and during her lifetime so many Florida springs have turned from clear-bottomed magic pools to weed-choked waters. I remember the day when Colleen and I went to have our usual Sunday swim at Wakulla Springs, finding it stained dark and covered with invasive hydrilla weeds. The glass-bottomed boats we loved were sidelined. She couldn't have been much older than seven when she said: "Mama, I'm glad I saw it when it was still blue!" That broke my heart. So thank you to all the Floridians working to heal and protect our springs so they run blue once again.

Wes Skiles

Catalog of Works

PHOTOGRAPHY

Featured in Magazines

"Huautla Cave Quest," *National Geographic*, September 1995.
Bucky McMahon, "Florida Springs: Deeper," *Outside Magazine*, 1996.
Karl Shreeves, "Journey to the Center of the Earth," *Skin Diver Magazine*, 1998.
"North Florida Springs," *National Geographic*, March 1999.
"Antarctica: Life at the Bottom of the World," *National Geographic*, December 2001.
Mark Schrope, "Deep Transmissions," *Outside Magazine*, October 2003.
"Watery Graves of the MAYA," *National Geographic*, October 2003.
"Deep Dark Secrets: Bahama Blue Holes," *National Geographic*, August 2010.

Featured in Books

Ernst Waldemar Bauer, *Wunder der Erde – Feuer und Wasser* (Hamburg: Hoffmann und Campe, 1989).
Robert Burgess, *The Cave Divers* (New York: Aqua Quest, 1999).
Anne M. Todd, *Caving Adventures* (Mankato, MN: Capstone Press, 2002).
William Stone and Barbara am Ende, *Beyond the Deep: The Most Deadly Descent into the World's Most Treacherous Cave*, with Monte Paulsen (New York: Warner, 2002).

Greg Stone, *Ice Island: Expedition to Antarctica's Largest Iceberg* (Piermont, NH: Bunker Hill Publishing, 2003).

Martyn Farr, *The Darkness Beckons: The History and Development of World Cave Diving* (Sheffield, UK: Vertebrate Publishing, 2017).

FILMS AND TELEVISION

Original Programming

Water's Journey: The Hidden Rivers of Florida, Wes Skiles, director, Jill Heinerth, producer, 2003.

Water's Journey: The River Returns, Wes Skiles, director, 2005.

Ice Island, Wes Skiles, director, 2002.

IMAX

Journey Into Amazing Caves, Wes Skiles, director of underwater photography, Mac-Gillivray Freeman, executive producers, 2001.

National Geographic

"Into the Labyrinth," *National Geographic Explorer,* Wes Skiles, field producer / cameraman.

Mysteries Underground, Wes Skiles, underwater cameraman, 1997.

A&E

"Polluting the Fountain of Youth," *New Explorer Series,* Wes Skiles, producer / writer / director, with Bill Kurtis, 1998.

"The Most Dangerous Science," *New Explorer Series,* Wes Skiles, producer / writer / director, with Bill Kurtis, 1998. Winner of The Telecine Golden Eagle, 1st Place for best science/adventure film; The International Film Festival Gold Camera Award, 1st place for science exploration films; The Chris Award, 1st place for exploration and cinematography.

TravelQuest, 13 Part Series, Wes Skiles, director of photography, Cinetel Productions, executive producer, 1992.

PBS

The New Explorers, with Bill Kurtis (7 years, 8 awards).

Discovery Channel

Predators of the North, Wes Skiles, director / underwater cameraman, 1992.
Adventure Crazy, Wes Skiles, underwater cameraman, Peter Faiden and Peter Howden, executive producers.
Florida: Window to a Hidden World, Wes Skiles, director, The Beyond Group Int., executive producers, 1991.

TBS/Columbia Tristar

Ripley's Believe It or Not, Wes Skiles, director of photography, segments.

CBS Special

The Searchers segment, Wes Skiles, producer / cameraman, LMNO Productions, executive producers, 1997.

Paramount

Wild Things, (21 segments, 2 years), Wes Skiles, field producer / cameraman Rhino Productions, executive producers.

The Learning Channel

SEATEK segment. Wes Skiles, segment producer / cameraman, GRB Entertainment, executive producers.
The Cave, Bruce Hunt, director, Sony Screen Gems, 2005. Trailer can be found at: www.sonypictures.com/movies/thecave/

WRITINGS

Wes Skiles, "Travel the 'World's Longest Underground River,'" *Florida Environments,* February 1987.
Wes Skiles, "Close Call in the Outback, Pannikin Plain Cave," *National Speleological Society News,* August 1989.
Wes Skiles, "Wakulla," *Ocean Realm, Magazine of the Sea,* Summer 1990.
Wes Skiles, "A Different Drummer," *Rodale's SCUBA Diving,* June 1994.
Wes Skiles, "Grand Illusion," *Rodale's SCUBA Diving,* June 1996.
Ken Ringle and Wes Skiles, "Unlocking the Labyrinth of North Florida's Springs," *National Geographic,* March 1999.
Wes Skiles, "Gilbert, Mangoes, and No Windows," *SCUBA Times,* 1998.
Andrew Todhunter and Wes C. Skiles, "Bahamas Blue Holes: Dive into Beauty, Danger, and Discovery," *National Geographic,* August 2010.

Wes gearing up and grinning about a dive. Courtesy of Terri Skiles.

Notes on Sources

Where a personal name and a date are given alone, the source is understood to be an interview conducted by the author.

OPENING EPIGRAPH

I was adding it up . . . . : Wes Skiles, quoted in Tom Mayer, "Natural Explorer," *Currents* 4.4 (May–June 2010).

INTRODUCTION

"Such adventures were the reason . . .": T. Rees Shapiro, "Wes Skiles, Photographer Who Captured Vivid Worlds Underwater, Dies at 52," *Washington Post*, August 5, 2010, www.washingtonpost.com/wp-dyn/content/article/2010/08/04/AR2010080406805.html.

"There was nothing to indicate . . .": Elliot Kleinberg, "Noted Photographer's Death Will Remain a Mystery," *Palm Beach Post*, November 1, 2010.

"You lose a good friend . . .": Brian Kakuk, July 8, 2013.

"Dopamine helps elicit . . .": Peter Gwin, "The Mystery of Risk," *National Geographic*, June 2013.

"Think of dopamine like gasoline . . .": David Zald, quoted in Gwin, "The Mystery of Risk."

"Generally, if you had . . .": Tom Morris, September 19, 2012.

It's a state . . . : Mihaly Csikszentmihaly, quoted in John Geirland, "Go with the Flow," *Wired*, September 1996, https://www.wired.com/wired/archive/4.09/czik.html.

"The alligator brain . . .": Woody Jasper, January 11, 2013.

Cave diving is really . . . : Wes Skiles, unaired video interview for *National Geographic*, May 24, 2010, courtesy of Terri Skiles.

CHAPTER 1. SWIMMING UNDER SONNY'S BARBECUE

"I think they're going . . .": This quote and other events of this chapter are transcribed from *Water's Journey: The Hidden Rivers of Florida*, Wes Skiles director, Jill Heinerth producer, Karst Productions, 2003.

CHAPTER 2. WATER BOY

"Mom not only drove us . . .": Jim Skiles, August 2012.

"The hardest thing . . .": Shirley Spohrer, January 2013.

"One of the surfing trips . . .": Jim Skiles, August 2012.

The craft was space-age cool . . . : Kevin V. Brown, "Build Yourself This One-Man Sports Submarine," *Popular Mechanics*, June 1968.

"I think he had two daughters . . .": Jim Skiles, August 2012.

"Because Wes was so disappointed . . .": Jim Skiles, August 2012.

"The photographer had five or six . . .": Wes Skiles, unaired video (see Introduction).

CHAPTER 3. THE CAVES BELOW

"I ran in there . . .": Stef DiPietrantonio, "Seffner Man Disappears into Sinkhole under Home," FOX 13 News, March 1, 2013, www.myfoxtampabay.com/story/21433117/2013/03/01/brandon-man-swallowed-by-large-sinkhole. Accessed December 9, 2014.

Two years later . . . : Katie Mettler, "Sinkhole Reopens Two Years after It Swallowed Seffner Man Sleeping in His Bed," August 19, 2015, *Tampa Bay Times*, www.tampabay.com/news/publicsafety/report-new-hole-opens-at-site-of-2013-fatal-sinkhole-in-seffner/2241865.

"She just heard this sound . . .": Jonathan Arthur, 2014.

Florida's so-called basement rocks . . . : Florida Geological Survey, *Florida's Aquifer Adventure*, video, 2004, https://www.youtube.com/watch?v=b62DICn8RLg.

"As much water as . . .": Cynthia Barnett, *Mirage: Florida and the Vanishing Water of the Eastern U.S.* (Ann Arbor: University of Michigan Press, 2007), 33.

All told, the Floridan aquifer . . . : Harley Means, Assistant State Geologist, Florida Geological Survey, e-mail to author, April 22, 2014.

"Basically, Florida is one giant . . .": Gary Knight, quoted in Julie Hauserman, "Pollution Threatens Purity of Florida's Spring Water," *St. Petersburg Times,* June 20, 1998.

Every day, the springs pump . . . : Ginnie Springs website, ginniespringsoutdoors. com/dive.php.

"There was a young man . . .": Bobbie Wray, January 2013.

"We asked Wes . . .": Bobbie Wray, February 2013.

"Inside Ginnie Spring . . .": Bobbie Wray, February 2013.

"Until he took his scuba . . .": Jim Skiles, August 16, 2012.

"In his senior year, Wes . . .": Allen Skinner, April 2014.

His sister Shirley drove him . . . : Shirley Skiles, January 12, 2013.

"When Wes didn't go to college . . .": Allen Skinner, April 2014.

"I got to Haiti . . .": Wes Skiles, quoted in Scott Carroll, "A Natural Photographer, Wes Skiles of High Springs Has Landed a Career Taking Pictures Underwater," *Gainesville Sun,* September 1, 1996.

Exley was a natural-born . . . : Robert F. Burgess, *The Cave Divers,* (New York: Aqua Quest, 1999), 318.

"Sheck had to average . . .": Ibid.

"Of course Sheck was older . . .": Spencer Slate, September 24, 2013.

"I was using flash-bulbs . . .": Wes Skiles, quoted in Jean Pierce, "Image Maker," *SCUBA,* November–December 1996.

"There was no literature . . .": Paul DeLoach, July 22, 2013.

"We've banged on the well . . .": Hauserman, "Pollution Threatens Purity."

"In Europe, Jacques Cousteau . . .": Woody Jasper, April 4, 2014.

In France, a German diver . . . : Burgess, *The Cave Divers,* 320–21.

"Here we have unexplored caves . . .": Woody Jasper, April 4, 2014.

As Exley writes . . . : Sheck Exley, *Caverns Measureless to Man* (St. Louis, MO: Cave Books, 1994), 40.

"The most ominous thing . . .": Ibid., 38.

"Wes got attracted to exploring . . .": Woody Jasper, April 4, 2014.

CHAPTER 4. CAVE BOOTY

"He's seizing there . . .": Tom Morris, September 19, 2012.

"So I'm lucky I'm alive . . .": Tom Morris, September 19, 2012.

"His body style, his technique . . .": Jeffrey Haupt, July 9, 2013.

"I don't think I knew . . .": Tom Morris, January 11, 2013.

"He had put a camera on layaway . . .": Terri Skiles, August 15, 2012.

"It was cold, cold . . .": Terri Skiles, August 15, 2012.

"If you were part of the elite . . .": Jeffrey Haupt, July 9, 2013.

"He told me when we first got married . . .": Terri Skiles, August 15, 2012.

"Wes tells me about this cool place . . .": Woody Jasper, April 4, 2014.

"We were competitive," . . . : Tom Morris, January 11, 2013.

"We had leads going . . .": Woody Jasper, April 4, 2014.

"It's really fun . . .": Tom Morris, January 11, 2013.

"You're exploring," . . . : Woody Jasper, April 4, 2014.

"In Wisconsin," . . . : Pete Butt, January 10, 2013.

"Me and three friends . . .": Pete Butt, January 10, 2013.

"In '83 I show up . . .": Pete Butt, January 10, 2013.

"Wes had the fever," . . . : Tom Morris, June 27, 2013.

"We're an elite circle," Wes told . . . : Bill Belleville, "Dark Passage: A Journey with Florida's Cave Divers," *Sunshine: The Magazine of South Florida*, November 27, 1988.

Legendary global cave explorer Bill . . . : William C. Stone, ed., *The Wakulla Springs Project* (Austin, TX: Raines Graphics, for United States Deep Caving Team, 1989), 1–2.

It might as well be . . . : Sheck Exley, "The Search for Wakulla," *NSS News* (National Speleological Society), April 1981, 87, 93–96.

CHAPTER 5. EXPEDITION WAKULLA SPRINGS

There had been inklings . . . : USDCT (United States Deep Caving Team), "Wakulla Springs Geology," usdct.org/wakulla2-geology.php.

The next officially sanctioned dive . . . : W. C. Stone, *The Wakulla Springs Project*, 2–3.

"Given the limited number . . .": Ibid., 12.

"When we got to Wakulla . . .": Bill Stone, September 25, 2014.

"Redundancy, the cave diver's favorite word . . .": Wes Skiles, "Wakulla," *Ocean Realm: Magazine of the Sea*, Summer 1990.

"When Wes showed up . . .": Bill Stone, September 25, 2014.

"Let's just say that thinking . . .": Tom Morris, June 27, 2013.

They decided to use heliox . . . : Bill Stone e-mail to author, November 4, 2014.

"Financing of this expensive experiment . . .": W. C. Stone, *The Wakulla Springs Project*, 10.

Because Wakulla Springs was a sensitive . . . : Ibid., 71–93.

We had set up our headquarters . . . : William C. Stone, "Carry On Brother," *Underwater Speleology* 37.4 (2010), nsscds.org/content/carry-brother.

Looking back on it . . . : Bill Stone, September 22, 2014.

"He could actually kind of scream . . .": Kenny Broad, August 15, 2013.

"Never before had I been . . .": Skiles, "Wakulla."

"It was raining hard . . .": Ibid.

"There it was," Wes told . . . : Burgess, *The Cave Divers*, 111.

"Inside the habitat . . .": Skiles, "Wakulla."

"That's how I went through . . .": Burgess, *The Cave Divers*, 112.

"After all those grueling trips . . .": Ibid., 115.

"At first I just sat inside . . .": Ibid.

Skiles' next reaction . . . : Ibid., 115–18.

"Equipped with a *National Geographic* . . .": Skiles, "Wakulla."

"We felt confident . . .": Ibid.

"Wes did most of the laying . . .": Paul Heinerth e-mail to author, October 29, 2014.

"The last thing . . .": Burgess, *The Cave Divers*, 120.

Skiles began mapping his way . . . : Ibid., 120–21.

"Fourteen hours later, at 2 a.m. . . .": Skiles, "Wakulla."

"Basically, we had the bad timing . . .": Bill Stone, September 25, 2014.

Wes's video became a documentary . . . : Bill Stone, September 25, 2014.

"His shot 'Phantoms of the Cube Room' . . .": Stone, "Carry On Brother."

CHAPTER 6. BURIED ALIVE

The Nullarbor Plain . . . : This quote and most of the account in this chapter are drawn from Wes Skiles, "Close Call in the Outback, Pannikin Plain Cave," *National Speleological Society News*, August 1989, 184–90.

"I just sat there and prayed . . .": Terri Skiles, January 11, 2013.

CHAPTER 7. HOW TO SUCCEED IN BUSINESS

"Wes would say, 'If people . . .'": Kenny Broad, August 15, 2013.

"It's the right time . . .": Mitch Stacey, "Waterflow, Cave Diving, See Skiles," *Gainesville Sun*, August 1, 1988.

As it turned out . . . : Terri Skiles, August 15, 2012.

"I remember asking Wes . . .": Tom Morris, September 19, 2012.

"We were instrumental in developing . . .": Woody Jasper, January 11, 2013.

"Wes worked hard to make . . .": Tom Morris, January 11, 2013.

Every New Year's Eve . . . : Bill Belleville, "Down Deep Danger Zones," *Newsweek*, August 15, 1988.

"He says he rarely ever . . .": Stacey, "Waterflow, Cave Diving."

"I didn't have any problem . . .": Tom Morris, June 27, 2013.

"I've gone from a sport . . .": Sara Hamilton, "Reaching for the Record Book; Adventures in Wetsuits," *Gainesville Sun*, June 14, 1987.

For hours we travelled downstream . . . : Wes Skiles, "Travel the 'World's Longest Underground River,'" *Florida Environments*, February 1987.

"It was a very good relationship . . .": Bobbie Wray, January 10, 2013.

"We were at the Diving Equipment . . .": Jeffrey Haupt, July 9, 2013.

Vulcan hired Karst Environmental . . . : Pete Butt, Tom Morris, 2013.

Wes and Morris were diving . . . : Wes Skiles, "Gilbert, Mangoes, and No Windows," *SCUBA Times*, 1998.

CHAPTER 8. SOMEBODY RESCUE ME

"Wes kept telling the *Rescue 911* . . .": Jeffrey Haupt, July 9, 2013.

"Wes wanted to tell *Water's Journey* . . .": Woody Jasper, 2013.

CHAPTER 9. LIONS AND RHINOS

We couldn't get out . . . : Wes Skiles journal, September 1991.

Going crazy on the boat! . . . : Ibid.

If you could only bottle . . . : Wes Skiles journal, February 13, 1992.

"He used to say to me . . .": Tom Morris, June 27, 2013.

a spiritual place . . . : Wes Skiles journal, October 1992.

We took time to stop . . . : Ibid.

CHAPTER 10. AND SHARKS, OH MY!

She immediately contacted Wes . . . : Terri Skiles, January 12, 2013.

If things go as planned . . . : Wes Skiles journal, January 5, 1993.

Well, the day has come . . . : Wes Skiles journal, January, 1993.

I've made what has to be . . . : Wes Skiles journal, February, 1993.

Not until I've captured five . . . : Ibid.

The sea around the boat . . . : Ibid.

Dive gear check, cameras loaded . . . : Ibid.

The great white's head "hit . . .": Carroll, "A Natural Photographer" (see chapter 3).

CHAPTER 11. SWIMMING WITH RAYS

"really good magic with animals": Bill Kreutzmann, June 28, 2013.

"After a couple days playing . . .": Fred Garth, "Wes Skiles: Cave Dweller," *Technical Diving*, December 2012.

Kreutzmann says the team . . . : Richard O'Brien, "Lowering Our Consciousness," *Sports Illustrated*, December 1994.

"I knew that some dive boats . . .": John Dwork and Sally Ansorge Mulvey, "An Interview with Bill Kreutzmann," Documenting the Deadhead Experience, *Dupree's Diamond News* 30 (Winter 1994).

"Wes is the one who . . .": Bill Kreutzmann, June 28, 2013.

"I just played as hard . . .": Dwork and Mulvey, "Interview with Bill Kreutzmann."

Wes told Kreutzmann: "For filming's sake . . .": Ibid.

"Wes was a big influence . . .": Bill Kreutzmann, June 28, 2013.

"I could feel their heartbeat . . .": Dwork and Mulvey, "Interview with Bill Kreutzmann."

Even though they were doing free diving . . . : Wes Skiles, "A Different Drummer," *Rodale's SCUBA Diving*, June 1994.

"He was free diving by himself . . .": Dwork and Mulvey, "Interview with Bill Kreutzmann."

In his journal, Wes wrote . . . : Wes Skiles journal, undated.

CHAPTER 12. SWIMMING WITH WHALES

Kurtis's roots run deep . . . : Christopher Borelli, "Bill Kurtis: An Anchorman's Journey to 'Anchorman,'" *Chicago Tribune*, December 17, 2013.

"Wes was an explorer . . .": Bill Kurtis, October 11, 2012.

From 10,000 feet . . . : Wes Skiles journal, 1994.

They would be filming . . . : Wes Skiles, "Grand Illusion," *Rodale's SCUBA Diving*, June 1996.

I was instantly sure . . . : Wes Skiles journal, January–February 1994.

These were pilot whales . . . : Kate Madin, "Pilot Whales the 'Cheetahs of the Deep Sea," *Oceanus*, May 19, 2008, www.whoi.edu/oceanus/feature/pilot-whales-the--cheetahs-of-the-deep-sea.

From out of the gloom . . . : Wes Skiles journal, January-February 1994.

"We had found, not four . . .": Skiles, "Grand Illusion."

CHAPTER 13. THE HATED CAVE

To even reach the water . . . : William Stone and Barbara am Ende, *Beyond the Deep: The Deadly Descent into the World's Most Treacherous Cave*, with Monte Paulsen (New York: Warner, 2002), 119.

The team would live . . . : Bill Stone, "Cave Quest," *National Geographic*, September 1995; Stone and am Ende, *Beyond the Deep*, 119.

"I don't much like vertical caving . . .": Craig Vetter, "The Deep Dark Dreams of Bill Stone," *Outside*, November 1992.

Once assembled for the diving . . . : Stone and am Ende, *Beyond the Deep*, 87.

During Stone's expedition, a six-mile . . . : Stone, "Cave Quest."

Cloaked in clouds and mist . . . : Wes Skiles journal, April 1994.

"Everybody, I think, has contemplated . . .": Stone and am Ende, *Beyond the Deep*, 164.

Exley was also in Mexico . . . : Bret Gilliam, "Zacaton: The Tragic Death of Sheck Exley," *Undercurrent*, November 15, 2013, https://www.undercurrent.org/blog/2013/11/15/zacaton-the-tragic-death-of-sheck-exley.

Low point of all recent . . . : Wes Skiles journal, April 1994.

"Not only did I feel . . .": Garth, "Wes Skiles: Cave Dweller." Broad also contemplated leaving Huautla.

"I've been on some really . . .": Stone and am Ende, *Beyond the Deep*, 223.

I'm deeper in the earth . . . : Wes Skiles journal, April 1994.

Wes later called the expedition . . . : Jean Pierce, "Image Maker," *SCUBA*, November–December 1996.

CHAPTER 14. HIGH ANXIETY

When *Outside* magazine called Wes . . . : Bucky McMahon, "Deeper," *Outside*, October 1996.

How wondrous the life . . . : Wes Skiles journal, January–February 1994.

"When the magazine calls . . .": Wes Skiles, unaired video (see Introduction).

"Wes would command everyone's attention . . .": Jeffrey Haupt, July 9, 2013.

Through singular focus over eight years . . . : Dave Plank, "Exploration: Gentlemen, Start Your Regulators," *Outside*, May 2, 2004, https://www.outsideonline.com/1845141/exploration-gentlemen-start-your-regulators.

"After 'The Most Dangerous Science,' . . .": Jeffrey Haupt, July 9, 2013.

CHAPTER 15. EXTREME ATOMIC DIVING

"We found this spot . . .": Greg Stone, October 25, 2012.

This will be a chance . . . : Wes Skiles journal, n.d.

Later he would write . . . : Wes Skiles journal, March 11, 1996.

He told a reporter . . . : Carroll, "A Natural Photographer" (see chapter 3).

"What I do is very hard work . . .": Ibid.

"Wes and I were at our peak . . .": Jeffrey Haupt e-mail to author, July 28, 2014.

They were the first film crew . . . : Ibid.

Three dives . . . : Wes Skiles journal, May 23, 1996.

Much to everyone's excitement . . . : Wes Skiles journal, May 1996.

Here today and now . . . : Wes Skiles journal, May 1996.

CHAPTER 16. CRUSADER

Today, some local leaders in Perry . . . : Julie Hauserman, "Florida's Forgotten River," *Tallahassee Democrat*, March 17, 1991, and "Plan to Pipe Waste into Gulf Applauded," *St. Petersburg Times*, March 20, 1997.

Aquapenn got a permit . . . : Ron Matus, "Liquid Asset: National Bottler Taps Ginnie Springs despite Fear of Rising Nitrate," *Gainesville Sun*, May 11, 1998.

"We have prided ourselves . . .": Ibid.

Already, manure from dairies . . . : "Gilchrist Commission Waits on Written Draft from Zoning Board before Acting on Moratorium," *High Springs Herald*, May 7, 1998.

"When he started to find . . .": Terri Skiles e-mail to author, June 26, 2012.

Wes Skiles has been diving . . . : Hauserman, "Pollution Threatens Purity" (see chapter 3).

"We have been blessed . . .": Ibid.

"People were drawn to Wes's energy . . .": John Moran, March 11, 2014.

"Being in an agency . . .": Jim Stevenson, February 4, 2013.

In a canoe flotilla . . . : Julie Hauserman and Craig Pittman, "An Unnatural Silence," *St. Petersburg Times*, October 14, 2002.

On that trip, Struhs directed . . . : Jim Stevenson e-mail to author, November 3, 2014.

"When Wes began attending . . .": Ibid.

"Everybody on the task force . . .": Pam McVety, March 2013.

"We went out and did some testing . . .": Russ Frydenborg, March 2013.

CHAPTER 17. THE AQUIFER'S SECRETS

"There are very few places . . .": Ken Ringle and Wes Skiles, "Unlocking the Labyrinth of North Florida's Springs," *National Geographic*, March 1999.

She says one of Wes's secret . . . : Georgia Shemitz, June 2013.

In the end, it took eight days . . . : Hauserman, "Pollution Threatens Purity" (see chapter 3).

Wes warned: "Life in the underworld . . .": Ibid.

"The fact that there is so much water . . .": Ibid.

"There was so much going on . . .": Bill Stone, September 25, 2014.

"He had his own team . . .": Bill Stone, September 25, 2014.

His longtime diving buddy Paul . . . : Paul Heinerth, "Peace, My Old Friend," *Underwater Speleology* 37.4 (October/November/December 2010): 28.

"When it came time to film . . .": Jill Heinerth, August 16, 2012.

"According to fellow Wakulla 2 . . .": Sue Cocking, "Finding Out the Cause of

Henry Kendall's Death while Diving Reminds Us of an Important Lesson, Safety First, Always," *Miami Herald*, July 18, 1999.

"The night after that happened . . .": Bill Stone, September 25, 2014.

After the expedition, Stone calculated . . . : Stone and am Ende, *Beyond the Deep*, 307 (see chapter 13).

"There was a lot of new technology . . .": Brian Kakuk, July 8, 2013.

"I modified some gear . . .": Brian Pease, 2014.

"The first time we tried . . .": Jill Heinerth, August 16, 2012.

"I'm not aware of anybody . . .": Brian Pease, 2014.

The Springs Task Force recommended . . . : Florida Springs Task Force, *Florida's Springs: Strategies for Protection and Restoration*, November 2000.

Wes also caught a county government crew . . . : Jill Heinerth, March 16, 2013.

"People were in total denial . . .": Mark Wray, March 28, 2014.

CHAPTER 18. ICE ISLAND

"Every day the ocean got rougher . . .": Gregory S. Stone, *Ice Island: Expedition to Antarctica's Largest Iceberg* (Piermont, NH: Bunker Hill Publishing, 2003), 21.

"We really hit it off . . .": Greg Stone, October 25, 2012.

"I think the biggest waves . . .": Greg Stone, October 25, 2012.

Jill Heinerth remembers . . . : Jill Heinerth, September 20, 2012.

Shackleton hadn't had good luck . . . : American Museum of Natural History, "Shackleton," http://www.amnh.org/exhibitions/shackleton/the-exhibition.

Wes hatched his idea . . . : Emory Kristof, February 23, 2013.

The B-15 iceberg was a half-mile . . . : G. Stone, Ice Island, 1.

At the time, it was "the largest . . .": Ibid.

"When Wes saw that story . . .": Terri Skiles, September 21, 2012.

"That's the kind of guy . . .": Greg Stone, October 25, 2012.

"I still can't believe we . . .": Greg Stone, October 25, 2012.

The more she learned . . . : Terri Skiles, September 21, 2012.

The amount of specialized equipment . . . : Paul Heinerth, Jill Heinerth, Greg Stone, and Terri Skiles, 2012, 2013.

"We had been warned . . .": Jill Heinerth, September 20, 2012.

The experience was one of those things . . . : Jill Heinerth, September 20, 2012.

"The captain said . . .": Jill Heinerth, September 20, 2012.

Three days into their crossing . . . : G. Stone, Ice Island, 20–21.

"I thought we were going . . .": Greg Stone, October 25, 2012.

"Wes, to his credit," . . . : Jill Heinerth, September 20, 2012.

"It took me a whole day . . .": Jill Heinerth, September 20, 2012.

Wes enthusiastically started putting . . . : Jill Heinerth, September 20, 2012.

The only communication the ship . . . : G. Stone, *Ice Island*, 27.

"I remember I was up on deck . . .": Greg Stone, October 25, 2012.

"I decided to film . . .": Jill Heinerth, September 20, 2012.

"Wes and our audio guy fixed . . .": Jill Heinerth, September 20, 2012.

With icebergs all around . . . : G. Stone, *Ice Island*, 44.

"There's nothing you can do . . .": Jill Heinerth, September 20, 2012.

"Wes had electric boots . . .": Jill Heinerth, September 20, 2012.

"We knew this was the most dangerous diving . . .": G. Stone, *Ice Island*, 50.

Wes was still shaken . . . : Jill Heinerth, September 20, 2012.

The iceberg had been stationary . . . : G. Stone, *Ice Island*, 55.

"I was in wonderment," . . . : Paul Heinerth, February 5, 2014.

"I think the biggest discovery . . .": Greg Stone, October 25, 2012.

The dive that Wes and the Heinerths . . . : G. Stone, *Ice Island*, 56.

Everyone was disappointed . . . : Paul Heinerth, February 5, 2014.

"We had moved our boat . . .": G. Stone, *Ice Island*, 57.

CHAPTER 19. MAKING *WATER'S JOURNEY*

"It all started with a roll . . .": Jill Heinerth, August 16, 2012.

"I thought that when I brushed . . . : Wes Skiles file, handwritten notes from students at Fort Clarke Middle School in Gainesville, 2004.

CHAPTER 20. HYDRILLASAURUS

"We'd start the interview . . .": John Tindall, July 7, 2013.

The very assumptions that state regulators used . . . : Todd Kincaid, August 2014.

"As cave divers, we knew . . .": Todd Kincaid, August 2014.

"All the models were reaching . . . : Rodney DeHan, August 2014.

"Early on," Kincaid says . . . : Todd Kincaid, August 2014.

"I was blown away," . . . : Todd Kincaid, August 2014.

"What we're saying with our laws . . .": Wes Skiles, 1998.

"That film, *Water's Journey*, changed . . .": Todd Kincaid, August 2014.

CHAPTER 21. *WATER'S JOURNEY* GROWS

When Wes was at home . . . : Nathan Skiles, July 7, 2013.

"Dad would give us all . . .": Tessa Skiles, February 23, 2014.

"In his mind, there was never a roadblock . . .": Nathan Skiles, July 7, 2013.

"Whether it was a politician . . .": Ross Ambrose, October 3, 2013.

As in the Fenholloway River . . . : Steve Patterson, "With Mill Pipeline Still in Doubt, Old Dioxin Haunting Rice Creek Research," *Florida Times-Union,* August 9, 2010, www.jacksonville.com/news/metro/2010-08-09/story/mill-pipeline-still-doubt-old-dioxin-haunting-rice-creek-research.

"I was just dying to go . . .": Nathan Skiles, July 7, 2013.

The government was actively enabling . . . : Joel Moroney, "Lake Okeechobee: Farm Pumps Kick Up Foul Matter," *Fort Myers News-Press,* July 6, 2007.

To film an avalanche . . . : Ronald Dupont Jr., "The Cave: Local Filmmakers Help Sony Create Latest Movie," *High Springs Herald,* January 6, 2005.

One movie critic called it . . . : Neil Smith, review of *The Cave,* BBC, August 19, 2005, www.bbc.co.uk/films/2005/08/19/the_cave_2005_review.shtm, accessed November 22, 2014.

CHAPTER 22. MELTDOWN

"He couldn't get away from . . .": Terri Skiles, August 15, 2012.

High-speed photography is technically challenging . . . : Andrew Zoz Brooks, September 4, 2013.

"We were very often around . . .": John Tindall, July 2013.

"Of course, Wes wants . . .": Jeff Lieberman, July 16, 2013.

"I remember Wes saying . . .": John Tindall, July 16, 2013.

Everything is so new . . . : Wes Skiles journal, December 12, 2008.

First cave I've ever filmed . . . : Wes Skiles journal, December 7, 2008.

I find myself returning . . . : Wes Skiles journal, January 1 and 7, 2009.

"Wes and I teamed up . . .": Kenny Broad, August 15, 2013.

"I'm surprised someone didn't keel . . .": Nathan Skiles, July 7, 2013.

They also found deposits of red dust . . . : Andrew Todhunter and Wes C. Skiles, "Bahamas Blue Holes: Dive into Beauty, Danger, and Discovery," *National Geographic,* August 2010.

"This was one of my most challenging . . .": Wes Skiles, unaired video (see Introduction).

One of the most intriguing . . . : Ibid.

"This is easily the most important . . .": Ibid.

After a long process . . . : Wes Skiles journal, June 2010.

He told a reporter . . . : Tom Mayer, "Natural Explorer," *Currents* 4.4 (May–June 2010).

CHAPTER 23. MAKING THE COVER

"It gave me some relief . . .": Sadie Quarrier, February 2013.

Editors were so enamored . . . : Kurt Mutchler, 2012.

"I think it is one of the best . . .": Kurt Mutchler, 2012.

Wes told the *National Geographic* . . . : Wes Skiles, unaired video (see Introduction).

"I'm speechless about the photograph being selected . . .": Ibid.

CHAPTER 24. LEGACY

The epigraph quoting Wes Skiles comes from Christopher Percy Collier, "Florida's Flow of Cool, Clear Water," *New York Times*, April 11, 2008.

In the months before Wes died . . . : Kenny Broad e-mail to author, November 7, 2014.

"It's my passion," . . . : Michael McLeod, "Aquifer's Advocate," *Orlando Sentinel*, September 23, 2007.

A month before Wes died . . . : Pete Butt, August 30, 2013.

The Palm Beach County medical examiner's . . . : Kleinberg, "Noted Photographer's Death" (see Introduction).

"Wes died doing what he loved . . .": *Congressional Record* 156, no. 128 (September 22, 2010).

"Wes did more to educate . . .": Florida Department of Environmental Protection press release, November 16, 2010.

The more Terri looked into the circumstances . . . : Terri Skiles, various dates, 2012.

That raises the specter . . . : Craig Pittman, "Florida's Vanishing Springs," *Tampa Bay Times*, November 23, 2012.

Ginnie Springs' owners went to court . . . : Mark Wray, March 25, 2014.

Index

Exley, Sheck, 22, 36, 47; death of, 117; declining Huautla expedition, 115; world records for cave diving, 23–24
Extreme environments, 3
Ezell, Joy Towles, 139

Fakahatchee Strand, 193
Fake underwater cave, 194–95
Faulkner, Gwen, 138
Fear, 4–6
Fenholloway River, 137; during droughts, 138; Fenholloway spring water bottling company, 140; special "industrial" label of, 139
Ferrite, 8
Fertilizer, 63, 212; slow-release, 192; sugar corporations and, 164
Flares, 176
Flash technology, 46
Florida: aquifer cave systems of, 183; aquifers in, 9; Arthur, state geologist of, 16; "basement rocks" of, 17; bucolic homespun routines in, 62; bureaucracy in, 144; Capitol Complex of, 17; crisis in groundwater of, 148; karst geologic region of, 16; land-use policies in, 76; limestone substrate of, 17; *National Geographic* and springs in, 148; polluters political influence in, 186; polluting Florida industries, 139; pollution in underground drinking-water conduits in, 136; public service videos about springs protection, 194; Silver Springs, 188; sky in, 11; South Florida Water Management District, 211; springs in, 17; St. Petersburg, 16; taking springs for granted, 140. *See also* Gainesville, Florida; High Springs, Florida
Florida: Window to a Hidden World (1991), 75, 147
Florida Department of Agriculture, 192

Florida Department of Environmental Protection, 142, 143; Don't Expect Protection nickname for, 164; Stevenson at, 158
Florida Environments, 66–67; second issue of, 68
Florida Game and Fresh Water Fish Commission, 144
Florida Geological Survey, 17, 187, 212
Florida Legislature, 138
Florida Museum of Natural History, 40
Florida Natural Areas Inventory, 17
Florida Springs Institute, 212
Florida Springs Task Force, 146; final report by, 163
Florida spring water, environmentalists and, 62
Florida State University, 16, 28; American Academy of Underwater Sciences, 43
"Flow" state, 5
Fontaine de Vaucluse, 23
Fort Clarke Middle School, 184
Fossils: fossil hunters, 15; marine, 17
Free diving, 104; Kreutzmann and Haupt, J., 109
Fresh water, 85
Freshwater caves, 136
Frydenborg, Russ, 146
Funeral, 2

Gainesville, Florida, 8; Alachua County Commission in, 141; Fort Clarke Middle School, 184
Gainesville Sun, 21, 66, 130; letters to the editor in, 142
Galápagos Islands: landing in, 109; *The New Explorers* segment about, 108; surfing on, 108
Garcia, Jerry, 102
Gay Jane (boat), 96
Geology, 16; Florida Geological Survey,

United States (U.S.), 59
University of Florida, 18
University of Miami's Rosenstiel School of Marine and Atmospheric Science, 200
University of Wisconsin, 64
"Unlocking the Labyrinth of North Florida's Springs" (*National Geographic*), 156
U.S. *See* United States

Vadon, Tabb, 105–6
Vanderbilt University, 4
Video work, 48–50, 55; filming African wildlife, 88; filming at Devil's Eye, 78; film loaded wrong in camera, 96; footage of Hurricane Gilbert, 72; sharking eating video camera, 93–94; Sony high-definition camera, 173
Vietnam War, 12; Agent Orange in, 107
Virgin exploration, 4, 30, 36, 85, 133, 203
Vocations, 64
Vortex Spring, 33
Vulcan Industrial & Mining, 69

Wait Wait . . . Don't Tell Me, 107
Wajanaa spirits, 60, 61
Wakulla Springs, 36–37; B tunnel of, 47; disorientation from nitrogen narcosis at, 42; diving conditions in, 161; farthest-ever exploration inside, 51; Grand Canyon of, 39, 53; Monolith Chamber in, 47–48; problems for expedition at, 43–44; "safety stations" in, 46; sensitive ecosystem of, 43; specialized equipment for, 40; three-dimensional images of, 159; Wakulla 2, 84, 159, 160, 163
The Wakulla Springs Project (Stone), 40
"Walking Among the Sharks" (*The New Explorers* episode), 128, 168

Washington Post, 1, 98
Water's Journey: Everglades, 193
Water's Journey: Hidden Rivers, 209, 213; conception of, 166; creative engineering in, 183; events leading to, 139; follow ups to, 191; fundraising for, 181; Heinerth, J., in, 160; impact of, 184, 188; Jasper on, 75; PBS airing, 10, 182; shown in schools, 190
Water's Journey: The River Returns, 191, 192
Weeki Wachee Spring, 157
Weir, Bob, 105
Wellheads, 10
Wes Skiles Peacock Springs State Park, 210
West Palm Beach, 34
Whale Conservation Institute, 109
Whales, 104; *Odyssey* search for, 110; pilot whales, 110–11; pods of, 111. *See also* Sperm whales
Wheat, Penny, 141
Wight, Andrew, 57, 75, 85
Wight, Liz, 75, 85
Withlacoochee River, 30, 36
WKPP. *See* Woodville Karst Plain Project
Wood cellulose, 138
Woodville Karst Plain, 36
Woodville Karst Plain Project (WKPP), 159
World War II, 138, 196
Worldwide Travel Quest, 87
Wray, Bobbie, 15, 18, 19, 68, 142
Wray, Mark, 165
Wray, Robert, 16, *81*
Wrongful death suit, 211

Yager, Jill, 96
Yucatán Peninsula, 70, 124

Zacatón, 117
Zald, David, 4
Zebras, 108

JULIE HAUSERMAN is a longtime Florida writer who has written for many publications, including working as a Tallahassee bureau reporter for the *St. Petersburg Times*. She was a national commentator for National Public Radio's *Weekend Edition Sunday* and *The Splendid Table*. Her work has been featured in such magazines as *Family Circle, Hip Mama,* and the *Apalachee Review* and the essay collections *The Wild Heart of Florida, The Book of the Everglades, Between Two Rivers,* and *UnspOILed*. She is editor-in-chief of an online state news operation, the *Florida Phoenix*.